The
Great Trek

Studies in
Anabaptist and Mennonite History

Edited by

*Ernst Correll, Cornelius J. Dyck, Melvin Gingerich, Leonard Gross, Guy F.
Hershberger, John S. Oyer, J. C. Wenger, and John H. Yoder.*

° Out of print. Available in microfilm and Xerox copies.

STUDIES IN ANABAPTIST AND MENNONITE HISTORY

No. 18

The Great Trek of the
Russian Mennonites
to Central Asia,
1880-1884

Fred Richard Belk

Herald Press, Scottdale, Pennsylvania, and Kitchener, Ontario, in cooperation with Mennonite Historical Society, Goshen, Indiana, is publisher of the series "Studies in Anabaptist and Mennonite History." The Society is primarily responsible for the content of the studies, and Herald Press for their publication.

The Great Trek

of the
Russian Mennonites
to Central Asia
1880-1884

Fred Richard Belk

HERALD PRESS
Scottdale, Pennsylvania
Kitchener, Ontario

Library of Congress Cataloging in Publication Data

Belk, Fred Richard, 1937-
 The great trek of the Russian Mennonites to Central
Asia, 1880-1884.

 (Studies in Anabaptist and Mennonite history; 18)
 Originally presented as the author's thesis, Oklahoma
State University.
 Bibliography: p.
 Includes index.
1. Mennonites in Russia. I. Title. II. Series.
BX8119.R8B44 289.7'47 75-28340
ISBN 0-8361-1103-6

THE GREAT TREK OF THE RUSSIAN
MENNONITES TO CENTRAL ASIA, 1880-1884

Copyright © 1976 by Herald Press, Scottdale, Pa. 15683
  Published simultaneously in Canada by Herald Press,
  Kitchener, Ont. N2G 4M5
Library of Congress Catalog Card Number: 75-28340
International Standard Book Number: 0-8361-1103-6
Printed in the United States of America
Design by Alice B. Shetler

10 9 8 7 6 5 4 3

INTRODUCTION

In this volume we have before us for the first time a detailed account of the migration of 600 Mennonites from their settlements in South Russia and the Volga River region to Asiatic Russia. The movement began in 1880 under the leadership of Claas Epp, Jr., and forms a part of the epic story of Mennonite migrations across the face of the earth "for conscience' sake" since their origin in six-teenth-century Anabaptism. The author tells the story with skill and empathy, basing his narrative on careful research and countless documents which have never been used before.

But this book is more than simply another chapter in the geography of Mennonite experience. It is a unique contribution to our understanding of the long history of millennialism and the church in the wilderness. *The Great Trek* had its roots in Epp's fascination with the writings of J. H. Jung-Stilling (1740-1817), a German physician and friend of Goethe, particularly his book *Das Heimweh*. Based on the books of Daniel and Revelation, especially 12:6 of the latter ("and the woman fled into the wilderness, where she has a place prepared by God . . ."), Jung-Stilling, and then Epp, taught that the ultimate place of refuge would be in the East. Many took this to be Russia, while Epp's vision led him to the very borders of China. In His providence God had provided just enough time for the faithful to reach that refuge before the Antichrist would break forth. The migration of 18,000 Mennonites from Russia to America at that time was obviously going in the wrong direction and a victory for Satan.

The church in the wilderness has been a strong and fascinating motif in all Christian history and even earlier in Judaism. Even as the people of Israel needed to experience the wilderness of the Sinai desert to be tested and purified before they entered the Promised Land (Deut. 8:2), so wilderness meant refuge, purification, judgment (Num. 14), hope (Hos. 2:14, 15) for countless ascetics, monks, and renewal movements from apostolic times to the present. The wilderness experience was central to John Bunyan's vision in *Pilgrim's Progress*, and in Epp's own era it was central to the nineteenth-century Adventist, Jehovah's Witnesses, and other millenarian movements in America. Undercurrents of this wilderness motif may be more present in the history of Mennonite migrations than has been recognized to date.

The Mennonite Historical Society is happy to see this volume included in its series of *Studies in Anabaptist and Mennonite History*. It presents both the story of a significant episode in Russian Mennonite history and a case study in the timeless search of the people of God for the kingdom of which the Scriptures speak and where their souls can be at rest. The granting of a publication subsidy by Mr. John Penner is gratefully acknowledged, as is the editorial help of Mrs. Elizabeth Bender of Goshen.

Cornelius J. Dyck

AUTHOR'S PREFACE

This work was first presented as a doctoral dissertation at Oklahoma State University under the title "The Great Trek of the Russian Mennonites to Central Asia, 1880-84." It was written under the direction of Dr. Douglas Hale of that university and owes much to his wise advice and scholarly encouragement. Others who made valuable suggestions on parts of the original manuscript or its revision include Dr. Cornelius Krahn, Dr. Cornelius J. Dyck, and Mr. John F. Schmidt.

The fine staff of the Mennonite Historical Library and Archives at Bethel College, North Newton, Kansas, were most helpful in granting the use of pertinent archival material needed to construct this work. Their technical assistance, especially on the part of the director, Dr. Cornelius Krahn, was invaluable. My wife and children gave excellent encouragement and showed great patience during the research and writing of this study.

In preparation for the second printing minor changes were made in the text and in some footnotes, particularly in chapter 1, in response to counsel received, which is here gratefully acknowledged.

Fred R. Belk
Sterling College
Sterling, Kansas
January 7, 1978

CONTENTS

10. NO-MAN'S-LAND: BETWEEN KHAN AND CZAR

11. FINAL TREKS OF 1881

12. NEW HOPE AT AULIE ATA

13. THE KHIVAN REFUGE

MAPS, ILLUSTRATIONS, AND PHOTOGRAPHS

ACKNOWLEDGEMENTS

Except as noted below, the maps and illustrations in this book are used by permission of the Mennonite Historical Library and Archives, North Newton, Kansas; Dr. Cornelius Krahn, director; John Schmidt, archivist. Reproductions were made by Oklahoma State University Photo Service.

The map on page 39 is from the *Family History of Siebert Goertz and John Harms*, by Helene Goertz, published privately at Newton, Kansas, 1965, prepared originally by J. Janzen.

The chart on page 57 by Cornelius Krahn is from page 743 of Volume IV of *The Mennonite Encyclopedia*, copyright 1959 by the Mennonite Publishing House, Scottdale, PA 15683.

The photograph on page 59 is used courtesy of R. J. Ensz, Washington, D.C.

The map on page 65 is from *Central Asia: A Century of Russian Rule*, edited by Edward Allworth, published by Columbia University Press, New York, 1967.

The illustration on page 67 is from *Turkestan: Notes of a Journey in Russian Turkestan, Bukhara, and Kuldja*, by Eugene Schuyler, published by Schribner, Armstrong and Co., New York, 1876.

The illustration on page 69 and the map on page 71 are from *The Heart of Asia*, by Francis H. Skrine and Edward D. Ross, published by Methuen and Co., London, 1899.

The portrait on page 73 is from *The Modern History of Soviet Central Asia*, by Geoffrey Wheeler, published by Weidenfeld and Nicolson, London, 1962.

The original of the diary page shown on page 93 is owned by H. W. Jantzen, Lodi, California.

The photograph on page 127 is from *Church History*, Beatrice, Nebraska.

The photographs on pages 125, 151, 181, and 185 are used courtesy of Mr. and Mrs. Ernst Claassen, Whitewater, Kansas.

A NOTE ON USAGE

The following abbreviations will be used throughout:

BM, Bartsch Map

CBB, Christlicher Bundesbote

DB, Der Bote

GB, Gemeindeblatt

HB, Heimatbuch

ME, Mennonite Encyclopedia

ML, Mennonitisches Lexikon

MHLA, Mennonite Historical Library and Archives,
Bethel College, North Newton, Kansas

MR, Mennonitische Rundschau

ZH, Zur Heimat

The *Mennonitische Rundschau* was entitled *Die Rundschau* between June 1881, and December 1883. It appeared in both weekly and semimonthly editions during the year 1883.

Dates referring to Russian or Russian territories are expressed according to the Julian calendar then in use.

Place names are spelled according to the accepted usage in *The Mennonite Encyclopedia* rather than following the newly developing, but not standardized orthography as, for example, Molochnaya instead of Molotschna.

1

MENNONITE BACKGROUNDS

Introduction

During the nineteenth century, a great exodus of European peoples to other parts of the world took place. Especially after the revolutions of 1848, tens of thousands of Germans joined this remarkable migration from their homeland every year in search of greater freedom and economic opportunity. But this was by no means a new phenomenon among Europeans. Beginning in the sixteenth century, many Germans migrated eastward from the Holy Roman Empire because of religious persecution.[1] The Mennonites, named after the Anabaptist (*Wiedertäufer*) leader, Menno Simons,[2] were one such group. Driven by deepening religious convictions which required separation from secular state control, they continued their restless search for freedom from Prussia to Poland to Russia. By the mid-nineteenth century thousands of Mennonites could be found in the Ukrainian colonies of Molotschna and Chortitza. To the northeast in the flourishing Volga River colony of Samara, the Trakt communities became outstanding agricultural settlements that were praised much by the Russians.[3]

Historical Perspectives

The Mennonite colonies in South Russia were regarded by the Russians as model organizations for other settlements because they became so well adjusted in their agricultural, social, and religious practices. Because of the harsh climate, they began as cattle and sheep raisers, but by 1850 they had overcome irrigation problems and raised fine grains; their contemporaries considered them "master farmers" who were both versatile and adaptable. Socially, they remained Dutch-German, both in language and in their village political structure. The radical differences between the colonists, their host country and the native peoples drew the Mennonite colony closer together. Religiously, they were congregationalists, but the autocratic trappings of Russian Orthodoxy and Islam, as we shall see, later caused them to adopt a more authoritarian leadership.[4]

On a journey to this area shortly after 1850, a visitor described the colonies as so thoroughly Dutch-German that he felt he was in the Vistula Delta region of Prussia as he walked through the streets and fields. He was much impressed with the leadership that inspired the people to work so diligently, as though the agricultural life were a religious duty. The visitor found in the Mennonite settlements strong proof of German industry, love of order, cultivation, and morality; of all Russia, this area seemed the most civilized.[5] This ordered stability was to suffer a setback, however, that would usher in the decline of these outstanding settlements.

After 1870, the Mennonites of South Russia found their freedom curtailed as hostile Russian influences moved into their local governments and schools. The promised exemption from the imperial armed services were replaced by a requirement that the Mennonites undertake alternative service for the state.[6] Because of this, approximately 18,000 Russian Mennonites emigrated to the United States and Manitoba, Canada, between 1874 and 1880 to avoid the obligation of state service to the Russian government.[7] After so many centuries of belief in nonresistance, these sturdy people moved on again to a place of greater freedom because of their faith.

Another group of Russian Mennonites, influenced by German mysticism, the prophecies of Daniel, and the Book of Revelation, came to the conviction that they must move farther to the East — *weiter nach Osten*.[8] They are the primary subject of this study. The majority of these people believed that Christ would soon come and that the Antichrist was about to appear in the West; to escape the Antichrist an eastward move to Turkestan was necessary. This millenarian impulse, combined with their antimilitarist attitude, prompted an episode in Mennonite history that has largely gone untold for almost a century. During the period from 1880 to 1884, this visionary band of people journeyed about 1,780 miles from the Ukraine to the wild, unknown, and barren land of Turkestan.[9] After their

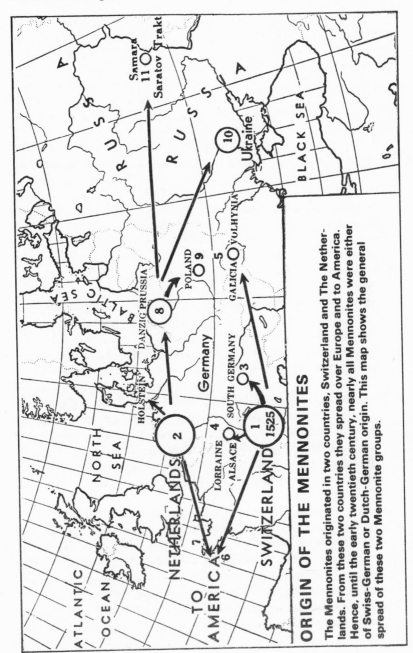

ORIGIN OF THE MENNONITES

The Mennonites originated in two countries, Switzerland and The Netherlands. From these two countries they spread over Europe and to America. Hence, until the early twentieth century, nearly all Mennonites were either of Swiss-German or Dutch-German origin. This map shows the general spread of these two Mennonite groups.

initial journey, the Mennonites underwent suffering, diverged from
their stable past, and fragmented into quarrelsome factions. Finally,
in 1884, many came to the United States to escape continued problems in Turkestan.[10]

The purpose of this work is to show the unique significance of
this Great Trek of 1880-1884 in Mennonite history and concomitantly
to the frontier history of Central Asia. Not only is it a story of the
hardships endured for the sake of their faith by a devout people, but
also the first chapter in the saga of German migration to Central
Asia. These first colonists of modern Turkestan became the vanguard of a German-speaking population which today exceeds two
million. Thus, this study should be of interest not only as an adventure of a small religious sect but also as a historical drama of the
settling of a vast frontier. Before examining this episode in detail,
historical perspective leading up to 1880 is necessary to appreciate
the event fully.

The story begins during the sixteenth century. The first Mennonites were a part of the radical left wing of the Protestant Reformation. When Martin Luther rejected the radical peasant movements
in 1525, a new and vital group arose. The Anabaptists, of whom the
Mennonites constitute a major segment, originated in Switzerland in
the beginning years of the great Reformation. There had always been
those who had rejected some phase of the Roman Catholic Church:
its "worldliness," its degeneration, its "unbiblical" practices, or more
specifically, some aspect of its doctrine, ritual, or government. Among
many other schismatic groups, there may be named the Cathari, Al-
bigenses, and the Waldensians. Either through direct connection with
these groups or their spiritual descendants, or because of similar
reaction to similar situations, or through the ever-growing independent
study of the Bible in the vernacular, the Anabaptists, too, came to
adopt "separatist" views.

As a branch of the Anabaptist movement, "Mennonites trace their
origins to a small group of youthful, impatient reformers gathered
around the leadership of Ulrich Zwingli in Zurich, Switzerland, in the
1520s."[11] Their leader, a believer in austere worship, believers' baptism,
and biblical authority, was not as forceful as Luther and sometimes
tempered his reforms in the face of opposition. A number of young
men, the future Mennonites, broke with their leader because of their
conviction that the Holy Spirit could lead them better than Ulrich
Zwingli. Impatient for change, they informed him, "You have no au-

thority to place the decision in the hand of my lords [the city council] for the decision is already made; the Spirit of God decides."[12]

On January 21, 1525, Conrad Grebel, one of the young men who withdrew from Zwingli's group, launched the Anabaptist movement by baptizing a priest named Georg Blaurock. Blaurock in turn baptized a number of others. Through their personal study of the Bible they adopted the following credo: Only those who had repented of their sins and were walking in newness of life could be a part of the church, and after repentance one was baptized on the confession of his faith. The church was a free institution, and no force was to be used against dissenters in matters of faith. Love was the prime New Testament teaching in life, and taking a human life through the military or civil authorities was outside the realm of a nonresistant follower of Christ. Finally, Christians should never swear an oath.[13]

These enthusiastic Anabaptists of the sixteenth century were the religious revolutionaries of that formative era; they planned for and attempted the renovation of contemporary society and church organization, both Catholic and Protestant. Their motives for revolutionary activity were not nihilistic but religious. Their purpose was the building of a new society, the kingdom of God on earth, which God would immediately inaugurate after the destruction of the old. It would be a new age.

And in many respects it was. There were striking changes in many areas — trade, travel, science, the arts, and religion. The Protestant Reformation is usually regarded as the most important religious revolt of this period, especially because it helped undermine the medieval church and stimulated the creators of modern society. This is a correct interpretation. Yet arising out of the Protestant Reformation was this more radical revolutionary movement, religiously motivated to replace all contemporary churches and society with new churches and a new society.

The Swiss authorities regarded the Anabaptist movement as a heresy of the worst sort, one that would destroy the foundations of the established Roman Catholic Church. Severe persecution began as early as 1525, and in a short while had all but annihilated the Swiss Anabaptist movement. In the canton of Bern, however, a small body of Anabaptists, called *Täufer,* managed to live on.

At about the same time in the Low Countries, Melchior Hofmann, a former Lutheran turned independent, established small secret groups throughout a number of Dutch communities. From these

"Melchiorites" arose a new movement, led by two brothers, Obbe and Dirk Philips, the adherents of which eventually came to be called "Obbenites." In 1536, Menno Simons, a man who had become converted through a personal study of the Bible and the writings of Martin Luther, joined the Obbenites and soon became their leader. For 25 years Menno worked toward uniting Dutch Anabaptists and wrote books and tracts which would help to strengthen his Anabaptist congregations. This work led to a united denomination that came to be called "Mennist." He taught the same basic principles as the Swiss Conrad Grebel — free church, baptism upon confession of faith, nonresistance, rejection of the oath, the principle of freedom of conscience, and voluntarism in religion and he insisted on high ethical standards of life and conduct.

Because of Menno Simons' personal charisma and his influential writings, all Anabaptists ultimately came to be called Mennonites, although until the twentieth century the Swiss Mennonites called themselves *Taufgesinnten* ("Baptism-minded"), and the Dutch used the equivalent term *Doopsgezinden*.

Theological Outlook

These Mennonites were a peculiar people. With their emphasis upon separation of church and state, the early Mennonites registered a strong protest against the leaders of the Reformation, such as Luther, Zwingli, and Calvin, who at first shared the belief that the church and state should stand apart, but later changed their view as to when political power could be used as a means of propagating their faith. Though never denying the legitimacy of civil government, the Mennonites taught that its duties were strictly secular and that it had no authority to enforce new religious doctrines or practices. [14]

Another attitude that was prevalent among early Mennonites was their otherworldliness. Hope for finding peace and security here on earth seemed remote to them. Persecution had accentuated the gulf between "the world" and the true people of God who had a heavenly home. The biblical denunciations of the world were emphasized in sermon and practice, while a strong effort toward a progressive holiness was continually stressed. [15]

Mennonite belief in the other world came from their supreme source — the Word of God. Scriptural authority was beyond question, final, and absolute. With a literal interpretation of all Scrip-

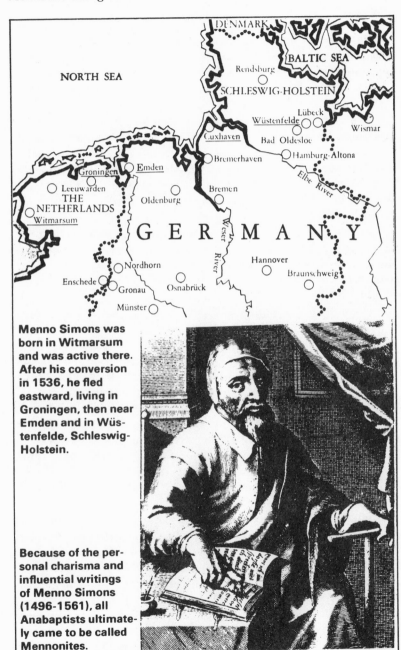

NORTH SEA

DENMARK

BALTIC SEA

Rendsburg

SCHLESWIG-HOLSTEIN

Lübeck

Wüstenfelde

Wismar

Cuxhaven

Bad Oldesloe

Bremerhaven

Hamburg-Altona

Elbe River

Groningen

Emden

Leeuwarden

THE NETHERLANDS

Witmarsum

Oldenburg

Bremen

Weser River

G E R M A N Y

Nordhorn

Hannover

Enschede

Braunschweig

Gronau

Osnabrück

Münster

Menno Simons was born in Witmarsum and was active there. After his conversion in 1536, he fled eastward, living in Groningen, then near Emden and in Wüstenfelde, Schleswig-Holstein.

Because of the personal charisma and influential writings of Menno Simons (1496-1561), all Anabaptists ultimately came to be called Mennonites.

ture, there was little room for analysis or disputation of its merits or adjustment to individual situational ethics. All social values were based on what was written, and any deviation from the Word was denounced as evil. To enforce this belief in the Bible, the church would excommunicate and ostracize anyone caught not adhering to the teachings of Holy Scripture.

With the Bible as their guide and authority, they had no need for a church hierarchy or priesthood. From the very beginning, ecclesiastical hierarchy was unknown, and equal rights were extended to all members, with the Bible as the court of appeals. Every member could study the Bible and form his own convictions.[16] According to the beliefs of early Mennonites, the sacraments were exclusively for the elect of God who had made a Christian profession and were thus qualified for baptism, admission to church membership, and access to holy communion. The qualification for communion rested upon whether the participant followed scriptural standards. These sacraments, then, were of a highly exclusive nature. Such were the cardinal tenets of the early Mennonites.

"Banned in Zurich, the Anabaptist movement spread with alarming speed into the Swiss Confederation, Austria, Bavaria, Wuerttemberg, the Palatinate, and the Netherlands."[17] The symbol of their resistance to state control was the sacrament of baptism for believers and their abhorrence of violence. Charges of radicalism and disruptive nonconformity were leveled at these Mennonites by Roman Catholics and Protestants alike. Intense persecution led some of them to become even more critical of the established churches. They began rejecting this present world in favor of winning Christ's kingdom with a sword.

The Kingdom of Münster which promoted the violent overthrow of government was condemned by most sensitive Christians. Here Anabaptist nonresistance gave way to an aggressive spirit of revolution. Anabaptists were invited to gather at the city to await the ushering in of the New Jerusalem. The Roman Catholic bishop of the city, alarmed by the audacity of these radicals, raised an army to expel them. In a siege of more than a year, horrible bloodletting on both sides gained Münster an unsavory reputation. After this those who opposed Anabaptism criticized the nonviolent along with the reactionaries. This hurt the entire Anabaptist movement.[18]

Political Ideas

The majority of Anabaptists, who rejected violence in any form, continued preaching the suffering of the cross as the way of revolution for Christianity. The Schleitheim Confession of 1527 taught love and peace as the only way of dissent. Menno Simons, who eventually became the directing force of the movement in the Netherlands, promoted communities of Christians which would eventually withdraw themselves from the society around them.[19] These Mennonites, then, were not frozen and forced into the political structure of a state church but remained entirely independent. A great problem in Mennonite history is the relationship between church and state. Because of their lack of allegiance to any state, they have been continually persecuted and this led to "migration fever."[20] But the majority have always believed in a higher authority than government on any moral matter. "The symbol of Mennonite dissent, in an age of intensifying nationalism and militarism, became their rejection of military service and their doctrine of *Wehrlosigkeit* (defenselessness) or nonresistance."[21]

The Mennonite view of the state sees two different worlds. The state and their churches belong to Satan; and their community of born again believers belong to Christ's kingdom. The state has no authority over Christ's kingdom, but they do admit God ordained the state to insure an orderly world. Thus Mennonites have come to believe that there is the kingdom of Christ and the kingdom of the world, which are separate and distinct. A true believer will seek the kingdom of Christ over the kingdom of the world.[22] As time went on, and Mennonites accommodated to state systems, a gradual erosion of their dualistic approach occurred.[23] Yet, when the Mennonites established colonies in South Russia after 1788, toleration and complete autonomy over religious and political affairs was still their primary motive for settlement. They endured so much persecution that the Russian immigration was a welcome event.

2

FROM THE VISTULA
TO THE VOLGA

Vistula Delta

Persistent persecution throughout the sixteenth century caused many Mennonite refugees to find their way to more tolerant lands. They followed the Rhine River into Germany and on to the Netherlands. In Spanish Flanders, where Catholicism finally prevailed, and where the Inquisition worked most perfectly, Mennonitism was practically rooted out by 1600. Many of the refugees fled to the northern provinces where opposition to Spanish Catholic rule was most determined. Religious toleration in these northern provinces was still a relative matter, however. Mennonites were still compelled to pay taxes to support the Reformed Church and to submit to humiliating restrictions. It was a most difficult process to initiate formal church congregations. Only in the late sixteenth century did Dutch Mennonites become clearly defined as a brotherhood, and even then, congregations in northwestern Germany and as far away as Danzig had close ties with the Dutch congregations. In the mid-seventeenth century a continual stream of Mennonite refugees expanded into England, East Friesland, and also to Poland and East Prussia, where a number of flourishing congregations had their beginning along the Vistula Delta.

Regarded as aliens and heretics, they met distrust and suspicion everywhere, and were only slowly accepted in their new homes. In 1686, the Elector of Cologne forbade his subjects to have any

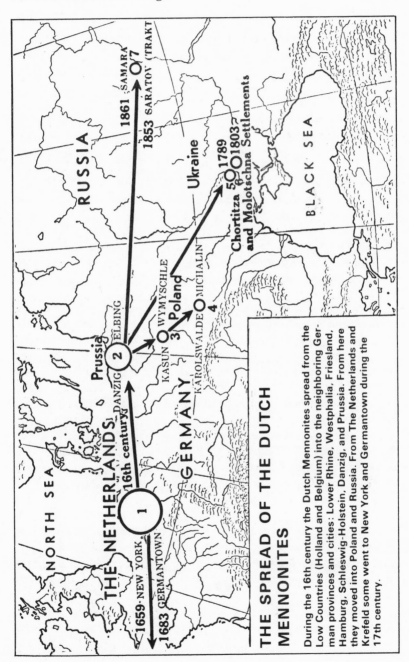

THE SPREAD OF THE DUTCH MENNONITES

During the 16th century the Dutch Mennonites spread from the Low Countries (Holland and Belgium) into the neighboring German provinces and cities: Lower Rhine, Westphalia, Friesland, Hamburg, Schleswig-Holstein, Danzig, and Prussia. From here they moved into Poland and Russia. From The Netherlands and Krefeld some went to New York and Germantown during the 17th century.

relationships whatever with these "ungodly vagabonds."[1] In 1694, the Elector of the Palatinate cruelly persecuted the new settlers at Rheydt. And even as late as 1818 the Prussian prefect of Braunfels still distrusted them because "they had long beards and no buttons and attended neither state church worship nor religious instruction."[2] The Dutch-German heritage of the Mennonites, taken for granted today, involved a slow process of adaptation.

Dutch refugees were among the earliest of Mennonites to locate in the region of the Vistula Delta and the Baltic coast to the east, settling on lay and church estates near Danzig, Elbing, and Königsberg. Slowly they began taking on the customs of their adopted land. One important phase of Mennonite development was their gradual acceptance of the German language rather than the Dutch.[3] This language essentially became a Low Dutch dialect. By 1671, Georg Hansen, an elder of the Danzig Church, was lamenting that the young people read German rather than Dutch; a hundred years later all ministers in the Danzig area were preaching in German. When the immigration to Russia began a short time later, the original Dutch language had been all but obliterated — a fact that is very important for the subsequent history of Mennonites, not only in Russia but also in North and South America.

In 1772, West Prussia was united with East Prussia under Frederick the Great. The Mennonites of the region were delighted with Frederick because of his reputation for religious toleration, and showed their loyalty to him by giving him 2 oxen, 400 pounds of butter, 20 cheeses, 50 chickens, and 50 ducks on the occasion of the annexation. Frederick was pleased with their demonstrations of loyalty and their gifts and in return granted them freedom of worship, the right to erect new churches, permission to establish schools, freedom from military service, substitution of an affirmation for an oath, the right to enter any line of industry open to others, and the right to bury their dead in their own cemeteries.

By establishing large independent settlements in the Vistula basin of Prussia, far removed from main transport routes, the Mennonites kept their religion, customs, and language unadulterated. They were not allowed to seek the conversion of others to their philosophy of life so no new blood found its way into their closed society in subsequent years. A study of names made in 1912 proves that Prussian Mennonites descended almost without exception from Dutch refugees who came from other areas. Investigations revealed that

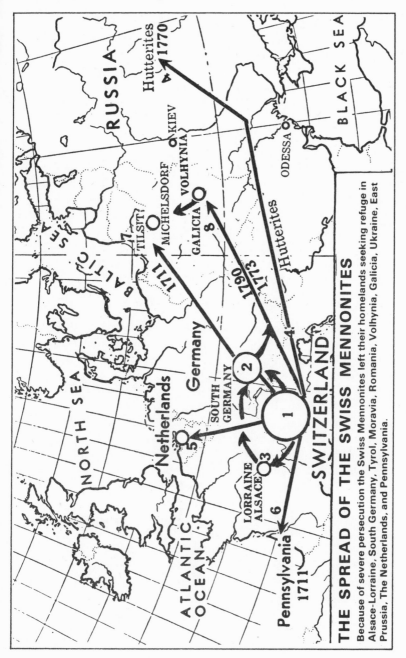

THE SPREAD OF THE SWISS MENNONITES

Because of severe persecution the Swiss Mennonites left their homelands seeking refuge in Alsace-Lorraine, South Germany, Tyrol, Moravia, Romania, Volhynia, Galicia, Ukraine, East Prussia, The Netherlands, and Pennsylvania.

among approximately 10,000 Mennonites in these Prussian lands, there were 369 families, among whom the following names predominated: Penner, with over 527 persons, Klassen with 409, Wiebe with 434, Janzen or Jantzen with 292, Friesen with 140, Reimer with 140, Epp with 131, and Peters with 109. These names are some of the best known, and those who bore them comprised almost one half of the entire population.[4]

The marshy wastelands in the Vistula Delta were soon turned into fertile farms through the skillful and untiring efforts of the Mennonites. They were accustomed throughout the decades of their settlement in West Prussia to acquire the unsettled marshy lands of the region for their descendants; when this area was occupied, they rented land in East Prussia. This outlet was soon exhausted, however, and Mennonites could only settle in wastelands and in communities with other Mennonites. Many turned to the crafts and trades. In these occupations few realized great accomplishments, however, for in their hearts they remained farmers.[5]

Toleration and Oppression

This territorial expansion of the Mennonites aroused the enmity of the Lutheran Church, since it received support from taxation of lands owned by Lutherans. The state church became greatly concerned by the growing prosperity of a rival religion and an alien people. In 1772 the Mennonites owned a total acreage of about six townships in West Prussia, which they expanded to approximately nine in the space of two years.[6] Prussian officials were sympathetic to the Lutheran pleas to restrict the Mennonites and looked with disfavor upon their pacifist convictions. The army could only tax persons who owned land, and the military also depended on landowners for conscription purposes. Thus, when the Mennonites bought more and more farms from their non-Mennonite neighbors, the number of farms taxable for military purposes decreased.[7] The rapidly multiplying people who steadfastly refused to fight in the army weakened the military potential of the Prussian state.

The state therefore resolved to force the Mennonites to pay dearly for their nonviolent convictions. On June 20, 1774, an order was issued compelling Mennonites to pay a lump sum of 5,000 thaler (about $3,500) in lieu of military service to support the military academy at Culm. This payment troubled the conscience of many dedicated Mennonites; they feared assimilation by the world and a reimposition of regulations and restrictions. In addition, their economic progress was hampered and their religion suppressed.

Near the end of the eighteenth century, the new king of Prussia, Frederick William II, reluctantly confirmed their ancient privileges of freedom of worship and exemption from military service. Soon, however, complaints from his recruiting officers concerning the sect prompted a royal decree prohibiting further land acquisition by Mennonites and requiring that they pay tithes to the Lutheran Church on land purchased from Lutherans. Finally, the Prussian government issued a decree on December 17, 1801, which forbade Mennonite land purchases from Lutherans or any other neighboring farmers.[8] Moreover, any Lutheran could buy back his farm from the Mennonites at the original price, regardless of improvements made on them. Henceforth, Mennonites could only buy from Mennonites, and thus all possibility for further expansion was halted.

Faced with this ordinance, the Mennonite settlements entered a time of hardship. Material progress was blocked, and expansion for the younger generation became only a shattered dream for the parents. As time went on, other annoying restrictions were placed on them. Mennonites were not permitted to hold public funerals; citizenship was granted to them only with great reluctance. They were asked to pay tribute money. Mennonite shops in Danzig were boycotted and their owners intimidated.[9] Consequently, a fertile field was provided for any external power which sought immigrants for new settlements. Imperial Russia was just such a power.

Prior to the accession of Catherine the Great to the throne of Russia in 1762, the Mennonites were virtually unknown in her country. This situation might well have continued if it had not been for the agrarian reform and colonization of depopulated provinces that the empress initiated. Catherine's proclamation of 1762, entitled "Instruction to the Commission for Drafting a New Code of Laws," stated that owing to insufficient population and the existence of large tracts of land that were neither inhabited nor cultivated, encouragement should be increased to lure farmers to Russia.[10] This proclamation resulted in an open invitation to all foreigners except Jews from all over Europe to settle in Russia. Liberal inducements offered to foreign settlers in the Ukraine, or New Russia as it was then called, attracted the attention of the Prussian Mennonites. Staunch pacifists, their convictions jeopardized by the Prussian military program, they were looking for a new land of opportunity.[13]

To the Steppes of the Ukraine

Mennonite agents were sent to St. Petersburg to confer with the government concerning the Russian offer. In 1788, the Russian Minister to Danzig notified the Prussian Mennonites that the imperial government was granting special privileges to them. Besides the concessions offered to all immigrants — free land and freedom of religion — the Mennonites were guaranteed for all time closed farming communities, freedom of religion, including complete separation of church and state, and freedom from military service.[12]

According to the ukase of March 17, 1764, each immigrant farmer coming to Russia was to receive a land allotment of approximately 81 acres, of which 40 were to be of arable land, 14 each of meadow and woodland, 9 1/2 pastureland, and a house and garden plot of four acres in the village. A subsequent ukase of February 20, 1804, granted each family twice the original allotment.[13]

The original settlement of West Prussian Mennonites in Russia began in 1789. Approximately 900 people reached the Ukraine in July of that year. Fifteen villages were founded on the Chortitza River, and the area was soon dubbed the "Old Colony" by later immigrants. In 1803, a "New Colony" was founded on the Molotschna River fifty miles east of Chortitza, and from 1789 to 1810, approximately 18,000 Mennonites settled in and around these two areas. After 1810, other colonies were set up in eastern Russia and Siberia. The Russian Government initially granted 280,000 acres to the Chortitza and Molotschna colonies. This area was gradually enlarged over the years until by 1914 they possessed 3,750,000 acres.[14]

In 1820, the Russian imperial policy of promoting foreign colonization en masse was officially halted, although the Napoleonic Wars and the increasing restrictions of the government had already reduced the influx. A new policy of restriction was applied to all immigrants except the Mennonites, of whom two hundred families could still enter the country annually "in view of the industriousness and the excellent state of farming prevalent among all the Mennonites in New Russia."[15] In 1841, Prussian authorities introduced military conscription among Mennonites, and additional numbers rushed to the Ukraine to emulate their earlier coreligionists. To the northeast in the Samara region two new colonies were formed along the Volga River. These were Am Trakt in 1855, and Old Samara in 1859.

Freedom, Problems, and Prosperity

These Mennonite colonies in Russia developed a close-knit community life and made no effort to fuse or adapt to the new culture. Both the colonists and the government encouraged this policy of separation. The Mennonites, desiring to avoid entanglement with "the world" and seeking only peaceful existence with the "believers," did not desire mixture with "foreign" ideas. The Ukraine enhanced separateness and clannishness, since the language, culture, and religion of the neighboring Slavs were strange to the immigrants. Separation was further enhanced by their settlement in closed farming communities rather than in cities.[16] These colonial communities consisted of from 10 to 40 homesteads with the entire village patterned after their Prussian homes in the Vistula Delta near Danzig. In this way, the Mennonites were never obliged to mix with Russians or other indigenous peoples, since the Mennonite settler never started homesteading alone but always with help from fellow colonists.[17]

Social Structure

Russian immigration law also created separate communities. The Russian Colonial Law of 1842, for example, provided for a traditional form of settlement and community organization familiar to most immigrants.[18] The civil authority in each village resided in the *Schulz*, with the *Oberschulz*, who was elected by all the villagers, responsible for the total settlement. This council worked with the inspector of the imperial government to provide local laws and administration.[19]

Though the colonies became directly responsible to Russian authority after 1870, these authorities sought only obedience to law and seldom encroached upon the internal life of the colonies. Village assemblies held administrative authority; they owned the land and allotted holdings of 175 acres to each homestead, while retaining several tracts for communal pasture, churches, mills, and other community establishments. The *Schulz* presided over the village assembly, similar to the *mir* of the native Russian village. The activities and relations of the Mennonite settlements with the imperial government were mutually satisfactory to both parties. Aaron Klaus, a high Russian official in the colonial administration, remarked that the government was pleased with the success of the Mennonite economy and that their institutions should be a "model for the organization of the majority of the other colonies of foreigners in the Ukraine."[20]

Seldom have Mennonites been involved in as much concern for mutual aid as they were during their time in Russia. They had a common pasture, a common granary for lean years and poor relief, common flocks, a communal ferry, a common distillery, and common ownership of registered breeding stock. They had money-lending societies, a very sophisticated fire insurance plan, and orphans' and widows' assistance. Not only was mutual aid evidenced in economic and social relations, but also in the political and educational spheres. Mennonites developed their thriving economy entirely upon the principle of mutual aid.[21]

This principle was much in evidence in the early years of the founding of both Chortitza in 1789, and Molotschna in 1803-04.[22] The original settlers of the Chortitza colony had a very difficult time in the early years. Disease and death took a heavy toll; government aid and building materials were slow in arriving, and dissatisfaction with their own leaders engendered a spirit of disunity. But by the turn of the century some 400 families had established 15 villages and were farming approximately 89,000 acres of land. Soon it became obvious that crown land allotments of 175 acres per family would not be sufficient to meet the growing needs of the colony. The government of the czar, therefore, made a large land purchase for colonization purposes. But the requirements of an expanding colony soon made new villages a necessity. The government again responded in 1836, and another colony was settled at Mariupol.[23] As the population grew, new families could settle on this land.[24]

The Molotschna colony, on the other hand, was an effort on the part of the Russian government to establish an experimental agricultural community. It was to serve as a model to the surrounding population in matters of grain farming, stock raising, horticulture, viniculture, and in the development of industries. It was situated about 75 miles southeast of Chortitza, and its settlers were generally more prosperous than those in the Old Colony. A good third of them were well-to-do, or even rich.[25] By 1840, 11,381 persons lived in the 45 villages of the Molotschna colony. This colony consisted of 344,000 acres, making it the largest Mennonite colony in Russia.[26]

Another colony developed because the Prussian constitution of 1850 abolished exemption from compulsory military service on religious grounds. Consequently, a considerable number of Mennonites from that country petitioned the Russian government to permit them to

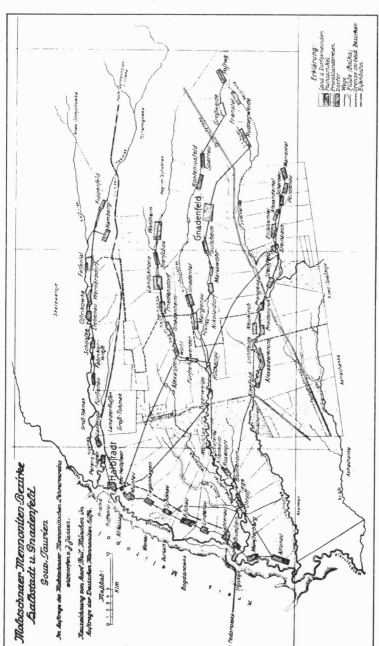

The Molotschna Colony was formed in 1803, fifty miles east of Chortitza.

settle in Russia. On November 19, 1851, permission was granted to 100 families to come into the country under substantially the same conditions as the earlier Mennonite immigrants, but with the following exceptions: first, exemption from military service was to be granted for a period of 20 years, after which the colonists had to pay a special fee; second, they were not to enjoy the right to brew beer, make vinegar, nor distill whiskey. Each family also had to deposit with the Russian embassy in Berlin a sum of 350 thalers to assure its establishment without any financial help from the Russian government.[27]

To the Volga

A tract of 17,301 dessiatines (about 46,712 acres) was set aside for newcomers in the province of Samara, in the immediate neighborhood of the great "Salt-Trakt," a road upon which the salt from the Elton Sea was conveyed to the interior provinces. Hence the settlement is known as the "Trakt Settlement." The actual settlement began only in 1855 and was not completed until 1873, during which period the following ten villages were founded: Hahnsau (1854), Köppental (1855), Fresenheim, Lindenau and Hohendorf (between 1856 and 1862), Lysanderhöh (1864), Orloff (1871), Ostenfeld and Medemtal (1872), and Valuevka (1875).[28] It is impossible to ascertain how many families originally settled in these colonies, but according to one authority, 120 families arrived in Russia between 1853 and 1857.[29]

The years from 1854 to 1873 saw the Trakt region growing agriculturally and economically. The raising of wheat, cattle, and horses provided important livelihoods. Red winter wheat made two crops possible yearly, thus increasing income. Dutch cattle brought from Prussia were crossed with the German "red cow" of the Ukraine, and the cattle industry developed. These "Menno-Dutch" cattle were noted for milk production of exceptionally high quality and quantity. The "colonist horses" were in quality and appearance superior to common horses. The breed was improved by crossing it with Belgian and Dutch sires and some Russian stock. By 1873, the Trakt community had a strong economic base.

Each village within the Trakt consisted of from 25 to 30 farms. Each family received a building site of about four acres in the village and a plot of several acres immediately behind it. These were commonly known as the "house-field" and were used as a meadow, for raising vegetables and grains, or for domestic use. The rest of

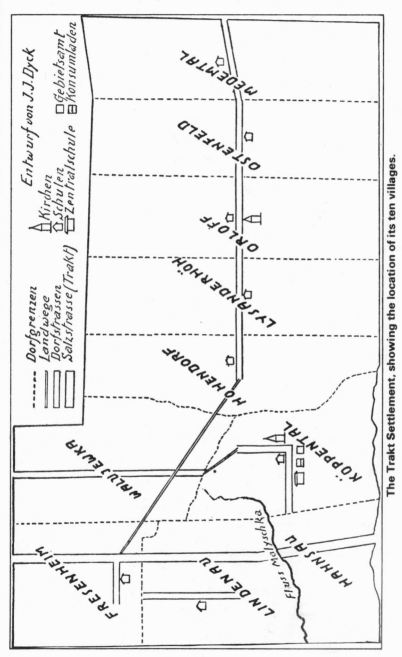

The Trakt Settlement, showing the location of its ten villages.

the land served as common pasture for village sheep and cattle. Only by the late 1850s, when farming began to supplant stock breeding, was this land divided into plots allotted to each farmer. [30]

There were a number of other provisions dictated by the government which were destined to influence the future of the Mennonites in Russia. The original family allotment was to be a perpetually hereditary possession, not personally for any one colonist, but to the colony as a whole, with each family enjoying the use of its allotted portion in perpetuity. The colonists were not allowed to divide, mortgage, or sell even the smallest part of their allotment. This restriction, however, applied only to the original allotment. Any land a farmer might subsequently buy or rent did not fall under the provisions of this decree. Lakes, rivers, and wastelands belonged to the whole village. Only the youngest son was allowed by law to inherit the land, thus encouraging the older sons to take up other farms or learn a trade.[31] This particular restriction was never rigidly enforced, however, and the Mennonites were generally permitted to follow their accustomed ways in matters of land inheritance.

Under these circumstances the Mennonites prospered in their new-found home. Their earliest efforts were mostly in cattle and sheep raising. Later this shifted to grain and other crops as the large pasture and grazing lands needed for cattle and sheep were gradually occupied by more immigrants. Industry and mercantile businesses began to play a significant role among the Mennonites by 1850, and steam-operated mills were introduced for grinding wheat and corn into flour and the manufacturing of tools and machinery.

Spiritual enlightenment was as important as these material gains if not more so. The church was the central institution of the Ukrainian Mennonites, since freedom of worship was the primary reason for their colonization. To become a member of the church and to receive full membership rights, one had to profess his faith in Christ as Savior and Lord and be baptized before the congregation. A church assembly, the *Bruderschaft*, held complete authority over all baptized church members. Duties of members were to live a simple Christlike life, shun the evils of the "world," and suffer persecution at the hands of the state rather than submit to armed service.[32]

With these Christian ideals firmly in mind the Mennonites flourished undisturbed into the late nineteenth century. Material and spiritual growth continued at such a rapid tempo that they became one of the leading minorities of imperial Russia.

3

COMPROMISE OR CONVICTION: AMERICA OR ASIA?

Prior to Reform

The undisturbed life of Russian Mennonites was brought into question by political developments in the imperial government. Ironically, the reforms of Czar Alexander II (1855-1881) proved a serious threat to the Mennonites because the effect of the reforms tended to extinguish the privileges of certain groups within Russia.

This abrogation of the privileges of the few began in 1861 with the liberation of some 22 million serfs, an act which pleased neither the landowners nor the serfs. Landowners, even though compensated by the government, did not like the interference with their pocketbooks. The serfs, after a disappointing denial of free land, first flocked to the cities, then due to the lack of suitable accommodations, many returned to the estates they had been working as paid laborers. In spite of this discontent, Alexander desired to try his hand at other reforms.[1]

The emancipation of the serfs inaugurated a new era in Russia. Censorship of the press and universities, a stifling tool of the government, was lessened and both were allowed a free hand in their own administration. Russians were once again allowed to travel outside imperial Russia and Western influence in the form of books and guest speakers were allowed to come into the country.

Not all of the czar's subjects were pleased by these new reforms, and a series of attempts to assassinate Alexander created the impression that he had allowed too much of an atmosphere of freedom of thought and expression.[2] Mennonites were not involved in these violent expressions of contempt for the czar's reforms. On the contrary, they had more reason for satisfaction than any other element of Russian society, because from the time of their settlement in Russia they had enjoyed extensive privileges. These privileges helped Mennonites to maintain social characteristics that were unique in Russia.

The Dutch-German character of their communities was undermined by the incursion of Russian influences after 1866. It was in this year that an imperial edict disturbed their way of life by decreeing mandatory use of the Russian language in all schools. Thereafter, the special privileges of local autonomy began to dissolve. By 1881, the Mennonite Board of Education had lost control of its schools completely; all education had been placed under the control of the government Department of Public Instruction in its intense effort to Russianize all national minorities. Eventually all school subjects except religion, German, and church music were taught in Russian.[3] Despite this attempt at russification, a census in 1897 found that less than one percent of all Mennonites in Russia used Russian as their mother tongue.[4] They remained steadfast in their cultural heritage and insistent upon their special privileges.

Reform Movement in Russia

In 1870, an imperial decree signed by Alexander as a reform measure put an end to the most important concession of all — exemption from military service. Henceforth, all colonists were to be placed under imperial administration, semi-autonomous local governments were curtailed, and military exemption was to be abolished. Within ten years they were to comply with the new law, after which the Mennonites would become "full-fledged Russian citizens with no special favors."[5] The new law was printed in June 1871, and published in the fall of that year. Though the law provided that Mennonites could perform hospital or medical corps services or act as railway engineers in lieu of bearing arms, the Mennonites still hoped that their privileges would be reinstated, or at least that they would be able to avoid military service. Five delegations were sent to St. Petersburg in an attempt to gain concessions but they all met with failure.[6] Their only recourse was that they had the liberty to emigrate until 1881. In that year they would have to comply with all laws affecting all Russian citizens.

Reform and the Mennonites

The War Department was not oblivious to this special people and actively provided for noncombatant service during wartime and forest service or industrial work in peacetime.[7] This meant that the Mennonites were no longer a privileged class and that their colonial privileges granted a hundred years before had been abolished. Still the Mennonites tried to get the laws revoked because they believed them to be a violation of the earlier law.[8]

The final delegation sent to St. Petersburg in 1874 obtained an audience with the president of the Imperial Council. This official expressed his dissatisfaction that the Mennonites, though having lived for generations in Russia, did not yet know the language of their country. The delegation was also granted interviews with Count Heyden, president of the Special Military Commission. These high officials, although friendly, refused to give any assurance of continued exemption from military service and explained that to do so would be unfair to other Russian subjects. They suggested, however, that they might be given the privilege of some substitute for military conscription, such as medical corps or hospital service, and promised that their religious scruples would be taken into consideration. But the delegates remained adamant in their refusal of any noncombatant role in connection with military service. They were told that their only solution, then, would be emigration to another country.[9]

Migration to America

Seeing no apparent relief from military conscription, the Mennonite leaders were inclined to give up their prosperous homes and emigrate, and a search began for a country where they could settle. Even as early as 1872 Cornelius Jansen, an outstanding Mennonite leader and Prussian Consul at Berdyansk, printed a collection of letters with the purpose of acquainting the Mennonites of Russia with the United States. With his preference well known, Jansen strongly urged his fellow Mennonites to emigrate. Russian officials began denouncing Jansen because many excellent settlers were beginning to follow his suggestions. He was forced to leave Russia in May 1873.[10] The Jansen case caused many Mennonites to reconsider whether they wanted to stay in Russia or not.[11]

After an unsuccessful attempt to appeal to the czar himself, about one third of the Mennonites of Russia, or approximately 18,-000 people, began seriously considering the United States as a new homeland. They knew compulsory military service did not exist in the United States, and they were aware of the homestead laws, according to which every person who had declared his intention to become a citizen would receive 160 acres of land.[12] Both the government and the American railroad companies were seeking new settlers for a vast frontier.[13] American Mennonite leaders, especially in Kansas, promised help in relocating new settlers from Russia.[14] President Grant, despite the fact that individual states retained conscription powers, assured Russian Mennonites that "we will not be entangled for the next fifty years in another war, where military service will be necessary." Grant's secretary of state, Hamilton Fish, assured them that conscientious objectors would always be granted noncombatant service.

In the United States Congress there was a mixture of feelings about Russian Mennonites. In a debate in the Senate some senators were in favor of being able to get "the very best farmers in Russia." Other congressmen, however, argued that a "closed community" would be created by their settlement. This, they argued, would be against the fundamental principle of equality of citizenship and freedom. The result of the debate was that no action was taken to forbid entry into the United States.[15]

In spite of differing congressional opinions, the immigration from the Ukraine of Russia was in full swing by the end of 1874. The Mennonites of America joined together to organize for financial aid to the Russian immigrants. The majority of the immigrants, numbering about 18,000, arrived in America in 1874, and smaller groups came during the last years of the nineteenth century.

Those who came to the United States and Canada from Russia settled primarily in the plains states of mid-America, which resembled the Ukrainian land they left. Many settled and prospered in the states of Nebraska and Kansas before moving farther westward. Still others went south into Oklahoma or north into the Dakotas. Approximately 8,000 settled in the rich valleys of Manitoba. Wherever they settled their farming techniques not only brought them prosperity but set an example for other settlers.

Among the many interesting features of the Mennonite economic

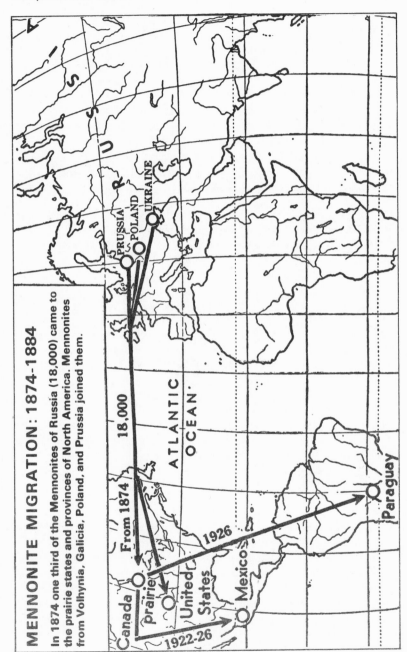

MENNONITE MIGRATION: 1874-1884

In 1874 one third of the Mennonites of Russia (18,000) came to the prairie states and provinces of North America. Mennonites from Volhynia, Galicia, Poland, and Prussia joined them.

development in America is their introduction of Turkey Red Wheat into their adopted land. Knowing that the American plains were similar to the Ukraine, they brought with them various seeds. Among these was hard winter wheat, "Turkey Red Wheat," which would later be of enormous significance not only for their own farming but for the whole of wheat production in the United States. As one interpreter explained it,

> It is therefore natural that the center of hard wheat production in this country should be in Kansas, since in Russia it is in the Crimea. The climate of the Russian district is a little more severe, which fact makes Crimean wheat all the more satisfactory in Kansas.[16]

The history of hard winter wheat in the United States, therefore, is closely related to the movement of Russian Mennonites to the middle great plains. The first crop of Kansas hard winter wheat, for example, was grown just after the new settlers brought in the new seeds. Their deep plowing and thorough surface cultivation was a boon to dry farming in the United States.[17] Wherever they went they contributed to the development of the region, and in a few years thousands of Mennonites were prosperous farmers.[18]

Those Left Behind

Meanwhile in Russia, the czar was greatly concerned that many of his most productive farmers had settled in the United States and Canada. The law of 1874, which made noncombatant service possible for Mennonites, had gone into effect and temporarily checked emigration. Many Mennonites of military age went to work for a two-year period in the Russian crown forests, the hospitals, and the Russian Red Cross.[19] However, some of the remaining Mennonites who opposed noncombatant service still sought to leave Russia.

A concerned Russian government feared that there would be a general exodus, so the government invited Mennonites to settle in Siberia in the Amur Valley. Here they could retain their special privileges as foreign colonists.[20] But a delegation to Siberia reported that the journey was too long and difficult and there was no railroad or market for their agricultural products.[21] After this discouraging report, those who opposed noncombatant service continued to look further into settlement possibilities in the United States, South

America, Australia, and the newly acquired Russian province of Turkestan.[22]

Among the approximately 36,000 Mennonites who stayed behind, the majority wanted to remain on their property, participate in alternative service if need be, and live out their lives as Russian Mennonites. But two small groups in Molotschna and the Trakt deviated sharply from the compliant majority. Fired by religious conviction, they decided to withdraw permanently from their present surroundings to seek a refuge in the East. From the deep reservoir of Christian theology, they took up the ancient doctrine of millennialism, which seemed to offer both a sanctuary from their present troubles and the promise of salvation for the future.

4

THE EMERGENCE OF CHILIASM

Background of the Movement

Though it is impossible to ascertain with exactitude how Turkestan became the place of refuge for a small group of Russian Mennonites, it is certain that a book written by Claas Epp, Jr., greatly influenced their decision to migrate. The entire book was concerned with belief in the doctrine of millennialism and its relevance to their plight

The belief Epp had in millennialism had deep roots in the Christian faith. The diaspora of the Dutch and Swiss Mennonites to the lowlands of Prussia, to South Germany, and finally to the steppes of Russia brought with it the possibility of a vital interaction with different faiths. Two centuries of comparative prosperity in Prussia gave them the opportunity to take on the cultural aspects of their surroundings. They retained this antimilitaristic faith but often failed to express the missionary zeal which they had previously exhibited. They became separatistic, quietistic, and chiliastic.

Chiliasm or millennialism, depending on whether one employs the Greek or Latin root, has been a theological problem for most Christians down through the ages.[1] In Christian theology this word had reference to the thousand-year duration of the earthly reign of the Messiah at the end of history. According to the writer of Revelation, Satan will be bound and thrown into the abyss, there to remain while "the saints of God and of Christ" reign with the latter in the messianic kingdom throughout this period of tribulation. There-

after Satan will be released for a season to war against "the saints
and the beloved city," after which he will be tossed into "the lake
of fire and brimstone" for his everlasting torment.[2] This passage is
the only one in Scripture that explicitly refers to a millennial reign
of Christ on earth, though some others[3] may plausibly be held to
refer to the same period. These passages have given rise to three
conflicting interpretations of the last days, known respectively as
premillennialism, postmillennialism, and amillennialism. In the first
case, it is held that Jesus Christ will return to earth before the
millennium. Postmillennialism anticipates His coming after the event,
while advocates of the third interpretation argue that the language
is too highly figurative to suggest the reality of a literal millennial
reign, but they do believe in the return of Christ.

Premillennialism, then, holds that Christ will raise the church and
return with her to reign literally a thousand years on earth. In this
age the Jewish nation will be reunited and the forces of evil bound
so as to render them impotent. Postmillennialism is a different
variation which has not enjoyed as much popularity in recent
times as the first interpretation. This view holds that Christ will return to set up His earthly rule after the kingdom of God has been
realized spiritually. The inhabitants of the earth will become increasingly more spiritually enlightened as the time of Christ's
appearing nears. The most commonly held view, however, has been
that of amillennialism, which recognizes no special period in history
in which an earthly reign will be established. Moreover, amillennialism rejects the "golden age" theory, which postulates a gradual
betterment or amelioration of society. God Himself will usher in the
end times, which includes the second coming, judgment, and the beginning of the new creation. One or another of these three prominent views of millennialism has been held by small groups of Mennonites, as well as members of other sects and churches throughout
the centuries. The death of Christ, His resurrection, and second coming
have been central themes of faith ever since the founding of the
Christian church, but the intricate character of the second coming has
usually been the object of mere speculation.

The followers of second-coming eschatology are most dedicated
among premillennial groups. According to Revelation, they believe,
a tribulation of the entire world will take place before the second
coming of Christ. Satan will come on earth in the form of a dragon
to persecute Christians. In this, he will find his revenge for his fall

from heaven. Multitudes of people will deny Jesus Christ because of the false promises of this Antichrist.[4] When things look darkest, Christ will come from heaven with a majestic appearance.[5] The antichristian empire will be destroyed, and the dragon will be thrown into the lake of fire for 1,000 years.[6]

Dreamers through the years have sought utopias and "golden ages" connected with this thousand-year period. Although it is mentioned seven times in a few verses of Scripture,[7] it is very incomplete in its description and detail. This left open doors for fantasy and misunderstanding. Early Christians sought a quick return of Christ. Exact dates for His return were predicted as the years progressed. The medieval emperor Otho III (983-1002) believed that the second coming would be during the year 1000. When it did not occur, the monarch became deeply depressed.[8] Joachim of Floris, a Roman Catholic abbot, said Christ would return in the year 1260. He even called Emperor Frederich II (1215-1250) the Antichrist.[9] Other theological persuasions saw the Roman papacy as the Antichrist. During the Reformation a new millennial fervor began because of the translation of the Scriptures into the language of the people. One Michael Stifel foretold the exact year, day, and hour Christ would return to set up His kingdom: October 19, 1533, at 8:00 a.m. In the sixteenth century the elector of Brandenburg, Joachim II, went to Kriegsberg near Berlin to be a firsthand witness to Christ's second coming.[10]

However, in the face of national catastrophes interpreted as divine judgment; millennialism has occasionally taken on the attributes of concrete practice rather than mere belief. This was true in the case of the radical Münsterites and of Melchior Hofmann in the sixteenth century, as well as in the initial movement of the Mennonites to Russia in the late eighteenth century. These radical millenarians emphasized escaping the tribulation of the Antichrist and the finding of a "place of refuge" for themselves and the rest of the remnant who escape the dragon. They claimed to know the exact place and time of the return of Christ, as in the case of Hofmann, or attempted to bring in the kingdom by force, like Münsterites.

Thus millennialism may be invoked as a general escape mechanism for those Christians who experience enormous spiritual and physical conflicts with hostile forces in the world. Their hope must take some tangible form to resolve the conflict. In some cases, it may involve economic factors, such as the landless aspiring to future prosperity. In other cases, political oppression has triggered the impulse to prepare for the second coming. But that does not explain all millennial movements. The phenomenon is one of the most complex, persistent, and interesting in all of religious history.

Millennialism was not indigenous to the early Mennonite faith but found its expression during the Russian experience. Cornelius Krahn, a contemporary Mennonite scholar who has specialized in the teachings of Menno Simons and the history of the Russian Mennonites, states that Menno does refer to the millennium.[11] Another recent authority holds that the early Mennonite leaders, such as Simons, Grebel, Philips, Michael Sattler, Hans Langenmantel, Pilgram Marpeck, Thomas von Imbroich, Leenaert Bouwens, and Peter Riedemann were free of chiliastic leanings, and that millennialism, although introduced by the German Mystics, Pietists, and Baptists, became an important part of the credo of some Mennonites only after the Russian migration.[12] He claims that Russian millennialism came first, after which it filtered to Germany, America, and Switzerland.

The Influence of Jung-Stilling

The same scholar emphasizes that the writings of Johann Heinrich Jung, or Jung-Stilling, Pietist physician and economist, had a profound influence on Russian Mennonites.[13] Jung-Stilling was born in 1740 near Hilchenbach, Westphalia, the son of a tailor and schoolmaster. At the age of fifteen he came to Litzel, where he was influenced by religious separatists, worked as a teacher and tailor, and learned eye treatment from a Catholic priest. He studied this same treatment at Strasbourg between 1770 and 1772, where he met Goethe and Herder. He became well known for his treatment of cataracts, lectured at Kaiserslautern, and became a professor at the universities of Marburg and Heidelberg. Though Jung-Stilling was a prominent figure in the higher circles of society, his first interest was always the service of God.[14]

Jung-Stilling was invited to visit Russia (1812-1813) by Czar Alexander I, and Russian students studying under him at Marburg University insisted that he visit their country. After meeting the czar, Jung-Stilling kept up a lengthy correspondence with him for several years. He became so famous when five volumes of his novel *Der graue Mann* were published in 1812, Russians, including Mennonites, began to study his works with intensity. Mennonites enjoyed his popularity because it gave expression to many of their own

beliefs;[15] for there already existed a number of contacts between
Mennonites and Heinrich Jung-Stilling.[16] He felt a spiritual kinship
with these people because of his early training and sympathy for their
separatist views. Among the scholarly influences on Jung-Stilling was
the historian of the Reformation, Gottfried Arnold, whom Jung-
Stilling frequently relied upon in his writings.[17] In his *Taschenbuch
für die Freunde des Christentums* (1813), he published a biography of
Menno Simons taken from Deknatel's edition of Menno's writings,
which he concludes with the admonition: "It is time to remove from
between the sects the obsolete walls of paper which have hindered
the unity of the spirit and brotherly love for so long a time."[18]

In addition to Jung-Stilling's scholarly knowledge of Mennonites,
he came into personal contact with many individuals. While a professor at Kaiserslautern (1777-1787) he lived in the midst of a Mennonite settlement, and his university lectures detailed their excellent farming techniques, integrity, and industry. He took many study
tours and field trips to their homes and model farms as a part of his
classwork.[19] In the *Stammbuch* of David Mollinger, the grandson of a
Mennonite immigrant from Switzerland, with the date 1767, are two
personal notes from Jung-Stilling.[20] Some personal letters to Mennonites are still extant,[21] and they fully corroborate Goethe's description of Jung-Stilling's absolute dependence upon God.[22] In Jung-
Stilling's autobiography, *Heinrich Jung-Stillings Jugend* (1780), he
recounts many kindnesses he experienced from Mennonite friends.
These friendly gestures by Mennonites greatly influenced his later
writings.[23]

An example of Jung-Stilling's attitude toward Mennonites is
found in his most famous allegorical novel, *Heimweh* (Homesickness-
Nostalgia), published in 1794. This book uses the story of a great
Oriental monarch as the vehicle for a theme similar to that of Bunyan's *Pilgrim's Progress*. In fact, Jung-Stilling's reading of that
novel prompted his own work.[24] The novel concerns an empire
stretching over all of Europe and Asia which is endangered by a secret conspiracy in France. The followers of the emperor form a
counterorganization to protect him. Throughout *Heimweh* there is a
yearning by the monarch's true subjects to reach the final kingdom
of peace in the East among the Tartar tribes of the region of
Samarkand and Bukhara in Central Asia.[25] Eugenius, the hero of
the novel, is reared for this cause by very religious parents, and
ultimately becomes a "prince" in the kingdom. Eugenius begins his

journey to the East accompanied by his faithful servant and has many adventures along the way. These adventures on their eastward journey is a continuing theme of the book. On one such adventure Jung-Stilling pays tribute to Swiss Mennonites by having Eugenius meet his wife in a Mennonite home.[26]

Jung-Stilling expresses a definite belief in millennialism and "withdrawal chiliasm" throughout *Heimweh*. Very passionately he declares that Eugenius "will gather the small band of protected believers from all nations and lead them . . . until the kingdom of our Lord begins. He who has ears let him hear!"[27] That this is a theological injunction is quite evident. Jung-Stilling's fanciful Pietism and chiliasm became an encouragement to certain enthusiastic Mennonites. In *Heimweh* their biblical faith was enhanced. There they learned of the time when the Antichrist will come, rule, and tempt the world, and then according to Revelation 12:4, the only refuge which the Antichrist cannot reach will be Central Asia, the region south of Samarkand.[28]

Not only was *Heimweh* well known among Mennonites, but South German Mennonites adopted one of his hymns, and Jung-Stilling's works were widely read by all Mennonites in general.[29] They were impressed by his deep insight. For example, in the *Taschenbuch*, he calls for a merging of the sects; the Mennonite principle of nonresistance he considered of little hindrance, because if all people became Mennonites coercion would be unnecessary.[30] While showing genuine appreciation for Mennonite faith and life, Jung-Stilling never completely agreed with their belief in pacifism in a world of continued warfare.[31] His admiration for Mennonites could not win him completely to their principles of religion. In spite of these differences, Jung-Stilling's chiliastic influence on the Russian Mennonites was very significant.[32]

After the death of Jung-Stilling, in 1817, his ideas lived on among Russian Mennonites. As the years passed their fervor only increased. One of the first Mennonite teachers in Russia, Tobias Voth, mentions a trip in 1818 to acquire the writings of Jung-Stilling. Through these writings he experienced a religious conversion; to what extent he was further led to accept Jung-Stilling's theories is uncertain. Influenced by these earlier pietistic scholars, Martin Klaassen, a Trakt teacher from the village of Köppental wrote, in 1873, a history book that urged continued belief in nonresistance and the importance of the second coming of Christ. Klaassen's work added to the fever that a move to the east was an absolute necessity for the true believer.[33]

Claas Epp and the East

Among the many who were powerfully touched by Jung-Stilling's *Heimweh* and other works was Claas Epp, Jr., a young farmer of Hahnsau, in the Trakt colony. The Epp family had been a famous one in Prussia, and they had originally come from the village of Fürstenwerder, twelve miles east of Danzig.[34] The family had migrated in 1853 as part of the last major influx of German Mennonites to Russia. Indeed, Claas Epp, Sr., had been the organizer and leader of that expedition which established the Trakt settlement, as well as the founder of Hahnsau, the first and oldest Mennonite village in the Volga region.

Senior Epp went about making Hahnsau a model agricultural village for peasants in the surrounding Volga Valley to emulate.[35] In exchange for their exemplary skill and industry, the Mennonite farmers of Hahnsau were promised free exemption from military service for 20 years, after which time they were expected to pay taxes in lieu of exemption. Each family received 160 acres of land.[36] The village itself was named after Edward von Hahn, a Russian statesman in charge of German migration, and was located in Malyshevka district (*volost*) on Terlic Brook. The original village had 25 families and a total population of 163. Every inhabitant farmed for a livelihood. Though one reason for the migration to the Trakt colony was the exorbitantly high land prices in the Ukraine, most of the inhabitants of Hahnsau, including Epp, had brought considerable capital with them from Prussia. Important to Hahnsau's later development were the traits of diligence and good business sense of its inhabitants and its superior opportunities for education.[37]

Nearby lay the district village of Köppental, founded in 1855, and named after a Russian state counselor who had promoted the settlement. Originally the village consisted of 25 families, each farming 175 acres. The Russian administrative headquarters for the district of the Trakt was located here.[38] Typical of most of the Mennonite villages of the Volga, Köppental was pleasantly situated in the valley of Malish Brook, along which the separate farms were located. High poplar trees lined both sides of the stream so that one could not see from one side to the other. In spring, the Malish would overflow so that the streets and basements were underwater, but for

TRAKT MENNONITE SETTLEMENT, 1897

Village	Year of Settlement	No. of Families	Population 1897
1. Hahnsau	1854		
	Settlers moved to Central Asia in 1880-81		
2. Köppental	1855	36	201
3. Lindenau	1856-59	26	174
4. Fresenheim	1856-59	21	103
5. Hohendorf	1862	18	96
6. Lysanderhöh	1864	22	119
7. Orloff	1871	17	80
8. Valuyevka	1875	8	57
9. Ostenfeld	1872	19	127
10. Medemtal	1872	30	219
		197	1176

youngsters it was joyous for playing in the water.[39] Köppental's schoolhouse was at the south end of the village on the east side of the road, and at a higher elevation than the rest of the houses. At the school the street took a turn and led eastward. Across the road from the school was the district office.

The church, built in 1866, stood immediately east of the district office[40] and was called Köppental-Orloff Mennonite Church after the two villages that cooperated in its construction.[41] The first elder of the congregation was Johann Wall, a companion of Epp, and David Hamm, important in later controversies, became minister. This church left a strong impression on one young man who later wrote:

> I always entered the church with a great deal of awe. It was so quiet and awesome especially when the elder came out of the vestry (Ohmstübchen) into the church with the words, "The peace of God be with you all," and when the procession of venerable ministers took their places. How dignified it all was and what an impression it made on the whole congregation. . . .[42]

Senior Epp, whose family belonged to this congregation, Wall and Hamm, all had strong convictions concerning nonresistance and adhered to the pietistic-chiliastic teachings of Jung-Stilling and others.[43]

The two little villages of Köppental and Hahnsau were centers of millenarian enthusiasm. For the very development of the colony from the beginning, millennialism was as important a factor as was escaping military service. Senior Epp later reminisced about the migration and the "fanatic admixture that came from Prussia."[44] A serious controversy arose early when Elder Wall became so fanatical that Senior Epp had to try to dissuade him from his position to avoid a premature dissolving of the community over the millennium. The reason he gave was that Wall had become too fanatical about the millennium and was illogical in his biblical presentations. Hamm, later a close friend of Claas Epp, Jr., and Martin Klaassen, on whose property the church stood, resented Epp's attack of Wall and began preaching Wall's views. Prophetic messages on Daniel and Revelation were proclaimed each Sunday in the Köppental-Orloff Church. So intense was Hamm's campaign that even Senior Epp had to join the rest of the community in studies of millennial prophecies.[45]

The elder Epp had four sons; Claas, Jr., born on September 9, 1838, was the oldest. Even as a boy, he avidly read and quoted Jung-Stilling's *Heimweh*, which had by this time become a second

Claas Epp, Jr., age 38, and his wife, Elizabeth (nee Jantzen), with their daughter Margareth in 1876. Mrs. Epp is pregnant with Bernhard.

Bible to the chiliasts of Russia. Like his father, Claas, Jr., had a pronounced gift for leadership and was an attractive personality, although he occasionally exhibited ruthless severity. He was successful in agriculture and apparently owned three farms in the village of Orloff in addition to his land in Hahnsau. In 1862, he married Elizabeth Jantzen, a daughter of Abraham Jantzen, and a daughter was born to the young couple that same year, followed by a son, Claas, in 1864.[46] Little is known of Epp's career until a decade later.

In 1874, the great decisions involving the Mennonite migration to America disturbed the normally happy Epp household. Claas Epp, Jr., after much soul-searching concerning the migration and plagued by disagreements with his 69-year-old father over theology and the leadership of the family, decided to stay in Russia, work in private circles, and emphasize the imminent end of the age and the premillennial return of Christ.[47] The Mennonites, he taught, were elected to please God, who had promised them an open door[48] in order to prepare a place of refuge[49] for other believers in the Christian church who were fleeing the tribulation. With a deepening sincerity he incorporated the ideas of Jung-Stilling and set the date of Christ's return so definitely that he could not help being discredited later. The date he said, would come before the end of 1889.[50]

South to Samarkand: A Chiliastic Hope to Meet the Lord

With this prediction of Christ's return the rivalry of the Wall and Epp families continued into the second generation. Cornelius Wall, unlike his father Johann, wholeheartedly embraced Claas Epp's chiliastic views and propagated them through his preaching. So popular did Wall become, that Epp came to regard him as a rival for leadership and realized that only more aggressive and dramatic action on his part would maintain his dominance over this faction. Thus he abruptly demanded that the group begin immediate plans for an eastern migration. The less decisive Wall responded by urging patience, and intense arguments ensued between the rival followers of Wall and Epp over the turnabout. The outcome of this tactical ploy was that Claas Epp and his followers rewon control of the theological leadership of the Trakt community.[51] Even intellectual leaders in the group, such as teachers and ministers, were attracted to Epp's speculations. Epp became their spokesman and prophet.

In 1877, he incorporated his ideas in a book entitled *The*

Die entsiegelte Weissagung

des

Propheten Daniel

und die

Deutung der Offenbarung Jesu Christi,

dargelegt

von

Claaß Epp
in Hahns-Au bei Saratow.

———

Zweite Auflage.

———

Alt-Tschau bei Neusalz a. O.
Verlag von Friedrich August Ruhmer.
1878.

The title page of Claas Epp's book, *The Unsealed Prophecy of the Prophet Daniel and the Interpretation of the Revelation of Jesus Christ.*

Unsealed Prophecy of the Prophet Daniel and the Interpretation of the Revelation of Jesus Christ.[52] This prophetic work not only used the Revelation but also went back into the Old Testament to the Book of Daniel for "unsealed" prophecies. This work is divided into three main chapters dealing with the prophecy to the Gentiles, the prophecy to the Jews, and the prophecy given to Christians, or new covenant people. The book contains a foreword by David Hamm emphasizing the second coming, the "little flock" of faithful followers, and his conviction that Epp was "compelled by the Spirit of God" to write this book. In the second and third editions the author brought his thinking up-to-date in revised prefaces. All three editions were distributed and paid for by Epp himself. The first edition of the book sold out in a few days. Epp's hope was that the book's startling contents, written as a witness in the last days, had awakened the brotherhood of the Trakt.[53] He was not disappointed in this expectation, for everyone read his book and began studying more intensively the doctrines of the judgment and the last days. The message that the coming of the Lord was near perhaps within the next decade, and that only the faithful would be saved[54] was a part of everyone's conversation. The destruction of all European governments except Russia's and the demise of all churches except the "great whore," the Roman Catholic Church, raised many eyebrows and caused hours of discussion.[55]

In the preface to the third edition, Epp explains Jung-Stilling's ideas as developed in *Heimweh.* He points out that before Eugenius went to the place of refuge, south of Samarkand, he went to Europe, joined a Mennonite family, then with his wife and a faithful servant, he searched for his utopia.[56] In this manner, Epp identified himself with the fictional Eugenius who led his followers to Asia. All Epp needed was a reason to implement his theological theories, and that justification was provided when the Mennonites faced the decision of the Russian government to cancel their special privileges.

While many Mennonites continued to plan for emigration to America, Epp's teaching and preaching offered them another alternative. Epp proclaimed that deliverance would be found in the East, south of Samarkand. By 1879, he was urging his followers to sell their possessions and move to Turkestan, a newly acquired Russian province in Central Asia. As the months passed, the fabled land of Turkestan became symbolic of refuge, hope, and salvation to a substantial minority of the families of the Trakt.

5

THE PROVINCE OF TURKESTAN

Geographical Features

At first glance, Turkestan would appear an unlikely candidate for the appellation of "promised land." The geographical setting was far different from the farmlands with which they were familiar. Indeed, it would be an entirely new world.

Turkestan or Central Asia comprises that territory now known officially as Soviet Central Asia or Kazakhstan. The area is bordered on the west by the Caspian Sea and the lower Volga River and extends eastward to the border of China and northward to Siberia. Today it comprises the Kazakh, Kirghiz, Uzbek, Turkomen, and Tadzhik Soviet Social Republics of the USSR.[1] The region covers more than 1,500,000 square miles — approximately one half the size of the United States. It occupies the same ranges of latitude as the territory from Denmark to Algeria or from the southern tip of Alaska to southern California.[2]

The only mountain ranges in Turkestan are the Tien Shan to the east and the Pamir-Alai systems to the south. These two ranges relieve the monotony of steppe and desert.[3] Except for these ranges, the area forms a great basin, once the bed of an inland sea, which was transformed over the centuries into an arid plain. Remaining vestiges of this prehistoric sea are the Caspian Sea, Aral Sea, Lake Balkhash, and some smaller lakes. Fed by melting snow from the mountains, the rivers Amu-Darya and Syr-Darya, the ancient Oxus and Jaxartes of the Hellenistic period, emerge from the mountains. Crossing the desert plains, they pick up a yellow-brown sediment, become wide and shallow, and empty into the Aral Sea.[4] Many dry riverbeds throughout the area testify to a more moist climate and greater plant cover long ago. Even now, snow fields and glaciers in the Tien Shan and Pamirs are diminishing, and the water supply of lakes and rivers is decreasing, though geographers disagree about the rate of further desiccation and whether an equilibrium has been reached. In northern Turkestan there is more water, and the steppe or prairie grasslands are quite different from the semidesert and desert of the south. Most of southern Turkestan, in fact, is desert. Less than three percent of the total land surface is arable without proper irrigation. Rainfall is sparse in all of Turkestan and never exceeds eleven inches per year.[5]

Climatically, the region is controlled by the continental conditions of the great Eurasion land mass of which it is a part. The lack of natural barriers and moderating effect of moisture exposes it to the full extremes of summer and winter temperatures. Winters are made cold and long by frigid air rushing in from Siberia. In January, the coldest month, the temperature on the steppes can drop to -60 degrees Fahrenheit. In the semidesert regions it can reach -40 degrees F. in the west and -57 degrees F. in the east. In the Volga Delta on the northeast border it is a little warmer, but temperatures reach as low as -22 degrees F., and the river is frozen for as many as 112 days each year.[6] Despite the cold weather, there is little snow, but the driving winds quickly pile it into drifts perhaps 25 inches deep in the north and from seven to eight inches in the semidesert region. Spring is very short, and winter cold quickly becomes summer heat. Winds that sweep the Volga become as hot as 104 degrees F. At Kasalinsk, near the mouth of the Syr Darya, the mean July temperature is 79 degrees F.; at Tashkent it is 82 degrees F. The Bukhara region has reached 122 degrees F. on an extremely hot day. The Kara Kum desert sand temperature was once reported at 174 degrees F. in July.[7]

This climate discourages most forms of plant and animal life. Plants are sparse except in the grasslands of the northern steppes; forest and meadows are confined to mountain slopes and river valleys. Only hardier animals such as camels, sheep, and cattle can survive the extremes. A pastoral economy has been practiced in Turkestan since ancient times, with flocks moving between lowlands and highlands following the grass and seasons. Agriculture has been actively practiced in all the river valleys since long before the Chris-

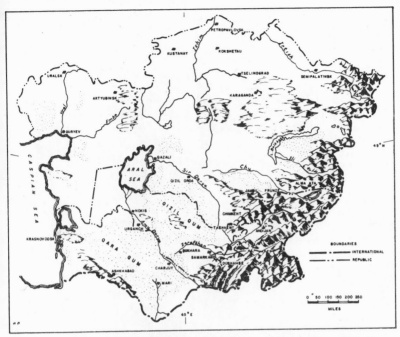

A map showing the topography of Turkestan, now known officially as
Soviet Central Asia or the Soviet Socialist Republics of Kazakhstan,
Kirghizia, Uzbekistan, Turkmenistan, and Tadjikistan.

tian era,[8] but in the desert no agriculture is possible without extensive irrigation.

The desert is an interesting phenomenon. Since the time of
the Kingdom of Bactria-Sogdiana, beginning in the fourth century
BC many geological changes have taken place. The major deserts,
Kara Kum (Black Sands) and Kyzil Kum (Red Sands), have expanded. They form a wilderness that is cracked and sun-blistered
with saline crystallization. In dry weather a camel will barely leave
the impression of its footprint.[9] The high sand dunes of other parts
of the desert are so bright when the sun is shining that one can
be blinded if the eyes are not protected.[10]

In some parts of the desert ancient ruins can be found which
tell of better days.[11] In fact, Central Asia has seen centuries of
better days, for it is here that the lover of ancient history may
wander in the settlements of primitive man, walk in the footsteps
of Alexander the Great, or retrace the scorching tracks of the Genghis

Khan.[12] This entire area came to be controlled by a desert-dominating people — the Muslims.

The Khanates of Bukhara and Khiva

During the sixteenth century two Muslim Uzbek khanates, Khiva and Bukhara, had come to dominate all of Central Asia. Bukhara, "the noble,"[13] became a cultural center, with its conglomerations of low flat-roofed houses of mud and cobbles clustered around the ruins of better days. In the middle of the sixteenth century, Bukhara became the capital of the Uzbek khanate because of the decline of Samarkand. A centralized government arose briefly under Khan Abdullah (1583-1598), a very cruel and brutal man, who used political murder to rid the khanate of his opponents. Khiva, also founded by Uzbek khans in the early sixteenth century, has a history similar to Bukhara's, with as much or more feudal splintering. Khiva became the seat of the Khan in the middle of the seventeenth century after many fights between Uzbek and the Turkomen lords. Bukhara and Khiva knew much trouble throughout their early development.[14]

Nevertheless, both khanates enjoyed a steady expansion of economic life.[15] Their farmers grew wheat, rice, cotton, silk, and a variety of vegetables and fruits that supplied the entire area. The nomads were breeders of horses, camels, cattle, and sheep. Very early in the sixteenth century Russia became dependent on these commodities from Central Asia. Guilds were formed to protect farmer and nomad alike from unfair exploitation, yet the khans remained authoritarian and controlled not only trade with all countries but also received taxes on all products leaving the country.[16]

Any semblance of a permanent centralized authority in Central Asia was impossible, however, and feudalism similar to that of medieval Europe began to develop. Independent provincial governors, called *beks*, ruled in a tyrannical, oppressive way like the nobles of Europe. Even the Muslim "clergy" became involved in feudalism. Caravan trade routes, in decline because of European sea discoveries, further pushed the area into backwardness. All real estate and water was owned by feudal lords, and thus the serfs were made very dependent upon them. For example, Sheik Khodshi-Ismail owned several hundred small and large manors all over Central Asia. He had huge herds and many slaves. Clerics were his caravan masters

The Uzbeks of Turkestan were Sunnite Muslims characterized chiefly by agricultural pursuits and life in towns, although some were nomads.

in trade with Russia, and he became one of the richest men of his day.[17] Class conflict was inevitable and plagued the khanates for centuries.[18] Entering upon a period of decline in the eighteenth century, the khanates became weak as intertribal wars destroyed cities, irrigation projects, and farmlands.

Russian Imperialism

This vacuum of authority permitted Russia, a great imperialistic power, to extend its control over Turkestan. One neglected topic in Russian history, and one of its most interesting, is the expansion of Russia's Central Asian frontiers and their colonization. Russian attempts to establish relations with Central Asia can be traced back to the sixteenth century when Robert Jenkinson, an English merchant in the service of Ivan the Terrible, went to Turkestan to begin trade.[19] From this small beginning, Russia was to launch a sustained effort to absorb Central Asia. After the accession of Peter the Great as czar in 1689, limited inroads were made into Central Asia, but he was far more active in expanding the empire in Europe and other parts of Asia. Upon his death in 1725, Russia controlled almost two million square miles in Europe and over four million square miles in Asia.[20] Russia's push to the southeast, a part of an irrepressible urge to expand, was primarily rooted in a predatory Cossack spirit, a merchant adventurism, and a messianism derived from Moscow's Byzantine Orthodox heritage.[21]

Many churchmen thought it their duty to spread their faith and they traveled with merchants and soldiers. Russian trade grew from its small beginnings in the sixteenth century and by the 1860s was still increasing steadily. Khiva, Bukhara, and Tashkent were involved in trading cotton goods for metal from Russian factories.[22]

As trade increased, so too did the desire for conquest. In fact, Russian conquest of Central Asia was achieved in a relatively short period of time with but a small number of troops. In 1864, an eastern Siberian Frontier Army joined its western counterpart, called the Orenburg Frontier Army. This combined force began preparing to push into Central Asia. The following year the city of Tashkent was stormed by fewer than two thousand soldiers, even though it was defended by thirty thousand men.

On June 15, 1865, near daybreak, a Russian Orthodox priest was the first man to climb the gates of the Sart fortress at

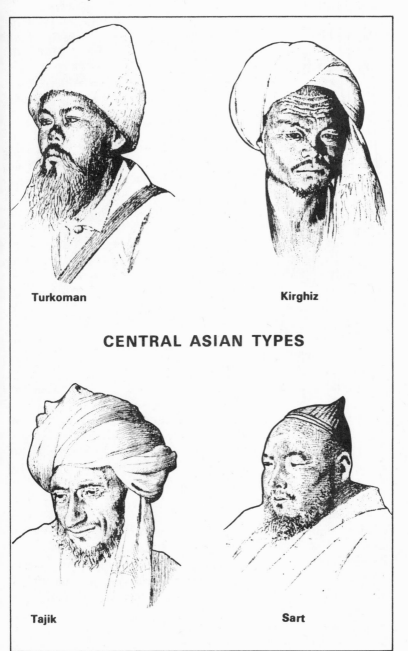

Turkoman

Kirghiz

CENTRAL ASIAN TYPES

Tajik

Sart

Tashkent, thus winning him a military cross because of his valiantly urging the troops to storm the gates for Christ while he waved an ecclesiastical cross over his head.[23] This courageous act was praised by the attacking soldiers because they believed Turkestan must be opened to Russian Christians. Prior to this battle no Christian community had ever existed in this Muslim city.[24] As one visitor at this time wrote, the lust for conquest of the Russians was cloaked in the garb of furthering Christian missions; they used conversion of the infidel as a pretext for extending their power.[25]

No other people were more convinced of their cultural superiority than the Russians, and in no other Muslim country had a non-Muslim encroachment been carried out on such a wide scale. The khanates joined forces to drive out the invader but were soon decisively defeated, and all Turkestan came under Russian dominance during the latter years of the nineteenth century. From tiny Kiev in the ninth century to a continental empire in the nineteenth century, Russia had become the largest nation on the globe.

Russian Provincial System

With the transformation of Turkestan into a colonial province of the Russian Empire, the people of the territory had not only to endure the oppression of local native exploiters but also the national and social oppression of a czarist provincial administration. When the Mennonites entered the province in 1880 they formed only a small part of the total colonization program of the Russians.[26]

It must be clearly understood, however, that during their advance southeastward the Russians did not directly annex all of the Central Asia territories in order to avoid provoking the animosity of Britain, their greatest rival in Asia. It was mainly the lands of the non-Uzbek nomads and the khanate of Kokand that were integrated into the Russian Empire, while the bulk of Bukhara and Khiva technically remained outside the Russian boundary. These continued to be ruled by khans, who, though vassals of the Russian throne, remained independent in their internal affairs. The annexed region was organized into the Turkestan governor-generalship (*guberniia*), headed, as were all other provinces in the Russias, by a military governor-general ruling from Tashkent. In the beginning, his authority extended over three provincial areas: Ferghana, composed of the lands of the former khanate of Kokand; Samarkand, which com-

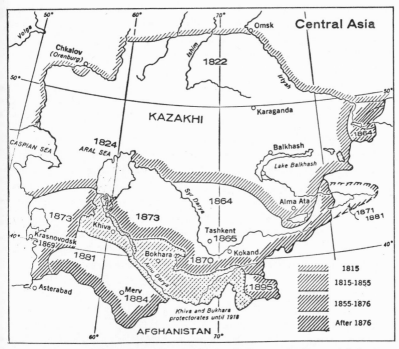

A map showing the expansion of Russian influence in Central Asia during the nineteenth century.

prised the former northeastern section of the khanate of Bukhara; and Syr Darya, which included various territories previously under the administrations of vassals of the khans of Bukhara, Kokand, and Khiva.[27]

No major changes were made in the social organizations of these native provinces in Central Asia after Russian conquest, and traditional features in the system of administration were preserved. While the higher officials — governors, their staffs, and district chiefs (*uezd*) — were Russians or European Russian subjects (Ukrainians, Tartars, or Germans), the subordinate officials of the Muslim villages and towns were native Uzbeks, Kirghiz, Sarts, or Tadzhiks, who were elected as before by the local natives.[28] The court system remained under local control except in lawsuits involving non-natives and criminal cases that were very serious — these were handled by Russian crown courts. This application of the principle of extraterritoriality seemed to work well. Civil suits between the natives were settled by Muslim judges *(kazi)*, also elected by the people.[29] The Russians, however, remained dominant. In the cities, Russians founded neighborhoods designed primarily for non-Muslim populations, but the natives were not prohibited from settling in the new towns *(novii gorodi)*, as the Russian districts were called.

Governor-General von Kaufmann

Russian control of the provinces began officially on July 11, 1867, when Czar Alexander II signed a decree creating the guberniia of Turkestan.[30] Three days later the military chiefs of the czar were summoned to administer the region,[31] and General Konstantine von Kaufmann was chosen as administrator and military commander of Turkestan. This servant of Czar Alexander had an intense zeal to russianize Turkestan.[32] Kaufmann sought to expand schools in the Russian language, increased trade with the Czarist Empire and bring in colonists who would help develop the region agriculturally.[33]

After deciding upon Tashkent as his provincial capital and putting down rebellions in Samarkand and Bukhara,[34] Kaufmann set about organizing his city to serve as a model for all administrative units in Turkestan.[35] Each city, in order to be governed properly, Kaufmann believed, needed a commandant aided by an assistant and office staff, a local garrison controlling a native police force, a surgeon general and a midwife for medical services, and a "town committee" to handle finances, give plots of land to colonists, levy taxes, and provide service such as street-cleaning and repairs, bridge-building, and tree-planting. Later he formed a powerful committee to control all economic administration *(khoziaistrennoi upravlenie)*; it defined city boundaries, laid out new streets, allotted homesites and received payment for these, set aside sites for public parks, listed legal inhabitants of the city, collected taxes, managed irrigation projects, and supervised any other program of development. These administrative units proved most effective as time went on. In fact, taxes were lower under this committee than they had been under native princes. One criticism, however, materialized when the committee allowed merchants to introduce alcoholic beverages.[36] Problems arose over the years, but until rebellious natives attempted to throw off the yoke of Russian imperialism, the administrations ran smoothly.

In 1873, Kaufmann led an all-out offensive against the khanate of Khiva because of continuing rebellions that had arisen there.

Konstantine von Kaufmann served the czar as governor-general of Turkestan from 1867 to 1882.

When victory seemed assured, Kaufmann asked the khan, who would never regain his prestige, to negotiate a settlement. Agreeing to talk, the Khan still feared he would be killed. Gratified to find himself still alive, the khan was even more surprised to learn that Kaufmann had no plans to interfere in native customs or restrict the Muslim faith. Strengthening Russian rule in the territory without antagonizing native customs or religion was Kaufmann's policy. The khan soon learned that native customs would not be altered in the area because Russian plans were more concerned about preservation of law and order than cultural reforms.

From 1873-1882, Kaufmann initiated many explorations and colonizations in Turkestan and became a popular and active governor-general. Although some could consider him a brutal imperialist,[37] others have called him one of the most efficient and enlightened of the military administrators of Turkestan. After fifteen years of service, Kaufmann was called the "founder of the country" (*Ustroitel Kraia*) by the Russians.[38] During the late nineteenth century the native storytellers of Turkestan spoke of three men most often — Alexander the Great, Tamerlane, and Konstantine von Kaufmann; Kaufmann, by all accounts, was the most popular of the three.[39]

But Kaufmann had far to go to transform the sterile, bleak, and forbidding wastes of Turkestan into a civilized and productive province of the Russian Empire. For one thing he needed colonists, skilled agriculturists who would bring their energies to this barren land. This is what first attracted his attention to the Mennonites.[40]

6

PLANS AND HOPES

Development of Migration Theology

Why certain pious Mennonites would consider the eccentric injunction of Epp, a self-appointed prophet, to abandon their fertile farms on the Volga and migrate to the inhospitable territory of Turkestan can be understood only in light of the threat to their faith which they saw in military conscription. While the millenarian teachings of Epp and others provided the inspiration for migration, further Russian efforts to abrogate special Mennonite privileges were the specific grievances which persuaded them to take this course of action.

To be sure, the Russian government had been remarkably indulgent in its efforts to palliate military service for the Mennonites and offered several alternatives which it hoped would satisfy these valuable farmers to the extent that they would not leave their homes. A decree of April 8, 1875, provided that Mennonite men of military age might serve in shipyards, fire departments, or forestry service in lieu of active army duty. But this was not enough to still their opposition to the whole idea. Mennonite leaders feared the corruptive influences of the big city on their youth; forestry service close to home seemed least objectionable. They were at least willing to negotiate on this point. They defined their position in a petition in early 1879, and sent it to Ambassador General Todtleben, a personal representative of the czar on German colonial affairs. They asked that their service have no connection, direct or indirect, with the military machine and that their own ministers be allowed to lead their young men both in their physical and spiritual welfare in the forests.[1]

On Sunday, April 14, 1879, General Todtleben arrived in Halbstadt, Ukraine, to meet with Mennonite representatives from all over Russia and persuade them, if possible, to remain where they were. Mennonite millennialists from the Trakt and Molotschna were at this meeting. Two days later he confidentially told them that the czar was quite concerned about their plight and that he believed an even more liberal change was forthcoming that would be in their favor.[2] A possibility still existed, however, that they would be used in workshops, as firemen, and in forestry service.[3] Whatever their area of service to the state, promised Todtleben, they would be under the supervision of Mennonite clergymen, and there would be no need to carry arms. In closing, Todtleben pointed out that they were already receiving special consideration in the matter. He added that if Russia had more Mennonites as citizens there would not be as many problems nor even a need for a military machine.[4]

Many at this meeting were moved to tears because of the apparent governmental compromise, and others, including some aspiring Turkestan migrants, abandoned their plans to leave European Russia. Nevertheless, many who trusted neither the Russian government nor its promises preferred to be free rather than be forced to serve the government. Particulars concerning their prospective journey were beginning to come into the news.

As early as April 7, 1880, a German-American newspaper, *Zur Heimat*, gathered reports about "migration fever" to Turkestan. About one hundred families on the Volga, led by Claas Epp, and one hundred families in the Molotschna, led by Abraham Peters, were preparing to leave their homes. They did not want to move to the west, nor did they want any kind of alternative service. Yet they had no official sanction to migrate anywhere. Consequently they appealed to influential people in St. Petersburg to obtain aid to go to Turkestan. Their requests were repeatedly denied.[5]

Deputation to St. Petersburg

Deputies from both regions had been elected by the people to seek advice and help. Johann Epp and Martin Klaassen from Köppental and Abraham Peters, a dedicated minister, and Franz Buller from Molotschna had earlier gone to the governor of the

Caucasus asking for an order from the czar granting them freedom from alternative service and the right to go to Turkestan. The czar, they were told, rejected their appeal.[6]

Then several other delegations were chosen to go to St. Petersburg to request specific permission to journey to Turkestan.[7] Hearing that Governor-General Kaufmann might speak in their behalf, they went to St. Petersburg to see him. He stated that he would appreciate their presence in Turkestan and promised to ask the czar to suspend the draft law for several years and give them the right to migrate to Turkestan. This first attempt failed, however.[8]

It was after this failure that they decided once again to petition General Todtleben, who had always been sympathetic to their needs. On November 1, 1879, they appealed to him for permission to go to Turkestan under the provisions of the migration law of June 1871. Todtleben is reported to have answered somewhat equivocally:

> I love and esteem the Mennonites. I represented them as if I had been a Mennonite and had a difficult time because of it. But now the situation is this: you now wish to escape army duty and establish a project like you wished to find when you came to Russia. Let the young men plant a forest under guidance of a clergyman as you desired before. Then come to me with a project and I will represent you in St. Petersburg. It will not be as up to now — everyone will be protected. I am not yet with you. Wait a year and you will see.[9]

In regard to their plans to migrate to Turkestan he explained that he felt military law would be introduced there within ten years and they could not escape forestry service there either, even if they did not enjoy planting.[10] Regarding migration, he believed it would be impossible to permit it because they would be unprotected in that strange land. In Russia, however, Mennonites could live protected in their belief, and, if they were clever, they might not be required to do very much. The most they would be used for was forest planting in Taurida Province, he said. Even before his general meeting at Halbstadt, he realized that Mennonites would not serve well in other services.[11]

Despite this contrary advice, and still without official sanction of their plans, Epp and his followers continued to prepare for their journey. During the late fall of 1879, these peaceful millennialists persisted in their efforts to obtain permission from St. Petersburg to move to Turkestan. A delegation made up of Jacob Toews, Johann Epp, and Martin Klaassen from the Trakt community, and Abraham Peters, the ministerial leader from Molotschna, traveled to the capital of the Russian Empire to obtain a firm answer to their many requests.

The situation was quite tense in St. Petersburg when they arrived because of several attempts to assassinate Czar Alexander, and the secret police were suspicious of these German Mennonites. After settling in their hotel they sought the help of a Mennonite sympathizer, a Pastor Hans of the Moravian Brethren Church. Through him they were introduced to Pastor Datton, the influential minister of the Reformed Church, and Baron von Mirbach, an active Christian layman and personal attendant of the czar. The Mennonites were much impressed by Mirbach's Christian attitudes.[12] Mirbach, however, cautioned that although he was sympathetic to their cause, he did not wield as much political power as they believed. He did say he would try to influence the minister of the interior in their behalf but very warmly urged them not to leave Russia because he had heard that Governor-General von Kaufmann only wanted them in Turkestan to help expand the silk culture. Mirbach said he believed Kaufmann wanted strong young settlers to help his own position.[13]

Despite Mirbach's warning, Toews and the others made contact with Minister of the Interior Ivanov, who very unexpectedly said he favored their cause completely and would help them all he could. After seeing Ivanov the delegation heard that Kaufmann was in the city and they decided to seek an audience with him.

Kaufmann was also very cordial and emphasized that there was plenty of free land for good farmers and freedom from military service in Turkestan. He could not promise, however, that young men over twenty could come, because Russian draft regulations required them to stay in their territory of registration. He did say he was planning to see the czar, who was in the Crimea, and agreed to ask him if this regulation could be reversed. Kaufmann then promised to meet with the Mennonite delegation on his return trip in two or three weeks. The hopes of the delegation were encouraged by this cordial reception.

After Kaufmann's return to the capital he informed the delegation that the czar had given permission for the Mennonites to emigrate to Turkestan, and that free land and exemption from military obligations would be the reward for their journey. Concerning

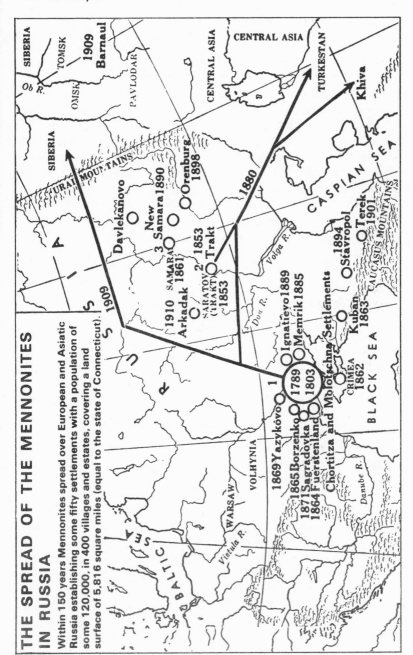

THE SPREAD OF THE MENNONITES IN RUSSIA

Within 150 years Mennonites spread over European and Asiatic Russia establishing some fifty settlements with a population of some 120,000, in 400 villages and estates, covering a land surface of 5,816 square miles (equal to the state of Connecticut).

the young men over twenty, however, he said he did not want to take away the prerogative of the minister of the interior on that subject. So the supplicants paid a second call on Ivanov. To their chagrin, the minister emphatically stated that all young men over twenty must stay and perform military service, but all others would be exempt. This, he declared, was his final position. Thus the encouragement by Kaufmann was negated by Ivanov's obstinacy.[14]

The delegation returned home discouraged about their prospects for migration; they believed the entire party would not favor leaving the young men behind, because the enforced service requirement was one of their major reasons for wanting to go to Turkestan in the first place. After telling the brethren of the favorable contacts with Kaufmann, they explained the major barrier to the migration. The congregations agreed with the delegation and decided to postpone any immediate plans for a trip until they could obtain influential help to get Ivanov to change his position. At this point many were very undecided about going to Turkestan.

A Secret Trip to Tashkent

In December 1879, during this period of doubt, two Mennonites, Jacob Hamm of the Trakt and Peter Wiebe of Molotschna, secretly and without permission of the entire group, decided to take the responsibility upon themselves to go to Turkestan, confer with Kaufmann on his home soil, view the settlement sites, and see if any new policy was forthcoming from Ivanov. After traveling to Orenburg, where the railroad ended, they decided to spend the Christmas holidays in that city. But an opportunity arose to travel with a Russian official on his mail service transportation permit, so they left for Tashkent on December 24, 1879.

Upon arrival, they were well received by Kaufmann and began seeking information about settlement plans and the military draft. While they were there, Kaufmann telegraphed Ivanov to request a decision on the draft status of the young men. Under this pressure, the minister reversed his earlier decision, granted permission for the young men of draft age to serve the government in Turkestan rather than their home province. He further granted fifteen years of exemption from service for those under twenty years of age and remitted taxation for all the Mennonites for that same period. Hamm and Wiebe were elated by this new development and questioned Kaufmann about the settlement sites. Responding to this, the governor-general ordered his real-estate counselor to prepare a location at Kaplan Bek, a former military post near Tashkent. Kaplan Bek was designated as a temporary settlement for a year until the Mennonites could find more suitable accommodations.[15] At last the way seemed open for the great migration.

Arguments Against Migration

Hamm and Wiebe returned to their home, eagerly relating what had occurred in Tashkent. Though Epp, Toews and the other leaders did not appreciate their unorthodox and secret trip, the enthusiastic emissaries insisted that Turkestan not only would offer a favorable land for settlement free from military obligations but (that they would also) be free to practice their millennial faith. After much debate the group decided to prepare to leave for Turkestan, and enthusiasm for migration was again at fever pitch.[16]

Government officials, hearing of the new situation, urged the governor of Samara Province to dissuade the millennial farmers from their plan to migrate, and this he attempted to do. After gathering Epp, Hamm, Cornelius Wall, and other leaders together, he argued that military conscription laws would soon be the same in Turkestan as in Russia and that it would do them no good to migrate because "as the Russian scepter goes so goes the law for military service." The Mennonites responded by saying that as long as there were fifteen years of freedom in Turkestan they would prefer to leave Russia.[17]

Then the governor attacked their millennial position. After studying intensively the prophetic passages of the Bible, reading Epp's book twice, and exhibiting a thorough knowledge of its contents, he praised Epp for his clarity of style. But he rejected Epp's arguments and urged the group to reconsider their position if they were motivated primarily by their millennialist convictions rather than merely their desire to aid their young men in evading the draft. The Mennonites responded that they knew it was the duty of the governor to dissuade them, but he could never discourage them from a millennial faith and nonresistance. Further, they admitted that some of his arguments would deter a few from making the trip, but they knew he would not tell them they *could* not go but only that he believed they *should* not go.[18]

Agreeing that he was limited in his power to forbid the migration, the governor then broached the subject of Kaufmann's commitment to them. He suggested that Kaufmann would be disappointed in them because he was expecting a thousand families, not the mere 200 which were gathering for the trip. He warned that not only would Kaufmann's goal of a fruitful Turkestan never materialize, but that the Mennonite communities left behind would be severely weakened as well. A settlement of 200 families, moreover, could not remain in Turkestan because the provincial government would not protect them as they would thousands of colonists. In answering these arguments of the governor of Samara, Epp and the Volga representation at the meeting declared that if need be, they would settle in the independent Islamic countries bordering Turkestan.[19] Besides, the Mennonite millennialists still had faith in Kaufmann's assurances, expressed in a telegram of December 31, 1879, that 200 families would gladly be accepted in Turkestan. Epp and his brethren claimed that the hand of God had favored their plans and that not even the governor of Samara or the czar could dissuade them.[20] Their theology was more important to them than human knowledge or reason.

In fact, confidence abounded in their "new revelation" which rejected so defiantly the ways of the world. Belief was strong that the Lord would bless them only if they did His will. Turkestan, moreover, seemed the only outlet for their plight. They could no longer follow a czar who would soon serve the Antichrist nor inhabit a modern state which was hostile to Christ, a product of the human mind, and devoid of spiritual insight. They would withdraw from this "worldly majority."

Not only did the Russian government oppose their plans, but fellow Mennonites were equally critical of their proposed trek. Many refused to accept millennialism as a valid biblical teaching and spoke out against the idiosyncracies of Epp. A vigorous opponent, Isaac Peters, is quoted in later years as having believed that the founder of the Mennonites, Menno Simons, "never believed in the millennium and whoever does is no Mennonite."[21]

Forming of the Bride Community

To answer these critics, the Epp faction wrote an elaborate vindication of its enterprise and had it published.[22] They justified their undertaking, first of all, as one which followed biblical revelation rather than the "worldly majority." They believed that both the Old and New Testaments revealed God's will that they must follow a higher calling as good disciples of Jesus Christ. Thus, the evil modern state had no right to control God's people. Secondly, they were unwilling to substitute state service in the place of army duty because both meant involvement in non-Christian activities. The kingdom of God, based on peace, could not be served if Mennonites became involved with a modern state that believed in warfare. The saving sword of the Spirit was needed more in the world than the killing sword of the state. Since a true Christian cannot serve two masters, the millennialists totally committed themselves to the Spirit of God; their opponents, they charged, were instruments of the Antichrist.

Finally, the Epp faction offered a vision of the future. They were seeking a utopia free from authoritarian rule, with freedom of conscience, strong church education, and freedom of belief foremost in their minds. They wanted safety from the "fire of war" and a place where the law of God ruled over all other laws. Since they believed that the "time of tribulation" had already begun, they worried about the "last days." They did not want to defy the Russian government, which had done much for Mennonites, but they decided they must first obey God because they were but strangers and pilgrims. These were their motives for emigration.[23] They decided to leave the Volga that summer.

In the late spring of 1880, two separate groups, one from the Trakt settlement led by Epp and another under Abraham Peters of the Molotschna colony, began final preparations to travel eastward. After much dissension within his congregation, Peters convinced his people to accept the chiliastic teachings, and they began preparations to join the Trakt community in their venture.[24] Several families from the Kuban region of the Caucasus who were of the same persuasion and had been forced to leave their homes also joined the Molotschna movement.[25]

All these people had reached the point at which they could no longer endure the demands of their society. They began to feel discriminated against by those in their respective communities who decided to remain. Tension, in fact, became so pronounced that even the millennial migrants separated into two parties. The division arose over whether to continue to follow Claas Epp and his teachings or to countenance the criticism by the government and fellow

Mennonites who tried to dissuade them from their plans. A few simply did not know what to do.

To restore unity of purpose, Epp called for a communion service at Hahnsau on June 25, 1880. Only about 35 families came, but only one would remain behind when the migration began.[26] This communion celebration led to the separation of the Epp faction known as the "Bride Community" — a body of believers totally dedicated to the goal of meeting Christ the Bridegroom in Central Asia. The Bride Community became the nucleus of leadership for the entire Turkestan migration, but their superpiety and intransigence would contribute to future schisms. In fact, dissension was exacerbated, not dispelled. Uncertainty about future plans caused great anxiety and the fear that perhaps God had forsaken them. Some said it was Epp's superpiety that would annihilate the movement. Others believed Epp to be the only leader who could restore hope to the group.[27]

Despite criticism, the movement inspired by Epp found many natural leaders who were ready to support the Bride Community on their proposed expedition: men like Cornelius Wall, the image of an Old Testament prophet with his long flowing beard, and Jacob Toews, a minister of outstanding ability. Franz Bartsch, a teacher with great intellectual capacity, and Martin Klaassen, who had written a book about Mennonites, also came to the fore. Other leaders were the Penner brothers, J. K. and Wilhelm, both ministers and teachers, and Hermann Jantzen, a strict disciplinarian and leader of men. All were ready and willing to follow Epp and his doctrine.[28]

During this period when new leadership came forward to support Epp, some American Mennonite voices raised a new protest against his movement. The editor of *Zur Heimat*, a pragmatic realist, warned that even with considerable support the Epp venture was destined to fail because of the dissension and splits in the movement. Prospects of peace and unity in a distant "utopia," he wrote, would never come to pass if Mennonites could not agree in their Russian homeland. The hardships of a trip to Turkestan, he warned, would only heighten dissension. Even the supposed cement of religious unity, he concluded, would only be torn apart by millennial controversy.[29]

In spite of this new criticism and increased divisions, Epp continued promoting plans for emigration. Through intense Bible studies he repeatedly emphasized the necessity of following revelation, escaping military conscription, and finding freedom in a place of refuge from the Antichirst.[30] Since Russian conscription law did not immediately affect Turkestan, it appeared the Lord was opening a door to Epp and his faithful followers.[31] For the remnant of Mennonites, he believed, moving eastward was the only hope for Christianity in the last days. The barren but promising land of their vision was Turkestan, where they hoped to meet the Lord.

7

BEGINNING THE TREK

As the summer of 1880 approached, the Mennonite millennialists of Russia began busily preparing for their impending trip. The first contingent left in July 1880; the last arrived in Turkestan in December 1881. The first two trains originated from the Trakt; the third came from the Molotschna colony; and the fourth and fifth left from the Trakt. Before this great trek was finished, the five wagon trains would make their way across steppe, desert, and mountain to the new Russian province. Some of the participants in this journey would remain in this new land, while a majority would leave a few years later to find a refuge in America.

In their preparations, new improvements to their wagons to equip them both for desert and winter travel were most important. New hoops were attached to the wagon bed; over these was placed a layer of felt blanket, a linen cover, and then a waxed cloth to make them dustproof, waterproof, and warm. These were large box wagons, some having a door with a window in the rear and in some cases even a nursery inside. Other wagons had the door at one side, the window at the other. The largest wagons had no rear door but a small compartment where articles used frequently were easily accessible. Usually a bundle of hay was stored on top of this compartment in case the travelers could not buy feed along the route.[1]

All but one family of the original 35 of the Bride Community would eventually desert Hahnsau to join the trek, but at first only 16 families were prepared to leave.[2] Though Epp had aroused their enthusiasm to a fever pitch at the communion service of June 25, six of the 16 families elected to delay their departure pending further preparations.[3]

First Wagon Train

Thus only ten families formed the vanguard of a migration that would eventually involve some 600 people. The families of this vanguard group had to postpone their departure briefly when the young daughter of Franz Bartsch, a future Turkestan leader, died, and Epp, out of sympathy for the grieving father, delayed the train for two days for the burial.[4] After the funeral, on July 3, 1880, this wagon train, composed of 17 wagons, some 20 adults, 29 children, and 40 horses left Hahnsau for a promised place of refuge in Turkestan.[5] Claas Epp, Jr., the chief inspirer of this adventuresome trip, accompanied the group for several days but returned to his home in Hahnsau after preaching a farewell sermon. He continued his custom of going part way with each group until he finally left with the fifth wagon train. Epp appointed two competent brethren, Jonas Quiring and Wilhelm Penner, to care for the temporal and spiritual needs of this first group until he could join them. Quiring was to be their minister and Penner the community teacher.[6]

Hardships of the Journey

This modest caravan, composed of more children than adults, began their trek into the unknown territory that lay to the east. Traveling along the mail road past the city of Uralsk, they forded the Ural River. Then driving along its left bank, they slowly approached Orenburg, the end of the railway and gateway to Asia. As they paralleled the river they noticed the change from Russian to Oriental civilization. On the narrow rutted roads they saw nomadic Kirghiz vendors bringing their goods to the Orenburg market on the backs of camels. Franz Bartsch, who spoke some Tartar, conversed with these vendors, and the young people learned many Kirghiz words, which later proved most helpful. In the city of Orenburg, they rested and were met by several Mennonite families who had come to bid them a last farewell. With each successive wagon train Mennonite friends exhibited their loyalty by at least coming to Orenburg to see the millennialists on their way.

Unlike the caravans to follow, this first group then turned south to the small town of Motzkaya Sashchita, where they bought supplies of rock salt which was produced there.[7] Turning eastward toward Aktube and Fort Karabutak, they rejoined the mail road running from Orsk to Kasalinsk, the route subsequent wagon trains would take. Here two infant sons of Henry Wiebe became seriously ill, died, and were buried together in one coffin at the military cemetery. Two simple crosses were left to mark their grave.[8]

As the journey progressed across the silent steppe, the only relief from the creaking wagons, jingling of harnesses, and an occasional whinnying of horses was the large handbell in the lead wagon. This bell was used for everything from a clock striker to a church bell. In the morning it was rung as an alarm clock, it called the pilgrims together for meals, and for morning and evening devotions. On Sundays, when the caravan rested, the bell summoned them for two worship services — one in the morning and one in the evening. After the bell sounded, either Wilhelm Penner or Jonas Quiring, the appointed leaders, generally led the service. Often, when the wagon train would stop at night, the landowner would ride up and ask them what they were seeking. The answer inevitably was, "We are Germans from the Volga. In faith we are going to Turkestan where freedom has been promised us."[9]

Until they reached the city of Irgis, sometimes by way of the mail road and partly using the caravan road running parallel to it, they had an uneventful trip. Now a challenge faced them in the form of a 135-mile stretch of the Kara Kum Desert, which they had to cross. To prepare for the upcoming desert ordeal, they purchased food, feed for the animals, and hired camel drivers and camels to help carry the extra load.

As the caravan proceeded, it presented a colorful sight. The Kirghiz drivers, clothed in multicolored robes and lofty turbans, were mounted on small mountain camels. With an air of dignity and solemnity, each led a column of ten camels in a slow but steady pace across the steppe. The Mennonites were impressed not only by the bearing of their guides, but also by their generosity and willingness to share their modest provisions. Soon after leaving, the Kirghiz milked their camels, prepared mutton with rice, and gave it to their employers. The camel drivers pointed out many Kirghiz tent villages (*au-uls*) as they continued into the desert.

In the desert, the caravan had to cut its own road through the sand dunes; the deep sand gave the horses much difficulty in pulling the wagons. Therefore, a relay system which would be used repeatedly was set up by which each wagon was pulled over a stretch of sand by five horses; men then rode these horses back, hitched them to another wagon and pulled it forward. During this long and painful crossing of about three weeks, water was very scarce, and if the Kirghiz drivers had not led them to deep wells they might have perished. In fact, the horses were continually thirsty, and many of the children became ill, probably because of the lack of good milk and water. As the children grew weaker from diarrhea and dehydration, the desert became a burning hell for the travelers. In all, the Kara Kum claimed eleven children among these ten families. In spite of the precaution of boiling all water, every child under four died before the journey was over.[10]

The Aral Sea was a welcome sight to these weary travelers, and the horses and remaining 38 people drank their fill of water from springs near its shores. After arriving at the city of Kasalinsk on the Syr Darya, they stopped for a week to give everyone a rest and to care for the remaining members of the group who were still ill. They then moved on toward Fort Perovsk. This journey was comparatively pleasant, because they followed the beautiful Amu Darya through a heavily wooded region where they found pheasants and many kinds of berries. They rested in Perovsk for a day, and after crossing the swift-running Aries River, they departed for the historic city of Turkestan, after which the province was named. From this point they hurriedly traveled to the city of Chimkent, where a festival was in progress. Here they purchased the necessary food for themselves, bought feed for the horses, and started for Tashkent and the final portion of their journey.

One evening while on this final leg of their journey, the travelers were startled by an unexpected visitor. During their nightly devotional meeting, a Russian troika drove up, and one of the two men inside asked them what type of meeting they were holding. When they answered, they discovered that one of the two men inside was Governor-General von Kaufmann himself! After recognizing some of the leaders, he became very friendly, advised them as to which road they should take, and suggested they should plan to winter in Kaplan Bek, a former military post about thirteen miles from Tashkent. Wilhelm Penner left the next day to make arrangements for their stay and returned with a delegation from Kaplan Bek. The Mennonites were overjoyed that their grueling trip was finally nearing an end.

Arrival in Kaplan Bek, October 18, 1880

Finally, after two more days' driving, they reached their goal on October 18, 1880.[11] The 1,780-mile trip thus far had consumed fifteen weeks, and fourteen children had died along the way. Exhausted, the band took up winter quarters in Kaplan Bek. The land formerly had belonged to a Kirghiz bek (or lord), who raised horses there, but Governor Kaufmann had requisitioned the land for temporary quarters for the Mennonites. Now they began to prepare for winter. Only two houses on the property were habitable, while the rest of the buildings were suitable for the horses. This meant that almost 40 people had to live in cramped circumstances. Finding this too inconvenient, the men purchased lumber to build more houses and to improve the horse stalls, and new doors and windows were added to improve the family dwellings.

While his brethren made the quarters suitable, Wilhelm Penner went to see the governor-general about future land hopes. When Penner described the length and perils of the journey, Kaufmann was surprised that they had completed the trip in only 15 weeks and expressed sympathy concerning the deaths of the 14 children. During the entire meeting with Penner, Kaufmann was most cordial and often reassured the hapless traveless, "The Lord will help you."[12] In the light of the previous warnings that they would never complete the journey and that Kaufmann would never receive them, this vanguard group at least had the satisfaction that they had completed one phase of their millennial dream. Though they were decimated by disease, they took heart in Kaufmann's willingness to help them. The immigrants believed the Lord was pleased with their plans.

The Second Wagon Train, August, 1880

As the weary travelers settled into Kaplan Bek for the winter, a second band of pilgrims was still making its way to Tashkent.[13] Under the leadership of Heinrich Jantzen of Köppental, this group consisted of some 13 families with about 30 wagons. They had set out from Medemtal village in the Trakt on August thirteenth, more than a month after the first wagon train.[14] As was the custom, they celebrated their leave-taking with a worship service; for a moment at least, all dissension and bitterness were put aside as the parting group bade a tearful farewell to their neighbors.[15]

As they traveled toward their destination they maintained the strict order that their wagon master, a right-hand man of Claas Epp, insisted upon. In fact, Jantzen's strictness was applauded, and his regulations were willingly followed. They made a colorful procession, as wagons in single file were joined by two large buggies, several smaller ones, and a green glass carriage.[16]

During the first stage of their journey, Jantzen tried to camp near settled areas at night. In the evening, they made a circle of wagons so that the rear wagon came to a halt immediately in front of Jantzen's wagon. Another custom that was rigidly observed was the holding of evening and morning worship services. The entire group stood in the center of the wagon circle, hymns were sung, Scripture read, and prayers given by either Jacob Toews, a minister, or J. K. Penner, the teacher brother of Wilhelm Penner, coleader of the first wagon train.

This wagon train was to be plagued by excessive rain from its first day on the trail. Muddy roads delayed its departure from the German Lutheran village of Gnadendorf the second day out, and after passing through a countryside dotted with German and Russian villages, the sodden procession pulled up at the district capital, Novo-Urensk, where they spent their first rainy Sunday. Notwithstanding the inclement weather, the pious pilgrims observed the Sabbath with their accustomed enthusiasm. A temporary pulpit was constructed, from which Jacob Toews delivered the sermon and J. K. Penner led the music. All songs were from the hymnbook *Die frohe Botschaft* (Glad Tidings) used throughout the journey and their favorite hymn became "Our Journey Leads Through the Desert."[17]

The following Sunday, J. K. Penner once again led the music and prayed that God would bless them as they broke the way for others to follow. And indeed, Mennonites all over the world were following with interest the progress of the trek.[18] A contemporary German newspaper predicted that many Mennonites would follow the example of this group. Unaware of this distant interest in their progress, the brethren on the wagon train were far more interested in their unfamiliar surroundings. These parochial people were fascinated by the camel caravans that made their horses shy and appalled by the squalid Russian farms where pigs rooted in the front yards of the unusual adobe-type homes.

Arriving at Orenburg, the group was strengthened by the unexpected arrival of several young men and some influential leaders,

and a host of letters from home helped to dispel the gloom attendant to traveling in the rain. Hermann Jantzen and Cornelius Quiring from the Trakt and Dietrich Peters and Peter Quiring from Molotschna arrived in camp at the same spot where the previous wagon
train had stopped — midway between the city and a Cossack military
post along the bank of the Ural River. They had come from St. Petersburg, where they had just received discharges from the army in order
to join the trek to Turkestan. The arrival of Elder John Wiebe and
relatives of Jacob Toews, who came from the Trakt to bid them farewell, cheered the travelers even more. The last mail had delivered
scores of letters from each family of the group.[19]

Unlike the first wagon train, which had turned south at Orenburg, this band continued eastward to Orsk by way of a good road
with excellent bridges and a telegraph line running parallel to it.
Haystacks dotting the countryside and fields of oats ready for harvest made these Mennonites homesick for the Trakt. When they arrived at Orsk, the weather was pleasant, Kirghiz natives were very
hospitable, and supplies were purchased for the long trip to Kasalinsk.
A camel caravan was hired to carry supplies, including four tons
of oats for the horses. Following the mail road, they arrived at
Fort Karabutak near the end of September, still in "good condition
and without casualty by death or accident" up to this point.[20] The
fort consisted of a few buildings, an armory, and several small
homes. Before leaving Karabutak, they paid their respects at the
grave of Heinrich Wiebe's two small sons.[21]

Over halfway between Orsk and Kasalinsk, the group had to
cross the dreaded Kara Kum Desert. Traveling through deep sand,
they sometimes had to search with the camel drivers for several
miles to find a well. The water was boiled, given to each of the 45
horses, and then shared by the people. Compared to the first
train, their sufferings on the desert were mild. In fact, they even enjoyed some festive days. The Martin Klaassens observed their twenty-
fifth wedding anniversary, and the group, led by J. K. Penner, sang
their favorite song, *"Es erglänzt uns von ferne ein Land"* ("There's
a Land That Is Fairer Than Day"). Later they celebrated the same
anniversary of Heinrich Jantzens. Indeed these events were brief
moments of joy amid adversity.[22]

After entering the province of Turkestan at the the sand dune
village of Tereki, they observed the Lord's Supper and all went to
the grave site of three children who had died on the previous

A page from the diary of Heinrich B. Jantzen, wagon master and right-hand associate of Claas Epp.

wagon train. Near the end of the desert, the elderly Mrs. Wiebe became very ill, and plans were made to hurry her ahead to Kasalinsk. However, with the assistance of Mrs. Jacob Toews, she improved, and the weary band made it through the desert without
a major mishap. As their first view of the Aral Sea told them that the
perilous desert journey was over, they rejoiced in their good fortune
at having withstood the ordeal so successfully.

Arriving at Kasalinsk, the first completely Muslim town, they
reached level ground again, and the weather was so pleasant that
the children ran barefoot alongside the wagons. The dwellings of the
town were all of adobe, and camels roamed the clean, beautiful
streets and marketplaces. All races of people were here: Russians,
Kirghiz, Sarts, Tartars, Bukharans, and Jews; here also the Syr
Darya flowed southeastward toward Tashkent. Governor Kaufmann
had left orders for the inhabitants to allow the party of Mennonites
to stay in Kasalinsk for the winter if they wished. In fact, the governor remained helpful and accommodating throughout the remainder
of the journey and always seemed well informed about their
progress.[23]

Upon leaving Kasalinsk, the train was delayed by a broken axle
and a camel falling through a weak bridge. But after this delay they
traveled parallel to the Syr Darya, and on the first of November
reached Fort Perovsk, still some 500 miles from Tashkent. Here they
encountered a terrain more difficult than any they had passed
through. Two wagons tipped over in the rocky road. Winter weather
set in, the temperature fell to near zero, and it began to snow so
hard that cooking in the open was impossible; wet clothes remained frozen for days, fuel was difficult to find, and the horses
were without shelter.[24] In mid-November the frozen group reached
the city of Turkestan, encamped near the Russian quarter of the
town, and bought needed supplies. While there, they were notified
that the first wagon train had reached Kaplan Bek, and that negotiations with Kaufmann were going well. With this encouragement they
hurriedly left the city and headed for Tashkent.[25]

In a few days they reached the turbulent waters of the Aries
River, from which they could see the Terek hills in the distance.
They had been told that when this range was crossed, their journey
was almost complete. Kirghiz natives helped the Mennonites across.
Half of the wagons were pulled across the dangerous river with the
aid of the teams of the rest of the group. One young man riding a

team of horses back across the river to the next wagon was suddenly swept into the current. Witnesses say he would have perished if it had not been for an alert Kirghiz who jumped from the steep bank into the water and with his long knife cut the lines and harnesses in which the horses had become entangled and pulled both the young man and the horses out of the water. It was not the first time that these natives had rescued the Mennonites.[26]

On the following day they reached the city of Chimkent, which was almost flooded from the rain. But here they found a friendly reception, food, and poplar trees which reminded them of their homes at Köppental. As they left the city for the south, the rocky foothills through which they had been traveling turned into a mountain range. The rain and snow continued, and they made only four miles the first day. Slushy roads impeded their progress, and once again they found soaked diapers and clothes frozen like chunks of ice. Crossing these mountains proved to be a more arduous task than the desert had been.

Arrival in Kaplan Bek, November 24, 1880

On November 24, they broke camp in the middle of the night in order to arrive at Kaplan Bek that day. With a Kirghiz guide leading the way, they branched off the mail route, crossed cultivated fields, hurried over shallow canals and rickety bridges, swayed along crooked roads, trudged through swampy areas, and finally forded the Keles River to arrive at their destination. The trials of their final day turned to joy when they met the brethren who had arrived four weeks earlier.

8

THE TREK CONTINUES

The new arrivals from the Trakt were soon to be joined in Kaplan Bek by a group from the Molotschna colony of European Russia. This group had long prepared for a rendezvous with their comrades in the faith with much enthusiasm for the entire venture.[1]

Preparations and Millennialism

But material preparations were not of primary concern to this band. More important to them, they believed, was their renewed emphasis on the prophetic passages of the Bible and their relationship to millennialism. These studies centered in the village of Gnadenfeld, where a conservative Flemish tradition had long emphasized evangelism, pietism, and a strong missionary impulse, and gave a new religious vigor and enthusiasm to the prophecy of the last days.[2] Moreover, a recent immigration of ardently millennialist Mennonite Brethren families from the Kuban regions, intensified the fervor of the entire colony.[3]

The most active promoter of millennialism and migration was Abraham Peters, who had become pastor of the Orloff-Newkirk congregation in 1860, the same year the Mennonite Brethren Church was formed. He had been deeply influenced by the pietistic sermons of a Lutheran pastor, Edward Wüst, and his church was a bastion of the conservative tradition — evangelism, total abstinence, and baptism by immersion. Peters was a dynamic speaker and won many followers through prayer and Bible study meetings as Wüst had done before him. In fact, as a newly ordained minister, he played a significant role in the religious revival which swept through the Molotschna between 1860 and 1870, and he was looked upon by many as the kind of charismatic personality who could lead the people to a promised land. Among his most devoted followers were three families of Mennonite Brethren who had been part of the influx from the Kuban.[4]

Peters' following was encouraged by the favorable reports they had received from the Tashkent delegation in January 1880. In the following spring, meetings were held in the villages of Prangenau and Friedensruh during which discussions of the advantages of the Tashkent area further heightened the enthusiasm of the Peters' faction.[5] They chose Peters to join the representatives of the Trakt colonists in their appeal to St. Petersburg, and efforts were made to gain draft exemptions for two young men in order that they might accompany the group.[6]

Third Wagon Train, August, 1880

In all, about 80 families began preparations for departure. Farms and property were sold at auction, huge wagons were constructed, and the many necessary implements for the journey were collected. On August 1, the Molotschna group gathered at Waldheim village, ready for departure. After a farewell sermon on the text of Hebrews 13:14 — "For here we have no continuing city, but we seek one to come" — the 75 wagons struck out across the plains toward the Trakt on the Volga, there to rendezvous with the second wagon train leaving that colony.

En route to the Trakt a strict traveling order was enforced because faster wagons tended to get ahead of the group and a separation of the party could result. This strict order, however, had its drawbacks because some of the single-file procession drove so slowly that large gaps occurred, and those behind a slow wagon often lost patience.[7]

The travelers from Molotschna spent their first Sunday in the Hutterite village of Johannesruh, where men wore long hair parted in the middle. Here it rained almost constantly, but it did not dampen the spirits of the young people, who ran barefoot through the thick mud. Later, these children would remember fondly their frolic in the mud, but at the time their enthusiasm dissipated as they developed large blisters on their feet.[8]

Each evening, after a full day of travel, they would drive their wagons into a circle for the night. The night watch was divided in half by four men who were assigned guard duty. About daybreak, two guards moved about the camp, beating on tin buckets to awaken the group. As soon as the horses were fed, morning devotions completed, and a hearty breakfast eaten, they would break camp.

A Suicide Reported

From the inception of the trip, Peters placed a strong emphasis on worship services, and he personally arranged morning and evening devotions by selecting one of four preachers with the group to be the speaker. The entire party was required to attend these devotions. On Sunday, they rested all day and added midmorning and mid-afternoon services, making four services each Sabbath, or a total of sixteen services per week![9] Day after day, traveling and worship continued. Then, just before the end of August, a lone messenger came galloping up to the wagon train bearing sad news of unrequited love. The sweetheart of one of the young men in the group had been forced by her parents to remain behind. She had committed suicide by hanging. The shocked young man, who had been compelled by his parents to leave Molotschna, suffered a nervous breakdown and had to be watched day and night for fear that he would try to take his own life.[10]

Despite a halt because of this startling situation, the wanderers soon reached the Don River, where they were ferried across, one wagon at a time. Sorrow confronted them once again when one of two pregnant mothers in the party gave birth to an infant already dead. Out of respect for her loss, and because Mrs. Cornelius Unruh was approaching the time of childbirth herself, the wagon train halted again for a few days. A baby boy was born to the Unruhs, and the whole group was lifted from its sorrow because a new life had joined their journey.

Peters Leaves for the Trakt

They reached the Volga River, but the unending downpour of rain made it so difficult to travel that they made camp. Peters and a companion decided to take a boat across the swollen river to the Trakt, where he hoped to meet brethren who were to accompany his wagon train and his son Dietrich, who, after an appeal of his draft status in St. Petersburg, was to wait at the Trakt for his father's arrival. Peters was disappointed in both hopes. The Trakt party had left without them days earlier, on August 13, because they did not know when Peters would come and they feared the approaching winter. His son, he was told, had not yet arrived at the Trakt. Later, happily, Peters learned that his son, as well as young Peter Quiring, had gone directly from St. Petersburg to join the second wagon train at the Ural River on September 5. Young Peters had been informed that his father's group would soon join the second contingent along the way.

The Molotschna party began to worry about Peters when he did not return to their camp on the Volga within the week. Fearing he had been lost in rising floodwaters, they prayed that God would return their beloved leader. Late one evening, at the beginning of the second week, the entire camp was suddenly awakened when they heard German hymns being sung. Approaching the circle of wagons was Peters with several Trakt people, including a minister, Jacob Janzen. They had brought their Molotschna brothers gifts of lard and large amounts of smoked meat, hoping to make up for their disappointment at not meeting the second wagon train.

The Auction

The next day, after the departure of the Trakt colonists, a member of the Molotschna party suggested that the smoked meat be sold at auction to the highest bidders to avoid squabbling over how the meat was to be distributed. Most of the group agreed, but while they were in the middle of their impromptu auction, one of the men who had brought the meat unexpectedly appeared and asked what they were doing. When advised of their proposal, he became very angry and said, "If I had known I would never have brought you any meat." He did not feel it a Christian act to auction gifts from sympathetic brethren. In fact, this incident so shamed the Molotschna people that the money was returned and the meat divided among the poorer members of the group. Some of the wealthy members, it was later reported, no longer thought of themselves as a little above the rest.[11]

Epp Begins a Revival

The day after this incident, Claas Epp arrived with several

preachers from the Trakt to bring encouragement to his Molotschna brethren and present a series of Bible studies on prophecy. Many Molotschna people had never heard Epp preach, and his startling predictions based on the books of Daniel and Revelation were new to them. Some of his premillennial studies in which he outlined what would happen in the "last days" were astounding revelations to the more conservative element. Peters had never been so specific or dramatic in his preaching. Consequently, Epp gained a deepening respect from many in the Molotschna party.

While in camp Epp also instituted a new communion service which he called a "Love Feast." Everyone shared their food and then participated in the Lord's Supper. The rich and poor sat together and ate the meat they had previously wanted to auction. Epp explained that Mennonites should share their sustenance equally because in heaven all would be equal. After this communion of sharing, Epp and his companions set out for the Trakt. Wishing Godspeed to his brothers going before him to Tashkent, he promised to join them as soon as he could conclude business and religious matters at the Trakt.[12]

It was mid-September when the Peters group left the Volga for the city of Orenburg. Supplies to last them until they reached the gateway city consisted of 3,000 pounds of white flour, 1,000 pounds of potatoes, 4,000 pounds of rye flour, horse feed, and hay. It took them a day and a half merely to load the supplies on the wagons.[13]

Stopped by a Magistrate

En route to Orenburg the wagon train was commanded to stop by officials at the small Russian village of Zaritzyn. They were told the local magistrate had been ordered by higher officials to detain them. The worried group elected Cornelius Unruh, who spoke fluent Russian, to be the spokesman before the magistrate. As he stood before the court, the authoritarian judge informed him that the wagon train should return home and asked perplexing questions about permits and travel papers. Unruh ably argued their case even though he could show no permits or other papers, and the magistrate dismissed him with a strong warning that the wagons camped near the town graveyard should have plenty of guards that night because of the hostility of the local populations. This hostility was a combination of fear and xenophobic mistrust of Germans. That night many local people did come to their campsite, but merely out of curiosity, and no incidents occurred. As a matter of fact, at least one Russian was ready to join their band. Later in the evening a young Russian boy approached Unruh about going with them on their journey. One of the men with Unruh suggested in Low German that they keep the boy overnight, since he was probably a runaway, and take him to the magistrate the next day. The boy immediately bolted and ran when he either understood the German or became fearful of the Mennonites. At daybreak the wagon train hurriedly left Zaritzyn.

Though disturbed by the experience of the previous day, the group decided not to turn back even though they had no permit to travel, but pressed on toward Orenburg. Arriving at Orenburg, Peters suggested that they stop for a week to take on supplies and rest. From their campsite on the bank of the Ural River, they could easily make short trips into the heart of the city.

During their stay, what most impressed the Molotschna people were the many church bells that rang periodically throughout the day. When they became better acquainted with Orenburg they asked merchants about this strange daily custom and were told that each time the bells rang it represented a funeral service for one of the inhabitants. No longer did the Mennonites enjoy the clanging of church bells. When the merchants learned they were the third group of Mennonites to come through their crossroad city en route to Turkestan, they were astounded that so many farmers would undertake such an enterprise.[14]

Leaving Orenburg behind, the wagon train took the same route as the second group through Orsk, Karabutak, Irgiz, and into the Kara Kum Desert. Like the previous caravans, they purchased extra supplies for the desert journey and hired camels and drivers to carry them. But the desert journey was surprisingly easy. Heavy rains had so packed the Kara Kum sand that the wagons passed through more quickly than the previous groups.

Even better time was made by the rumbling wagons from Kasalinsk to Fort Perovsk, but one family in particular suffered a series of mishaps. While camped near the fort, Grandfather Johann Wedel, in his dotage at eighty, wandered away from the group. This had not been the first time. But earlier, after considerable inconvenience, he had been found.[15] This time, however, an entire day's intensive search by his family proved fruitless. The next day a full report was given to authorities at the fort, and the wagon train moved eastward. Two days later a telegram informed them that old Wedel had been found ten miles from the fort at a Kirghiz village and that his hands and feet were badly frostbitten. His sons went back to pick him up, but when they arrived he was already dead and buried. The grief-stricken search party returned to their wagons, and immediately a respectful memorial service was held in Wedel's honor.[16] But the family's problems were not yet over. The following day, Tobias Wedel was thrown into the icy waters of a turbulent stream. Though he was able to swim to safety his wagon was so badly damaged that a new one had to be purchased. This placed a heavy financial burden on the poor family.

The Night in a Graveyard

Other families had similar hardships, and the group had by no means seen the end of unsettling incidents along the way. At Chimkent, after 16 full weeks on the road, even the routine process of making camp was transformed into a macabre experience. Late one Saturday evening, as they sought a site to spend the Sabbath, they found the city gates of Chimkent closed and bolted. After coaxing a town official to allow them to enter, they were led to a large open field covered by a number of earthen mounds. Very suspiciously the official warned the Mennonites not to leave their wagons for water or any other reason. Early the next morning, however, a young girl left her parents' wagon to relieve herself and get some water from a nearby canal. Suddenly, the entire party was awakened by her screams. It was discovered that as she had walked over one of the mounds it had given way, and she fell through up to her armpits. She was shaking with fright when one of the brethren pulled her out. It was then that they found they had spent the night in an ancient graveyard.

Peters, knowing that Muslims revere the dead, could not understand why they had been allowed to stay there, and he began looking around the site. Some of the graves had stone walls that were broken and fallen in so that one could see corpses through the holes in the ground. When Peters asked the city officials the reason they had been assigned this spot for the night, they replied that they had not been able to think of another area large enough for such a wagon train. No one, they explained, knew how old the graves were nor to what civilization they belonged. For some time the officials had wanted to destroy the graveyard, but because they did not know who was buried there, they hesitated doing anything. When the Mennonites arrived, the city fathers of Chimkent had become fearful because when large wagons entered their city before, they had been accompanied by Russian guns and cannons. Peters assured the officials that they were only peaceful farmers seeking a future hope. Never again did these Molotschna Mennonites see a graveyard like the one in Chimkent.[17]

Leaving this unique campsite behind, the travelers spent the latter half of November plagued by heavy rains, chuckholes, broken axles, and tracks too narrow for their wagons. As they approached Tashkent some of the brethren from Kaplan Bek came out to greet them, including Dietrich Peters and Peter Quiring from Molotschna who had come with the second wagon train. There was much rejoicing when these young men were reunited with their families.

Arrival in Tashkent, December 2, 1880

This third and longest trek had taken eighteen weeks; the pilgrims had left nine people buried along the trail. Instead of quartering this contingent at Kaplan Bek with their brethren, Kaufmann had arranged accommodations for them in Tashkent itself. It was no wonder then that after a brief but refreshing stay with their friends, the party was anxious to settle at their new home in the city. Arriving at Tashkent on December 2, they learned that their newly prepared dwellings would be in the Russian Exhibition Area of the marketplace.[18] The process of getting acquainted in their new cultural surroundings would prove most interesting.

9

TROUBLE AND DISPERSION
OF THE BRETHREN

By December 1880 some 400 Mennonites had arrived in Turkestan. Most of the first two wagon trains from the Trakt resided in Kaplan Bek, but the people of the Molotschna train decided to live in Tashkent, where there were more opportunities for housing and jobs. Within a year both of these groups would undergo disillusionment that would end in dispersion.

Getting Acquainted

In Kaplan Bek, a school and church were immediately built under the leadership of Wilhelm Penner and Franz Bartsch. These two ministers wanted the people to keep busy; when they were not improving their housing situation, many services and prayer meetings were held. When the dwellings were completely renovated to accommodate 22 families, they found they still lived in close quarters. This gave them many opportunities to practice the brotherly love they said they believed in. In fact, every Sunday, the evening meal was held in common — called the "love feast." At these meals they discussed Bible passages and letters from the Trakt, sang hymns, and had devotions. All of the families enjoyed these sharing experiences and sincerely believed it was God's will for them to be in Kaplan Bek.[1]

Immediately upon the arrival of the second train in Kaplan Bek, Wilhelm Penner, of the first group, and wagon master Heinrich Jantzen went to see the governor-general about land. Although nothing of significance was decided, they were assured they did not have to worry about taxes or the draft for fifteen years. This made all the Trakt Mennonites feel that this end result made the trip and its hardships worthwhile.[2]

The Peters' wagon train, after a brief stay in Kaplan Bek, moved to the city of Tashkent and their new home. Tashkent was a twin city, with a Russian and native Sart section. The first Mennonite homes lay outside the marketplace near the Russian Exhibition Ground, a noisy square full of bustling crowds and featuring even a shooting gallery. One of the dwellings assigned them was a compound surrounded by a high cement wall which had once served as a military barracks. It had no windows; its huge gate was locked and there were only a few small doors called "needle's eyes" because camels and humans had to crouch to go through them. There was a pond in the center of the yard and there were shade trees and drinking water provided. About twenty families settled there. Nearby were the shops of sugar and syrup makers; the children were delighted by the proximity of the stores. Not far away was the Chirchik River; its steep banks were covered with fruit trees, and a variety of fish could be caught in its waters. One Mennonite reported that apples, pears, plums, cherries, peaches, grapes, apricots, pomegranates, lemons, oranges, strawberries, raspberries, dates, figs, olives, watermelons, and muskmelons all grew in this lovely place.[3]

When the Mennonites arrived, they drove their wagons into the huge square courtyard that was to be their new home, unhitched, put their horses into a stable along one wall, unloaded provisions, and were assigned living quarters along the walls of the court. Early the next morning and every morning thereafter they were rudely awakened at 5:00 a.m. by several thousand Russian soldiers marching in morning review. A brass band accompanied the troops, and a few times each week they even shot off cannons during this morning exercise.

After settling in their new home, they began to realize that the commitment of the Russian government to the Mennonite migrants had been a very vague one; Kaufmann had spoken merely of making some land available in the Tashkent area. The newcomers, oppressed by their crowded quarters and anxious to begin the cultivation of their new land, were desirous of some immediate settlement of their grant. Consequently, shortly before Christmas, the Kaplan

Bek and Tashkent emigrants sent a delegation to wait upon Governor-General Kaufmann, request their land, and draw up a contract.

Though hospitably received by Kaufmann's secretary, the delegates were cowed by the formidable reputation of the man and intimidated by their own uncertain position as strangers in a strange land. The timid petitioners appointed Cornelius Unruh as their spokesman, owing to his fluent knowledge of Russian, and waited anxiously in an anteroom as Unruh went to confront the great man alone. He found the governor-general courteous and solicitous of the welfare of the Mennonite flock. Kaufmann, moreover, kept his promise and made arrangements for the Mennonites to be escorted to a tract not far from Tashkent which had been set aside for their use.[4]

On Christmas Eve the delegation inspected this tract. Though it lay conveniently near the city and could be had for a pittance, the ground was stony and the proximity of a Kirghiz village augured ill for the settlers there. To the experienced eyes of the Mennonite farmers, this land would not do. Kaufmann patiently heard their complaints and offered an alternative: 150 miles away, not far from the Siberian border, lay a tract of beautiful land near Aulie Ata. Would this be more suitable? The delegation accepted the invitation to inspect this tract, but they would not be able to make the journey until later in the spring.[5]

So the winter passed with no permanent haven in sight. To make ends meet, most of the sojourners in Tashkent were able to find work in a limestone quarry which produced stones for street construction. So hazardous were the working conditions that two Mennonite men were almost killed when the bank of a deep pit caved in.[6] Kaufmann, however, continued to evince his sympathetic attitude toward the Mennonites, even paying $1,500 out of his own pocket for court costs in registering the Mennonites as citizens.[7]

The Chinese Community

To escape the noise and congestion of the Russian Exhibition Ground, some of the Tashkent Mennonites moved from their barracks home to a spot adjacent to the Sart section of the city. Here 50 Chinese families lived directly across the street. The Chinese had many customs that puzzled the Mennonites; one in particular was the binding of little girls' feet. When the curious newcomers asked them why they did this, it was explained that it was an honor for women to have small feet. The Chinese girls, in turn, asked the Mennonite girls why they had such big feet! The Mennonite girls, not understanding this strict Chinese custom, told the young girls that their feet were larger so that they could run, jump, and play. This answer apparently disturbed the Chinese girls so much that they openly criticized the custom imposed upon them by their parents. One Chinese girl, who became acquainted with Elizabeth Unruh, the daughter of Cornelius Unruh, confided to her that she did not want small feet. Consequently, her elderly grandmother, feeling the Mennonites were leading her astray, did not allow her to associate with them any longer. When the Mennonite girls attempted to see her, they heard her crying and moaning because of the tightened bandages. Angrily the grandmother told them to never come to her home. They never saw her again.[8]

Typhoid Fever Epidemic

As the Mennonites were getting acquainted with new peoples and customs, a terrible epidemic struck the brethren both in Kaplan Bek and Tashkent.[9] The disease had apparently been brought to Kaplan Bek by several people in the first wagon train. Others soon began running a fever and suffered from severe diarrhea. A young woman in the first group died, and many others became extremely ill. In all, of the first ten families to settle in Kaplan Bek, 26 people died. At first, the surgeon major of the local army unit ascribed the disease to wet walls and damp quarters. But then the district surgeon, alarmed by the deaths and illness, came and pronounced it to be typhoid fever. Hearing this, the Russians feared a widespread epidemic and ordered all 22 families to go to the army supply headquarters for tents so that they could be moved outside the town limits and be quarantined.[10] This order was hurriedly issued on a Saturday, and the Mennonites had to pick up their tents promptly on Monday morning. In the meantime the more seriously ill were taken to Tashkent for treatment. The Mennonites could not understand the reason for the quarantine in tents because neither the surgeon nor other officials took time to explain their plight. After they expressed dismay, an official came late Sunday afternoon and explained that the doctors felt the tents would be better living quarters for them rather than having wet walls and damp conditions to contend with.[11] Living in tents seemed to improve the condition of the ill, and recovery was satisfactory in this first typhoid epidemic. The following summer, however, almost every family in Kaplan Bek was stricken. Wagon master Heinrich Jantzen was grief-stricken at the loss of his oldest sons.[12] A daughter of Martin Klaassen was among twelve additional Mennonites to die.[13]

Typhoid also raged among the members of the third wagon train in Tashkent, striking the young adults the hardest. As the winter of 1881 turned into a warm spring, even more people became ill. In fact, the natives had to warn the Mennonites about working in the heat of the day at the stone quarries. Instead of following the custom of the other workers and halting work between 10:00 a.m. and 4:00 p.m., they would work until lunchtime and resume labor at 2:00 p.m. The result of this mistake was that many strong young men contracted what the Russians called "climate typhus," and their conditions worsened as the spring and summer grew hotter. It is estimated that the number of deaths in the Tashkent contingency ranged between fifty and eighty people, even though they made full use of the best-known prescription for the disease — fresh fruit — which was plentiful in the region.[14]

In February 1882, *Die Rundschau*, an American Mennonite newspaper, published a very revealing list of those persons who were known to have died in this epidemic:

> Since January 1, 1881, three husbands died: Cornelius Wedel, his wife and eldest son, from Waldheim, Dietrich Wiens, on a trip to see brethren in Bukhara from Blumstein. Peter Wiens, newly arrived from Weinersdorf. Six wives died: Agnetha Pauls (nee Wiebe) from Weinersdorf. Wife of Johann Baergen (nee Wiebe) from Fischau, Wife of Cornelius Wedel (nee Pankrass). Anna Peters (nee Pauls), Maria Wiebe (daughter of Leonard Duecken from Blumenstein, her husband is a son of Peter Wiebe) from Weinersdorf. Wife of Isaac Koops (nee Kroeker) from Neukirch. Four young men died: John K. Wedel from Waldheim. Heinrich H. Graewe from Kleefeld. Abraham Kroeker, stepson of Cornelius Esau from Neukirch and our son Jacob (Jantzen). Also Wallentin (Vallentine) Braunen, 12 years old, from Alexanderkron, then several children under 2 years of age.[15]

This report gives a total of 27 deaths from all age-groups since the beginning of 1881. But not all the deaths are here recorded. In fact, by the most conservative estimates, between 15 and 20 percent of all the Mennonites died in the epidemic of 1881. No matter how one views the figures, the fact remains that a serious blow had been dealt the movement by this terrible epidemic.[16]

Czar Alexander II Assassinated

Another decisively important blow was the assassination of the friendly reformer czar, Alexander II. Alexander had honored Mennonites for their faithful nonmilitary service in the Crimean War (1854-56) and the Turkish War (1877-78); to the Mennonites of Chortitza colony he had given a handwritten document of his thanks; to the Mennonites of Molotschna he had expressed his gratitude for feeding and quartering some 600 Bulgar immigrants. Personally, he had sent his adjutant, Count Todtleben, to dissuade them from their mass exodus to America and had granted them permission to perform forestry service in lieu of military service. The Turkestan Mennonites had more appreciation for this czar than perhaps any other Mennonites in Russia because he had given his permission to migrate for social and religious reasons.[17]

Because of the repercussions on the Mennonites of Turkestan, the circumstances of the czar's death should be noted. On March 1, 1881, despite a warning from a close adviser, Alexander went to inspect the troops at Mikhailovsky Palace in St. Petersburg. While riding in his sleigh, a political terrorist threw a bomb at him. This first bomb did no injury to the czar, but as he stopped to inspect the damage, another shattered both of his legs and disfigured his face. His legs were amputated at the palace, but he died shortly after the operation without regaining consciousness.[18]

The Mennonites of Turkestan received notification by way of a telegram sent all over Russia the day following the assassination. They received the news with profound shock. Promptly they held a memorial service in his honor and a sympathy message was drawn up and presented to Kaufmann, who received it graciously.[19] Most of the Mennonites wondered what would happen now; with his passing, Russia lost a czar who had not only indirectly helped the Mennonites, but showed the most promise of flexibility.[20]

Harsher Policies of Government

Since Alexander's eldest son had died of tuberculosis, his second son, Alexander III, who had previously been destined for a military career, became czar. He took the oath of office the day after the assassination and in his coronation speech expressed the wish to continue his father's policies. Some interpreted these emotional words to be a promise of continued liberal policies, but they soon discovered that the new czar was too conscious of his father's murder at the hands of radicals to be tolerant of dissent. With his accession to the throne, the Russian Orthodox Church, which had played a relatively minor role during his father's reign, encouraged a program of anti-liberalism, and instituted a revival of monasticism. Education, long a stronghold of liberal thought, was subjected to closer scrutiny by the authorities. Local autonomy of schools was ended and student organizations restricted. Primary education was once again returned to the Orthodox Church.[21] These reactionary moves greatly affected the Mennonites in Turkestan. The new emphasis upon orthodoxy was not in accordance with their belief in complete religious freedom, and the new education program could destroy their German-language education. Some Mennonites sensed an impending change in policy toward them.[22]

Mennonite Patron Kaufmann Dies

The loss of their czar was soon compounded by the loss of their sympathetic patron. In May 1881, during negotiations for land, a special meeting with Kaufmann had been called. Because Kaufmann was ill with a sore throat and headache his secretary asked them to come the next day. When they arrived the surgeon general did not allow the meeting with Kaufmann because of his continued sore throat. The following day it was reported that he could not talk at all. Then they learned he had suffered a stroke and was partly paralyzed. The next day he died. The entire populace, including the Mennonites who had as yet not signed a contract for land, began a period of mourning for the beloved leader. A black flag flew at half-mast over the governor-general's palace.[23]

On May 16, 1881, the Mennonites attended Kaufmann's funeral to show their respects.[24] The funeral procession began at the palace where a great throng of people assembled. Two hearse wagons, one with the open casket and the other with the casket lid decked with flowers, began the slow procession as all the church bells of the city rang out. Following the wagon were Kaufmann's widow, young girls carrying wreaths of flowers, Cossacks on horseback, a large band, cannons, and a multitude of people: Turks, Sarts, Chinese,

Indians, Jews, Kirghiz, Turkomans, Armenians, Bukharans, Russians, and Mennonites. After a brief memorial service in the largest Russian Orthodox Church, the bells began to chime once again. The ringing itself was deafening, and then the cannons boomed a response at Kaufmann's graveside. The Mennonites were awed by the funeral and never forgot it.[25]

Successor's Attitude

After this elaborate funeral the Mennonites soon learned that Kaufmann's successor, General Vladimir Kolpokowsky, an ardent Russophile, was not sympathetic toward German Mennonites in Turkestan. When he met with Kaplan Bek and Tashkent representatives, he flatly told them they should not have taken such a long journey and that he would expect them to demonstrate their "superior abilities" before he decided what to do with them. This new official reaction toward Mennonites brought a new fear that perhaps this area was not the place of refuge they had hoped it to be. In fact, when Kolpokowsky further refused their pleas for assistance, they realized they must again move.[26]

Anti-Epp Dissension Causes Split

This change of attitude by the government only added fuel to a smoldering debate going in the Mennonite community. The community had hoped to be unified, but differences between the Epp and Peters factions proved a great stumbling block. Very often the Tashkent brethren traveled the thirteen miles to Kaplan Bek to discuss the possibility of a move to Aulie Ata. They even broached the subject of reorganizing into one congregation and electing a single elder. Both Cornelius Wall and J. K. Penner, however, questioned whether they could stay with a combined group because both men had had disagreements with Epp. Furthermore, they did not like Epp's weekly letters in which he told them the "Lord is writing to the church of Philadelphia," as they were called according to Revelation 12.[27] Although Abraham Peters essentially agreed with Wall and Penner, he cautioned them not to deny the need for Christian unity in a Muslim land.[28] But as Peters became more familiar with the radical theology of Epp and some of his followers at Kaplan Bek, he became disillusioned about the worth of unity for unity's sake and the cooperative settling of a frontier area with a man he believed to be a modern-day "false prophet."[29] Now Wall, Penner, and Peters believed Epp could bring their people only sadness and disunity.[30]

The Trakt people at Kaplan Bek disagreed with these three leaders. They believed Epp's letters urging them not to accept "worldly" elders or preachers who would lead them away from God's Word. Epp told them to be wary of following such men because it would not only lead to sinful alternative service for the government but also to a denial of the efficacy of their millennial faith. This correspondence suggested that the group consider leaving Kaplan Bek for the khanate of Bukhara, where Epp now believed the place of refuge to be located. Let the Peters' contingent go to Aulie Ata, where they would live in sin, argued Epp, but let the faithful millennialists go in search of the Christ.[31] The dream of settling the area south of Samarkand had long been an obsession of Claas Epp. This, said Epp in a letter to the group, was the open door spoken of in Revelation 3:8: "I know thy works: behold, I have set before thee an open door, and no man can shut it: for thou hast a little strength, and hast kept my word, and hast not denied my name." While plans were completed for the trip to Bukhara, Epp was planning his departure from the Trakt in order to join them as soon as possible.[32]

Deputation to Bukhara

In mid-June 1881, the Kaplan Bek Mennonites sent a deputation composed of Wilhelm Penner and another man to explore the country of Bukhara and ask its khan for permission to settle there. They left Tashkent on the mail wagon, crossed the Hunger Steppe, a waterless, treeless, extremely hot region, and came to the Zaravshan River near Samarkand. Here they left the mail wagon and transferred to an *arbas* (a high wagon) whose seven-foot wheels helped them cross the river easily. At Samarkand they exchanged Russian rubles into Bukharan money, purchased a ride on another mail wagon, and proceeded to the Russian border town of Katakurgan. Here they hired a Bukharan guide named Sultanbek, who promised for eleven rubles to get them to Bukhara within two days on his one-horse arbas. Sultanbek, however, did not carry out his promise because he soon intoxicated himself with opium. Penner then hired a Sart guide they met on the road, who successfully led them to the walled fortress city of Bukhara. Without delay, they went first to the Russian embassy and then on to the palace of the khan where the Mennonite deputies were graciously received. When they returned to Kaplan Bek a few weeks later the news that the khan granted permission for them to move to Bukhara overjoyed all the brethren.[33]

On hearing this report, some of the Molotschna people decided to go to Bukhara with their Kaplan Bek friends. In order to show their sincerity, however, they had to reconfess and rededicate their lives to Christ and go through a ceremony of laying on of hands by the Kaplan Bek elders. Some forty families decided to leave, but found out that they had to put up a 500-ruble bond in order to leave Russian territory. This bond was to protect the Russian government. who feared they would be killed by hostile natives en route. The bond emphasized that the Mennonites would be losing all protection if they left.[34] The rumor that slavery and "girl stealing" were the order of the day in Bukhara dissuaded several families from following up their plans.[35]

This indecision on the part of the Turkestan Mennonites led to a split into three parties. The Peters faction decided to accept Russian law and stay in Turkestan; the Epp group made plans to leave Kaplan Bek and Bukhara; and a small group seceded from the Kaplan Bek leadership and temporarily took up quarters in Tashkent. Some of this last group, including Cornelius Wall, later joined the Peters group when it moved to the Aulie Ata region of Turkestan.[36]

July 1881 Evacuation of Kaplan Bek

On July 25, 1881, in spite of warnings from other Mennonites and a new outbreak of illness, 26 families left Kaplan Bek for Bukhara. Barely had they crossed the Keles River when an omen occurred: two wheels broke on two different wagons. During the delay for repairs, old Heinrich Schmidt, a senior member of the party, died. The next evening the funeral was held, and early in the morning he was buried in Kaplan Bek. The train then decided to divide into smaller groups for faster traveling; Martin Klaassen commanded the first section and Hermann Jantzen the other.[37] A brief stopover at Tashkent found six Molotschna families ready to go along, and following a farewell service, eight or ten other families promised to try to follow later. Finally, on July 28, the two trains headed south in the intense heat of summer.

10

NO-MAN'S-LAND:
BETWEEN KHAN AND CZAR

The Claas Epp faction of the Mennonite millennialists were destined by their choice of Bukhara to undergo even more hardships
than they had encountered in Kaplan Bek and Tashkent. They would
soon find that their deep desire to meet the risen Christ would place
them in a dilemma that seemed insurmountable.

Seeking Shar-i-Sabs

In the midst of their many problems during their eight-month
stay in the Tashkent area, they became even more certain that Christ
was leading them step by step according to a divine plan to their
"place of refuge" south of Samarkand. In fact, by the time of
their departure they had become convinced that the actual place of
the heralded second coming of Christ would be in a small valley
called Shar-i-Sabs (Valley of the Carrots), just 100 miles inside Bukharan territory.[1]

So intense were their hopes for a refuge at Shar-i-Sabs that
they tried not even to think about the multiplying rumors they had
heard concerning slavery being practiced in Bukhara. Some in the
party dismissed the rumors and confidently relied on earlier Russian treaty commitments with the khanate that supposedly prohibited
slavery. Fears about slavery and barbarous natives, they contended,
were completely unfounded, because the Russian army had conquered
the area and completely wiped out the odious practice. Even with
this kind of reassurance, however, many members of the group still

shuddered at the embellished stories of slave traders operating in the khanate and feared that they were probably looking forward to the arrival of such a choice group of submissive Europeans to prey upon. As preparations for the trip were completed, a gnawing concern gripped every member of the party, and some could visualize the potential destruction of the people and the movement at the hands of Bukharan slave traders. Instigated by the Antichrist, these barbarians might bring a holocaust of hellish evil upon them. Would they ever reach Shar-i-Sabs to meet Christ?[2]

With such uncertainty did they leave Kaplan Bek behind that only the encouragement of letters from Epp and the leadership of men like J. K. Penner and Hermann Jantzen could give them new courage. If what they were doing was the Lord's will, exhorted their leaders, then they had no choice in the matter. Furthermore, with the Lord with them, they did not have to fear slave traders, bandits, Russian officials, or the Antichrist himself.

Journey Toward Bukhara

This was the setting for their midsummer exodus. The climate of Turkestan was at its hottest, driest, and dustiest. On July 28, 1881, the day they left, the temperature was 99 degrees F., and those in the van wondered if it was a portent of the hellfire they were trying so desperately to elude. Still the train of 48 wagons carried 153 hymn-singing Mennonites resolutely forward along the dust-choked roads south of Tashkent.

As they left the city, they resolved to look forward to the joy that would come in Bukhara. After taking the mail road, they decided to divide their journey in two by stopping for a time at Samarkand, the approximate midpoint. Late that first day, after crossing the Syr Darya by ferry, they camped on its sandy banks and held a spirited service on soil they believed untainted by the "world law" of the Russians. On this secluded spot they gained a new sense of freedom from the constraint that they had felt in Tashkent, a city controlled by "rulers of this world" rather than Almighty God, the Supreme Ruler of all men.[3]

The next day brought with it the ordeal of crossing the Hunger Steppe, so called because of its bleak and barren landscape. Leaving the mail road, they followed a wagon trail which offered a shorter route as well as more water along the way. The steppe, they found, was completely devoid of vegetation but extremely level, making it easier on the wagons and their occupants. The journey was proceeding more rapidly than they had expected. After several days of smooth going, they had covered some 65 miles, and they rejoined the mail road. Its deep ruts and evenly placed telegraph poles gave them some semblance of civilization at least.

Having safely crossed the Hunger Steppe without any serious difficulties, the caravan arrived at the little Sart town of Dishak, which offered a friendly and welcome respite for the weary travelers. After setting up camp, the Mennonites purchased needed supplies, including their first Sart bread — large, round, flat cakes called *sarcherni lapushai*.⁴ Leaving Dishak, they then followed the road through hills dotted with boulders as large as houses until they came abruptly to the fertile Zaravshan Valley. Here Kirghiz officers, employed by the Russian government to assist the mail wagons, helped them ford eleven tributary streams and the broad Zaravshan River. The emigrants tied several wagons together and harnessed all the horses as a single team to pull them through. The Kirghiz even loaned the travelers native carts to carry personal belongings that might otherwise be damaged. Four hours were required to ford these streams. On the other side the Mennonites found a veritable Garden of Eden: fields of waving grain, well-irrigated orchards, and rice fields dotted the landscape. In the valley they were met by officials who were ordered to accompany them to the "Pearl of the East," the city of Samarkand.⁵

Samarkand: Pearl of the East

Delayed by officials in Samarkand for two weeks, the party was assigned living quarters in a former prison that had only recently been vacated and remodeled. In spite of the former circumstances of their quarters, the Mennonites looked on the bright side, grateful for a place to stay while they rested before embarking on the second half of the trip. The children were the first to notice their pleasant surroundings — beautiful shade trees and a pond — and they all thanked God for their good fortune.

The Samarkand sojourn was not free from pressing responsibilities and worries, however. Several members of the party had become very ill on the journey. Martin Klaassen, author of a book on Mennonite history, appeared on the brink of death. Though he soon recovered, another of the brethren, Peter Pauls, died unexpectedly and was buried in a nearby cemetery. Moreover, the young men in the party were notified that they must register, indicating that if they ever returned to Russian soil from Bukhara they would be subject to the military draft. Despite these dreary aspects of their Samarkand stay, a number of the party found the ancient city fascinating. They were intrigued by the decayed aspect of Tamerlane's tomb and impressed by the four 200-foot towers facing the marketplace.[6]

After this variety of experiences they left Samarkand on the morning of August 26, 1881, and reached the Russian frontier garrison village of Katakurgan just one month after leaving Tashkent. The three-day journey to Katakurgan was the most difficult, because wind gusts caught the wagon canvas and caused the wagons to sway, while dust and dirt covered everything. In fact, one wagon was caught in a driving gust of wind and sent tumbling down a deep ravine. The occupants, a twelve-year-old-girl and her small sister, surprisingly enough, were unhurt.[7] Resting in Katakurgan for a few days, they gathered additional supplies and made necessary wagon repairs.

Arrival at Bukhara

On September 1, the Bukhara travelers crossed the border into the khanate. Though dreadfully rutted roads had been hard on wagon wheels and caused considerable delay, they passed across the frontier, which was simply marked by a wooden post with Russian lettering. After going eight miles into Bukhara, they camped for the night in their usual circle fashion in an area they later learned was called Cherein Chatun.[8]

At dawn the next day they were awakened by a band of armed officials who suspiciously wrote down facts and figures about the number of people, wagons, and the value of the property they had with them. Two of the emigrants were asked to accompany the officials to make their report to the local governor or bek. He received them cordially and told the representatives that he had to report their whereabouts to the khan and would let the group know what the khan said about their situation in about three days. Disheartened, the men returned to camp and told the rest of the group what had transpired.[9]

Expulsion from Bukhara

Fatigued as they were from their journey, the anxious pilgrims feared this to be a bad omen. Three days passed and nothing happened. Then eight days after the encounter, on September 8, seven sword-carrying soldiers arrived to inform them that they did not have permission to trespass on Bukharan soil and must return to Russia immediately. Even though a noon meal had been prepared, their wagons had been disassembled, and a young child, Anetha Fast, had died that very morning, the officers insisted impatiently that they pack up without delay. Fires were extinguished, the Fast child was gently placed in her parents' wagon, and wheels were thrown hurriedly and haphazardly into the wagon.[10] Then the officials, their swords and turbans glinting in the sun, personally escorted the wagon train back across the border to the small Sart village of Serabulak. Incongruous with their harsh expulsion of the emigrants, the soldiers delighted in giving the small children candy. Ordering the local natives to treat the Mennonites well, they returned to the bek to report.

Forced to return to Russian soil the brethren set up camp in gloom and despair. Promptly the next morning, two brethren went the eight miles to Katakurgan to consult friendly Russian officials about their plight. The sympathetic officers, knowing that it was now illegal to receive them after their determination to leave and their signatures having been affixed to documents in Samarkand, tried to placate them with stories of a tract of neutral land that might become their home. This tract lay along the border between Bukhara and Russian Turkestan and belonged to two Samarkand mosques. Here, they suggested, the Mennonites could live peacefully in a "no-man's-land" unmolested by Russia or Bukhara. Promising the two Mennonites that they would approach officials in Samarkand about arrangements, the Russian officers excused themselves, and the men returned to Serabulak.

After conferring with the entire group, it was decided not to rely solely upon the Russian officials but to send their own delegation to Samarkand. On September 20, Hermann Jantzen, Gerhard Esau, and Cornelius W. Penner left for the Russian Embassy in Samarkand to draw up a contract or lease agreement. Prior to their departure, they had learned that the khan of Bukhara must also agree to any lease or contract. Since he was gone on a trip, the Russian officials, they thought, could notify him later. While the three men were absent on their mission to Samarkand, those remaining in Serabulak were notified that the khan had said they would not be permitted to cross into Bukhara border territory under any circumstances; they would be shot if they tried to trespass in his country. He did not care what the Russians decided about them.[11]

Despite this attitude of the khan of Bukhara, the representatives of the Mennonites concluded a lease agreement in Samarkand. Without consulting the khan, the landowners and the Russians had set the rent at 1/13 of their harvest yield per year for the 108 acres (40 dessiatines) of land they would be working. Added to this was a stipulation that they would at least temporarily enjoy exemption from military service. But if Russia ever gained administrative control of Bukhara, the Mennonites would again be subject to Russian draft laws. This lease and its stipulations seemed fair to the negotiators, and they returned to Serabulak to share what they believed was good news.

One young man, Cornelius Quiring, was particularly happy after hearing about the negotiations in Samarkand. He was the only one of draft age that would have to serve if the exemption were abrogated. At least for a time that service to the state could be avoided.[12] While the Mennonites pondered what they had done in concluding the lease agreement, the Russian ambassador to Bukhara came through Serabulak and reminded them that they could not remain on Russian territory or young Quiring would be drafted immediately. Though aware of the khan's hostile attitude, this persuaded them to move on. They would go to explore the land under lease and make certain it was suitable for their needs.

Moving to No-Man's-Land

For a second time then, they plodded back across the border and camped the first night near a flowing spring. For two consecutive days, Bukharan officials came to their campsite and insisted that they move on to the neutral land because they were trespassing on private property. The next day, one unscrupulous official tricked them into believing that he would lead them to their new homes, but they ended up that evening back on the Russian side of the frontier.

Furious with the official, the emigrants crossed the border a third time on the following day. Here they had the misfortune to meet the same border official, who this time calmly allowed them to camp and then warned them of dire trouble in the future. With disaster impending, the Mennonites decided to pray, fast, and stand their ground. The next day the same border patrolman ordered them back across the border into Russian territory. Upon their refusal, he then implied that if they stubbornly stayed another day, 400 soldiers were coming to shoot them all — men, women, and children. The Mennonites could only retort, "Let them come!"[13] They spent the night in prayer and vigil. Steadfastly they vowed that they would neither oppose the soldiers nor defend themselves. If God wanted them to die as martyrs, they would follow His will.

Few in the camp slept that night. But to their surprise, daybreak did not bring 400 soldiers but merely a handful of insolent officials who ordered them to move nearer to the border where they said the local governor would graciously allow them to remain. Obeying this order the emigrants gratefully sent two brethren to personally thank the bek. Returning from the bek, however, they brought the dreadful news that on the following day 2,000 soldiers would come and shoot all the "impertinent" members of the wagon train! Later that day, however, they received word that the bek had decided on a more merciful course: the Mennonites would merely be bound hand and foot and sent as prisoners to Samarkand. The little band of pilgrims waited for the inevitable punishment and tribulation. But as the days passed, no one came to harm them.[14]

Ebenezer: A Refuge

The Mennonites believed they were on the neutral ground of the lease agreement, which lay only eight miles from Serabulak. Despite the uncertainty of their position, they had to make provision for the coming winter. They meticulously laid out a village site and began constructing sod houses on a high steppe they named Ebenezer.[15] While the construction was proceeding, however, many in the group became ill with the same massive diarrhea that they had contacted in Tashkent. Jacob Toews' wife, J. K. Penner's mother, and Martin Klaassen were the most critically ill.[16] On November 24, the beloved Martin Klaassen died. But the distraught emigrants were not even given time to bury their dead.

The sorrow and mourning for Klaassen were interrupted by the sound of hoofbeats. A detachment of Bukharan soldiers arrived with another order from the khan demanding that the Mennonites leave his country and return to Serabulak. He cared nothing for the Samarkand lease agreement nor for the promises of his subor-

Preacher Jacob Toews and his wife. He later served as minister at First Mennonite Church, Newton, Kansas.

dinate, the bek. The soldiers had brought 100 native carts to assist the families with their belongings. Victims of so many conflicting promises and orders, the leaders of the settlement stalled for time. Hermann Jantzen, the chosen mayor of Ebenezer, did his best to entertain the soldiers, and for two days the khan's troops ate with the Mennonites, camped on their street, and allowed their horses to eat their feed. In the meantime, Jantzen and others tried to reason with the commander. They must be allowed to remain at Ebenezer until spring because of their sick children, the coming winter, and their lack of food. The only concession allowed by the commander, however, was permission for four men to petition the local bek, who in turn would contact the khan. But the bek was inflexible. The petitioners were returned to the camp with their hands tied and under guard. Shortly thereafter, the bek himself arrived and ordered that the dwellings be destroyed and the village obliterated. The khan's orders must be followed to the letter.

Driven from Ebenezer

While some soldiers laboriously dammed the village water supply, others began tearing down the sod dwellings. The glass windows, which Mennonite housewives had painstakingly wrapped in linen before their departure and which had been brought so carefully along on their journey, were first shattered by the troops. They then drove the occupants out of the huts so that the rest of the sod structures could be dismantled. This slow house-by-house process of destruction continued all afternoon; by nightfall only half of the dwellings still stood. That night, the bek allowed the group to gather for a brief message by Jacob Toews and the burial of Martin Klaassen.

Serabulak for Winter

The next day the occupants were forced from the remaining dwellings and made to prepare to leave for Serabulak. Heinrich Jantzen, mayor and wagon master, saw the roof of his home torn off and his belongings thrown onto a cart. When his son Hermann tried to prevent some soldiers from rummaging through the household items, he was bound and roughly thrown on top of the baggage in one of the carts. Wagons, horses, carts, cattle, soldiers, and emigrant people were hurriedly directed by the bek to make their way to Serabulak. Bound and helpless, Hermann Jantzen was greatly troubled by the cold wind and his freezing limbs until one of the soldiers released him to run alongside the cart to keep warm. This forced march, the Mennonites later recounted, was the worst indignity they had suffered on their entire journey.[17]

Arriving again in Serabulak on the evening of November 26, they decided to rent property in the small village in order to spend the winter, hoping that Russian officials would overlook their undignified return. The immediate concern about winter weather was more important to them than the shame and despair they had experienced in this "final" trek. Four families stayed in a mosque they later used as a church; some found temporary quarters in stables; others wherever they could find extra rooms. The Klaassen family, for example, was one of the fortunate ones. Renting from a local landlord, they acquired lodging in an enclosed courtyard with a mud-brick dwelling.

Because of this forcible ejection from Bukhara, many of the brethren became convinced they had perhaps been mistaken in their theological predictions. In their first meeting after their return, it was concluded that Serabulak must be the collection site for the remnant of God's people during the tribulation; the actual place of refuge lay elsewhere.[18] This "gathering place" was but a small village with one main street. In Serabulak the pilgrims found no sympathy for their theology but a very simple and helpful people, nonetheless. Living in mud-brick huts, all the inhabitants of Serabulak were practicing Muslims and took their faith seriously. Yet they willingly opened their village to the Mennonites even during the sacred fasting month of Ramadan, when the natives ate no food between sunrise and sunset. One evening, in fact, young Jacob Jantzen was invited to a Muslim banquet with the village elder. In order not to offend his host, he hid bits of food he found unpalatable in his boot.[19] The brethren were also invited to hold their Sunday worship services in the local mosque, since the Muslims used it only on Friday and Saturday. This was gratefully accepted by the Mennonites. In this mosque both children of the Widow Wiebe, Anna and Bernard, were married. Anna's marriage was to Heinrich Toews, the son of Jacob Toews. The elder Toews, asked to perform the service, used as a marriage text John 14:27: "Peace I leave with you, my peace I give unto you: not as the world giveth, give I unto you. Let not your heart be troubled, neither let it be afraid." Bernard Wiebe was similarly united in marriage, and the young Mennonites began married life in a strange land and the alien atmosphere of a "heathen" mosque.[20]

Smallpox Epidemic

In this unfamiliar but hospitable environment, the two great curses of the Mennonite emigrants — epidemic disease and theological disputation — returned to ravage their community. Smallpox broke out late in the winter and claimed the lives of several Mennonite and native children and even a few adults. The epidemic subsided as quickly as it came, and many who had been seriously ill miraculously recovered.[21] Beginning in January 1882, the epidemic was replaced as the chief concern of the brethren by still another split in theology. Some, strongly believing Bukhara to be the place of refuge, argued that they should all return to Ebenezer. Others, who were equally convinced that they were following the Word of God, felt that going to Bukhara in the first place was the biggest mistake they had ever made. This faction urged that their initial error not be repeated.[22]

Discord and J. K. Penner

The proximate occasion for the new split, however, was a sermon preached by J. K. Penner in the mosque. Emphatically he had reminded his hearers that no man can know the time or place of the return of Christ. He based his homily on Acts 1:6 and 7. "They asked of him, saying, Lord, wilt thou at this time restore again the kingdom to Israel? And he said unto them, It is not for you to know the times or the seasons, which the Father hath put in his own power." This rousing message caused many to question Epp's contention teaching that he knew when Christ was coming and where He would appear.[23] Furthermore, they agreed with Penner's anti-Bukharan stand that had developed over a period of several months.

The family of Benjamin Dirks, as well as others, were influenced greatly by Penner's forcefulness and sincerity. They began questioning other teachings of Epp concerning the coming of Christ. Dirks and two other men even left Serabulak for three days to pray in the wilderness. When they returned they announced that they could no longer remain with the group in good conscience if they continued to follow Epp.[24] Before they could make any further plans, an opposing faction of ten families withdrew completely from the group and crossed the border to settle illegally at Ebenezer on April 21, 1882. They believed the end of the world was imminent, and while their action was against Bukharan law, it was not against the

Anna Toews (nee Wiebe) and her mother about 1875.

"higher law" of God, who was sending His Son soon to receive them.[25] This small group of radicals referred to themselves as "the elect" or "the righteous," and they decided they could have no more to do with a sinful world, including their former brethren. No ordained minister was with them, and so they placed great emphasis on the priesthood of all believers; weddings were no longer encouraged because in the kingdom of God there is no need for them; communion was held every Sunday because the end was at hand and communion between God and His faithful, they argued, was absolutely necessary.

Young Men Drafted

The day this small group left for Ebenezer a notice came from Samarkand that since Mennonites were living on Russian soil, young Jacob Jantzen, who remained in Serabulak, and Cornelius Quiring, the other possible draftee, who was with the ten families at Ebenezer, were to be drafted. Learning of this notice, the families that had arrived at Ebenezer called this coincidence a "sign from God." They were glad they had left and vowed not to return.[26] Jantzen, now the lone draftee within the reach of the Russians, sadly went to Katakurgan to the conscription authorities. Here he learned he would have to go to Samarkand to be formally tested and inducted. For this trip it was decided that two of the brethren would accompany him as moral support. When they arrived at Samarkand, they learned from officials that they must go all the way to Tashkent and see the governor-general himself if they desired to petition for exemption. No guard accompanied them, and Jantzen was on his own honor. After they made this arduous journey, a physician of the governor-general ruled that Jantzen had very bad eyes; instead of military service he was ordered merely to undergo four months' treatment in the Tashkent army hospital, after which he would be given a certificate of dismissal from the service![27]

Even though there was joy among the Mennonites because of Jantzen's apparent good fortune with the military, there was growing fear about what the group would ultimately decide to do. Since they could not gain the khan's permission to stay in Bukhara, and they could not return to Russia, what were they going to do? Furthermore, they knew the millennialist brethren still in European Russia

Under the preaching of Johannes K. Penner, people began to question if Claas Epp really knew when Christ would appear.

were coming to join them and would soon swell their ranks and perhaps heighten their dilemma.

11

FINAL TREKS OF 1881

With the Epp faction of the Mennonites floundering in indecision on the Bukharan border, the last contingent of the brethren were completing plans to journey to Turkestan from European Russia. These new wagon trains would undergo many hardships before they reached their destination. By the end of 1880, after three parties of emigrants had safely reached the Tashkent area and were trying to acclimatize to their strange new environment, two more widely separated groups had made the decision to migrate eastward to meet Christ. Although not all the participants were natives of the Trakt region, both of these millennialist parties departed from there.

Even receiving letters recounting the dire hardships and theological dissension in Turkestan did not deter these people from the task they believed was the Lord's will for their lives. This task, although dangerous and gaining new critics almost daily, was necessary in order to follow God's Word. After all, Christ would meet them at the place of refuge and give them eternal glory. How could they not respond to this holy mission?

Inspired by such convictions, a fourth wagon train left the Trakt sometime in August 1881. It included a strange mixture of people. In this small band, there were three families from Molotschna who had planned to leave earlier with Abraham Peters and six families from the Kuban region of the Caucasus. The Kuban Mennonite Brethren formed a close-knit group and fervently believed in the imminent second coming of Christ. Jacob Funk, one of the number, was chosen as the wagon master.[1] These Mennonite Brethren, believing themselves more pious due to their strict adherence to God's Word, had earlier left the Kirchliche Mennonites because, in their way of thinking, they were not following the entire Bible. The difference in background between these Kubans and their Trakt brethren presented no problem because of their total commitment to millennialism. In fact, they were so enthusiastic they decided to leave the Trakt, where they had gathered, before a larger train to be led by Epp himself was prepared to depart, and they could not be dissuaded. Even the death of a small child in their party just prior to their departure failed to discourage them.

New Wagon Trains Eastward

The members of the Mennonite Brethren Church on this wagon train knew they would be a minority faction when they reached Tashkent. But to them, belief in millennialism was far more significant than provincal or even denominational background. To be sure, Molotschna and Trakt Kirchliche Mennonites would outnumber them in Tashkent but this minority of Mennonite Brethren would later wield power and influence disproportionate to their numbers.

Fourth Wagon Train, August 1881

After overcoming their sorrow at the death of one of their children and setting aside their concerns over being in a minority, they left the Trakt in the late summer heat. Having already learned of the extreme hardships encountered by the previous wagon trains, they probably exercised great care to be well supplied and equipped. At any rate, they had a much easier journey than any of the other parties. Wagon master Jacob Funk, who was the leading inspiration of their group, led them admirably over a route similar to that that the Molotschna migrants had followed, and they arrived in the city of Tashkent on October 9, 1881. Most of these nine families later decided to join the Peters faction in a move to a completely new area.[2]

Fifth Wagon Train

The fifth and final wagon train, including the major portion of Claas Epp's "Bride Community," were very cautious about leaving the Trakt and decided to leave after the Funk party. Like the others, they were seeking Christ, the "Bridegroom," in Turkestan, but they had many affairs to settle before joining in the migration. In preparing for the trip, many problems had arisen; many within the inner circle of the Bride Community had doubts about the wisdom of leaving at all. Some frankly dreaded the expedition because of reports coming back from Kaplan Bek, while others cherished misgivings about the reasonableness of millennialism itself. Still a smaller faction could not withstand the criticism of friends and relatives who called it a "crazy venture." To compound their problems, moreover, permanent rifts had developed over these issues.

One of the most serious divisions that afflicted them from the beginning was over the conflict between Claas Epp and the respected Trakt minister, Jacob Janzen. Though he had planned to go with one of the first two wagon trains, Janzen had changed his opinions and did not leave. Courageously, because his was a minority opinion, he followed his personal convictions and began denouncing Epp as a "false prophet." He warned the people that only disaster would come to them if they stubbornly followed Epp and believed in his teachings as the only way. Epp reacted harshly to Janzen's open denunciation. He formally excommunicated Janzen and his family, as he would others in the future, because said Epp, he was no longer a worthy member of the Bride Community. Anyone who tried to challenge the authority Epp held from God was not suitable to meet Christ in Turkestan.

After this expulsion, the Janzen family were informed by the majority that "nobody will care for them or help them, no matter what happens." This rejection was such a shattering experience for the formerly well-respected Janzen that he made plans to leave his beloved home. Although he did not agree with Epp's pretensions to the role of prophet, he still believed in the second coming of Christ in Turkestan. Moreover, he did not want his sons to be forced to serve the Russian government, so he was forced to seek friends elsewhere. Joining the third wagon train from Molotschna when it passed through the Trakt in September 1880, Janzen and Peters became comrades in arms. Later Janzen would not only influence Peters' theological ideas but would even inherit an important leadership role.[3]

Janzen's departure from the Trakt did not eliminate discord. As the weeks turned into months, Epp was faced with increasing dissension. This strife, he realized, was not enhancing his leadership role nor the resolution of his people; it must be dispelled through honest toil. Therefore he stepped up the hard work of preparation in the summer of 1881. Though it was late in the year, he began advocating an immediate departure, confident, he said, that "the Lord will help us." Epp's tactic of pushing his flock to great effort seemed to work, and enthusiasm began to grow. Dissension abated and criticism disappeared because the people were working hard to avoid the approaching winter that could trap them before reaching their goal. The renewed conviction that they were part of a remnant to be used by God made many forget the previous issues that had caused division.

Dusty Departure of September 1, 1881

After concluding last-minute financial and family affairs, the large company assembled their wagons at Medemtal village, the same departure point as the second wagon train. One of the ministers gave a farewell sermon from Psalm 1, the whole assembly spent a lengthy time praying, first standing then kneeling, and Claas Epp forcefully read Jeremiah 50 and led in a prayer of dedication.[4] On September 1, 1881, his party made its dusty departure. There were 47 families in all: 72 two- and three-horse wagons carrying a total of 277 people. Little did they realize that they were beginning a trek that would be a continuous story of broken wheels and axles, snowstorms, sickness, and death.[5]

Mennonite communities far from the Trakt, in Russia and abroad, were deeply interested in this adventure. Astonished by events already transpiring, they were divided as to the final outcome of the bizarre coupling of millennial theology and nonresistance. Claas Epp and the last of the millennialists were discussed at length by those left behind. Some wondered if they would ever be seen again; others questioned themselves: "What if they are right?" Pessimists averred that they would soon see their errant brethren hurrying back to the beloved Trakt. It would be years before a clear picture of what nonparticipants believed would emerge from these five treks.

At this time, however, Epp's party was not thinking about any negative possibilities but were only seeking to follow God's will. Epp sought to show the world how dedicated Christians could set an example for those who would follow them to the place of gathering and refuge. Therefore, he instituted a strict schedule throughout the trip. Driving only on weekdays, the wagon train was awakened each morning at 3:00 a.m. by the night guard. Fires were started, the 130 horses fed and cared for, everything was loaded on the wagons, breakfast was served, and then a bell summoned those who wished to go to morning worship. Johann Jantzen, the community teacher, would speak the words of a hymn, and then the group would sing after him. This was followed by a brief Scripture reading and prayer on their knees.

Strict Schedule of Epp

Depending on light and weather conditions, departure was usually between 5:00 and 6:00 a.m. Often it took more than half an hour for the entire train to get moving. In the early days, in fact, there was disorder and pushing toward the front, but that was corrected as they continued on their way. Before embarking each day, they rationed water and food in such a way that they could drive until noon before stopping to eat. By 2:00 p.m. they were on their way again and usually drove until just after sunset. When they stopped for camp there was much to do: the horses were looked after, water had to be found, meals were prepared, and wagons were repacked so beds could be laid out in the wagon bed or on the ground. The bell then sounded for evening worship. Their songs were taken from the *New Mennonite Handbook,* and prayers were always concluded with the Lord's Prayer and a benediction.

On Sunday, the schedule varied somewhat. After sleeping late until 7:00 a.m., they held a brief morning service. Breakfast and chores followed, and then everyone dressed in his best clothes and came to Sunday morning worship. After an hour or so of singing and kneeling in prayer, the message was delivered by Johann Jantzen, and with more singing and praying the worship concluded. In nice weather, Sunday school was held for the children in the afternoon from 2:00 to 3:00 p.m. Following this, the Mennonites held an afternoon service. Claas Epp presented a challenging message on an entire Bible chapter. In the evening again, if the weather cooperated, a song fest was held to the accompaniment of a portable organ, a flute, and a violin. Attracted by the songs, friendly Russians, Tartars and Kirghiz would flock to the camp for this service. The singing at the service, the participants would later say, was the most inspiring part of their week. Week after week, this strict schedule was followed no matter what other events were taking place.[6]

Rapid Travel and Its Problems

Traveling at a rapid pace, they were anxious to reach their destination as soon as possible. By September 16, they had arrived at Uralsk, about 115 miles from their starting point. Orenburg, 85 miles farther eastward, was reached after five more days of hard driving. While resting at Orenburg, the head of one of the families, L. Neumann, died of pneumonia and was buried along the road.[7] The 176 miles to Orsk were completed on October 7. Heading southward through the hard, flat steppes, they arrived at Karabutak on October 17, after driving through a heavy snowstorm most of the way. The temperature in Karabutak fell to -8 degrees F., but the natives of the city were friendly and helpful, and Mennonite children were invited into their warm homes. The Mennonites appreciated this gesture of friendship all the more because an icy north wind and drifts of snow temporarily halted their progress.[8] The wagons, white with snow, were so cold that the washing could not be dried, and mothers had to put wet diapers next to their bodies for warmth so babies could be changed. Although much better insulated than the previous wagons that had made the journey, they were still not adequate. By this time, four people lay seriously ill in the wagons.[9]

Arrival in Turkestan, December 15, 1881

Snowbound in Karabutak, the colonists conferred soberly about their future. A majority decided that they should join their brethren at Serabulak, the "gathering place" on the frontier of Bukhara, rather than settling permanently at Tashkent.[10] When the snowstorm subsided, they set off once again on the next leg of their journey — one which would be long, perilous, and bitterly cold. At Irgiz, 118 miles further south, they lined their wagons with additional felt, replenished their supplies, and hired Kirghiz camel drivers to carry their extra burden. As they entered the province of Turkestan proper, the snow changed to a freezing drizzle, but the hard-packed sand of their trail allowed them to move a bit faster at least. At Kasalinsk, the party halted for repairs for a few days, then pushed on across the frozen steppe. Arriving at Perovsk on November 27, they found the Syr Darya covered by a treacherous ice flow. Before they reached the city of Turkestan on December 17, the frozen party had encountered temperatures as low as 26 degrees below zero and had been plagued by a grand total of eighteen broken axles. In the four months of their journey they had covered 1,566 miles under the most appalling conditions.

Through it all, the children suffered worst. Six infants had been born along the route. One was dead at birth; another died soon after. In addition, Hermann Jantzen, a baby only one year old, and Franz Abrahams, who was five, succumbed to the murderous cold.[11]

The party had planned to spend only the Christmas holidays in Turkestan, but the snowdrifts made further progress impossible. Therefore on December 28, the Mennonites took up temporary winter quarters in the city and waited for a break in the weather. The respite was welcome, but the frugal pilgrims fretted over the added expense that winter quarters entailed. The Johann Jantzen family, for example, occupied a room which cost them fifteen rubles ($7.50) per month, an amount far in excess of what they could comfortably afford. Discouraged by the frustration of their plans and the incredible hardships of the journey, they were still far from despondent. Three teachers in the party, Emil Riesen, Hermann Bartsch, and a man named Sterkel, set up a school for the children, while the adults resumed their interminable theological disputation.[12]

Throughout the winter theological and social arguments increased and Claas Epp became the center of controversy. Some in the party desired to go directly south of the city of Turkestan to Bukhara because they believed God would have them hurry to the place of gathering; others wanted to see relatives in Kaplan Bek before carrying out the Lord's will; a minority faction, not wanting to join the Bukhara journey because they concluded Epp was a religious fanatic, made plans to go to the Aulie Ata region of northeastern Turkestan. These three factions argued constantly. Epp was unable to resolve their differences, and his popularity waned so much that his prophetic lectures had fewer and fewer people in the congregation. In fact, Epp's inability to provide inspiration and leadership for the entire dissident group during this hard winter proved a far more serious problem than any of their physical sufferings of the journey so far.

Trip to Serabulak

By February 1882, with indecision and dissension still growing, it was decided to send three men from Epp's train to Tashkent to inquire about a settlement. They returned without having obtained any firm commitment; many then wanted to bypass Tash-

Since the Muslims used their mosque only on Friday and Saturday, they invited the Mennonites to worship there on Sunday.

kent altogether and go directly to Serabulak to meet the rest of the Bride Community. Other counsels prevailed against this very long desert journey through the Kysil Kum wasteland, however. On March 31, the entire party left the city of Turkestan for Tashkent.[13]

Spring thunderstorms, melting snows, and flooded rivers made progress extremely difficult. With mud flowing over the wheels of the wagons, they decided to halt for a while in the little Kirghiz village of Ikhan to wait for better weather. Leaving Ikhan on April 27, they drove through fertile grasslands and had reached Chimkent by May 13. It was here that twelve families who were opposed to the settlement in Bukhara seceded from the party in order to join relatives in the newly formed settlement of Aulie Ata in northern Turkestan.

When Epp's party at last arrived in Tashkent, he began talking about traveling either to Afghanistan or the 100 miles across Bukhara to Shar-i-Sabs.[14] Hearing a rumor that his theological adversary at Serabulak, J. K. Penner, had recently likened his followers to the "dumb dogs" mentioned in Isaiah 56:10 and had complained that nothing in Epp's teachings had come true, he felt it imperative that he hurry to Serabulak and dispel any false accusations about his millennial faith or personal life. He made it clear that because of his audacity and intemperate speech, Penner would soon be excommunicated from the Bride Community Church. This, according to Epp, would be tantamount to missing Christ when He came.[15]

Traveling as fast as they could and following the approximate route of their predecessors, Epp's party crossed the Hunger Steppe at the end of May and passed through Samarkand at the beginning of June. On June 12, 1882, Claas Epp and some 40 families drove into Serabulak, where a joyful reunion celebration was held. Rather than excommunicating men like Penner, Epp hastily arranged Bible studies each afternoon and prayer meetings at night, because he was convinced that he had to win back his erring brothers. Expounding the books of Daniel, Isaiah, the Gospels, and Revelation with a new fervor, he likened their journeys to the wanderings of the children of Israel. A revived zeal soon captured a majority of the congregation, and they were now receptive to Epp's leadership and a new plan of settlement.[16]

They had to do something quickly, for the new influx of people made a very large group with seven ministers and two teachers. They could not impose much longer on little Serabulak; there were no more quarters available for them and the group was beginning to tax the hospitality of the friendly Sarts. Epp had an answer for this dilemma. While passing through Samarkand, he had been advised that the khan of Khiva might make a place for the Mennonites if Bukhara continued to deny them entry. Khiva now became the new promised land.

12

NEW HOPE AT AULIE ATA

As the Mennonite millennialists faced these perplexing circumstances on the border of Bukhara, the brethren they had left behind in Tashkent were actively engaged in a new enterprise, which would lead to the development of a new settlement in northeastern Turkestan. These Tashkent brethren were in a far more agreeable situation than their counterparts who had wandered to Bukhara. They were comparatively comfortable and secure in the center of an urban area. Working in the quarries, however difficult, still provided income for their families. Moreover, the early support of General von Kaufmann had given them renewed courage in their strange surroundings.

Tashkent Mennonite Plans

But as time went on, a series of misfortunes combined to render their position no longer tenable. The typhoid epidemic had decimated their ranks; Kaufmann's death had deprived them of a patron, and harsher governmental policies followed. Furthermore, these ardent farmers longed for country life; the city was no place to raise children. Also their more practical outlook on life tended to diminish their preoccupation with mystical chiliasm, and this led to a desire to start all over again.

Peters Dies in Tashkent

But by far the most discouraging development among the Tashkent Mennonites was the death of their beloved pastor, Abraham

Peters.[1] The trials of the journey, the rigors of settlement, and the
increasing problems all had taken their toll of this great leader.[2]
Growing weaker as the months wore on, Peters maintained an active
schedule of preaching, teaching, and negotiation[3] until he died in
January 1882.[4] Those who had been critical of the millennialist movement from the very beginning saw in his death a portent of the demise of the entire movement in Turkestan. While one group was
languishing in Bukhara, the death of the greatest man in the colonization effort would soon bring an abrupt end to a venture that
had been completely demoralizing and discouraging from the very out-
set.[5]

Yet amid these counsels of despair, a new leader and the
prospects of new land offered new hope. Jacob Janzen, a staunch
opponent of Claas Epp, succeeded to Peters' role of leadership. This
former Trakt resident, who had earlier rejected Epp's teaching, gave
able guidance to the entire Molotschna contingent when they needed
it most. Not only had he been Peters' first choice for the position,
but he had already demonstrated his capacities in handling the deli-
cate negotiations concerning a new settlement. In fact, he held out
for a provision in their contract which would give 15 years of exemption from any government service for their young men. Janzen's
dreams came true when an agreement was signed with the Russian
government in February 1882.[6]

Move to Aulie Ata, April 8, 1882

After the sealing of this contract, plans were quickly made to
leave for Aulie Ata, a region 150 miles northeast of Tashkent but still
within the borders of Turkestan. A scouting party composed of 13
families were the first to leave. Nine of these were probably those
included in the Jacob Funk wagon train, and the others consisted of
Cornelius Wall and relatives.[7] Following this small group of
pioneering brethren, a larger group of more than fifty families left
on April 8, 1882. They arrived at a spot about 40 miles southeast
of the city of Aulie Ata on April 23 and sent back favorable reports.[8]
Meanwhile, a third band, which had been corresponding with the
Janzen group and wanted to join them, formed part of Claas Epp's
contingent in the city of Turkestan.[9] This group of 12 families had
become completely disenchanted with Epp's brand of millennialism.
After being halted with Epp's train at the village of Ikan on April

11, they traveled directly eastward and reached Aulie Ata on May 4, 1882.[10] By this date, then, more than 80 families had arrived in the Aulie Ata region.[11]

Aulie Ata, or Yambil as it was called by neighboring Kirghiz natives, had once been considered as a possible capital for the guberniia of Turkestan. By 1882, it had grown to a respectable town of over 10,000.[12] Tashkent, however, proved the best city for the seat of government not only because of its strategic location in the valley of the Syr Daria, but because of its commercial interests, excellent fortifications, cultural heritage, and milder climate. Aulie Ata, on the other hand, was approximately 5,000 feet above sea level and usually discouraged colonists because of reported poor crops and cold weather.[13] It was learned by the Mennonites, however, that the Talas River basin could become a productive area for raising grain and cattle if enterprising farmers would diligently work the land.[14]

This valley, about 25 miles wide and almost 200 miles long, was enclosed by the perennially snow-covered Alexander Mountains, named after the great Greek hero. Out of the mountains each spring flowed several life-giving streams that emptied into the larger Talas River. The soil of the valley was composed of a yellow clay which needed this extra moisture for farming.[15]

On reaching the beautiful valley, each contingent began building dugouts for temporary quarters and promptly planted wheat crops with the seeds they brought with them. The first group leased 270 acres, or 100 dessiatines, at one ruble per dessiatine. Overhead for grain and sowing raised this expenditure to 250 rubles. The first small harvest of the Mennonite vanguard later yielded 200 rubles' profit, an encouraging sign to those who followed.[16]

With the initial group's sowing completed by the end of March 1882, they awaited the arrival of more brethren to help clear the land and increase the productivity of the area. As newcomers arrived, each family was allotted 35 acres to begin farming. As manpower increased, a network of irrigation canals were ingeniously constructed which would divert the waters of the Talas to the grass, trees, and grain fields. In fact, these Mennonite pioneers soon discovered that with proper cultivation, irrigation, and some fertilization everything that grew in European Russia could be produced in the Talas Valley. In this veritable garden spot of Asia, four Mennonite villages grew up: Gnadenfeld, the smallest; Köppental, begun by the leader Janzen; Gnadental, and Nikolaipol.[17]

From the very beginning of the colony, the neighboring Kirghiz natives were very friendly to the new pioneers. During the lonely months of beginning a settlement in a strange land, they were most helpful and shared their knowledge about the area with the strange "invaders." Owing to the isolation of their settlement, these Kirghiz natives interacted with the Mennonites in a degree unparalleled in the Turkestan experience. No other native group so influenced Mennonites as did the Kirghiz.

These Black Kirghiz (*Kara Kirghiz*) living in and around the Alexander Mountains and near Lake Issy-kul, totaled in number about 300,000. The new settlers found their neighbors fascinating and were especially intrigued by their living quarters. The Kirghiz circular tents, or *kibitkis*, were held up by rods and had walls and a roof covered with felt to soak up water. A small opening at the point of the roof let out smoke from the communal cooking fire. These dwellings were regarded by the new settlers as superior to their own dugouts. During the summer the Kirghiz would take their tents high into the Alexander Mountains, where they could be near their grazing cattle.

Although their main livelihood was cattle breeding, they did practice some agriculture, especially rice growing. Their methods of plowing and planting seemed rather strange to the systematic Mennonites. Two animals — either horse and camel, bull and horse, mule and cow, or any other combination — were hitched to a simple wooden plow which crudely tore up the ground. The brethren were equally amused when they first saw the primitive mode of transportation among their neighbors. They rode horses, camels, donkeys, mules, bulls, or even cows with apparent indifference. They did not use wagons, but loaded whatever they wished to transport upon the backs of their poor beasts. These horses, camels, cattle, and smaller animals provided a staple diet of meat which the Kirghiz ate from a common pot without the use of salt, pepper, or bread. The poorer Kirghiz, however, were far more destitute than even the most poverty-stricken Mennonite because they never had sufficient meat to eat. Instead, these poor natives subsisted on a simple diet indeed: a kind of gruel consisting of camel's milk and roasted millet. With the exception of one small Russian hamlet to the north, the Kirghiz were the only neighbors the Mennonites knew; they formed the sole German settlement in the vast region between Tashkent and Aulie Ata.[18]

A vast uncultivated prairie frontier faced these dedicated colonists. As more people continued to arrive from Tashkent and the number of mouths to feed increased, their early days were full of hardship and deprivation. Some villagers had neither grain to sow nor money to buy any; strong men were eager for hard work, but they needed immediate assistance and did not know where to turn for help in a new land. Fortunately, a rich Russian merchant named Ivanov loaned many of them seed and arranged for a generous installment plan calling for repayment over a five-year period with no interest. He was happy, he told them, to have new farmers in the area. The Mennonites, who had learned to distrust "unscrupulous" Russians, were astonished at his generosity.[19]

Harsh Winter

The approaching winter weather signaled the time for moving out of their dugouts and building more permanent structures. Although adobe or clay loam served as the primary building material, wooden beams could be secured in a pine forest high in the mountains. When the settlers used the forest, however, they were required to replant a seedling for every tree they felled.[20] In August 1882, Jacob Mandler, of the new village of Gnadental, wrote his relatives that houses were going up even though the summer harvest had been generally poor owing to the lateness of planting in the village area. With the village still mourning the deaths of six people from undiagnosed illnesses, Mandler begged his brethren abroad to pray for the poverty-stricken people of Gnadental.[21]

Even with the use of these native materials, the new houses began to give their village the appearance typical of Mennonite settlements everywhere. Homes were plotted in an east-west orientation; along the streets canals brought water to the individual homes in order to alleviate the expense of a number of separate wells. Two rows of poplar trees were planted along the larger canals, and each householder dug a smaller canal into his garden at the rear of his house for irrigation purposes. Varying according to the owner's financial status and skill, the houses were neatly spaced and well constructed. They were usually 30 to 50 feet long with some having attics over a seven-foot-high flat roof.[22]

After most of the homes were constructed, harsh winter weather caught many farmers unprepared, their crops still in the field. In fact, on October 3, 1882, a heavy snow and hard frost froze even the grain for the horses, and the bulk of the crops in the field at that time were ruined. Then, as suddenly as it had snowed, a bright sun came out, and the weather remained pleasant long enough to give them a chance to finish building their homes.[23] Despite this respite, several families became completely discouraged owing to their extreme poverty and a new smallpox epidemic. Desperate, they moved to the city of Aulie Ata and later to Tashkent in order to find work. Each of them hoped to earn enough money in the city so they could come back and begin a profitable farm.[24] But troubles continued to dog them. One such family, the Siebert Goertzes, lost two sons to a renewed outbreak of typhoid fever in Tashkent. Another young man, Bernard Wiebe, was threatened by conscription, had to appeal his case to St. Petersburg, and was finally put on probation for a year.[25]

Meanwhile, the Aulie Ata settlers came through that first winter in better condition than they had entered it. Actually, only one child died of smallpox, and the pioneer farmers believed things were improving.[26] The snow ended in early February 1883, and they were anxious to begin sowing. Friends in Nebraska and Kansas had sent money, as did *Die Rundschau*, an American Mennonite newspaper. Jacob Janzen, the leader of the Aulie Ata settlements, subsequently credited this change in the weather and financial aid from America as those critical factors which gave them a completely new outlook on life.[27]

Spring Improves Situation

That spring saw gradual economic improvement, a majority of the inhabitants could now eke out a meager living at least. The breeding of swine and horses coupled with all types of grain production promised a subsistence income for many. As the population grew, the need for more dairy cattle increased. Milk and cheese soon became an important source of income, and some of the farmers became so involved in this activity that they moved with their cows into the mountain pastures every summer like their Kirghiz neighbors. Camels were purchased to carry food, supplies, and mail periodically from the four villages to the "cowboys" in the mountains; they would then return loaded with milk and cheese.[28]

Help from Abroad

But the poorer members of the community, with their life savings spent long ago and no cow to depend on, had to rely on friends who had extra food or on relatives in America. Janzen and Peter Pauls, a settlement social worker, were responsible for seeing that the gifts from neighbors and America were equitably distributed. Older people and families with children were given preference, but if any family received a designated gift from relatives, they saw to it that the proper family received the money. For example, on July 16, 1883, Janzen received $310.00 from American brethren. Soon the whole community knew about the money donation, and one after another of the needy came to the Pauls' home for aid. He carefully instructed them to be frugal with the money, because he did not know when any more would arrive. By noon the money was gone, and the late arrivers left with empty hands and "empty hearts."[29]

The following day, Janzen and Pauls were stopped repeatedly on the street and asked when more funds were coming. They found that many of the very poor were at the end of their resources, but Janzen could only counsel them to continue to look upward to God and eat the mixture of flour, water, and salt they were growing accustomed to. One man informed Janzen that he could not continue much longer because his children were waking up at night and screaming that they were hungry.[30]

With pleas such as this ringing in his ears, Janzen explained to American friends the dark future of his colony. Some, he said, could expect a small harvest of hay, oats (sufficient for a short time), and a meager crop of wheat and barley. But others had plowed too deeply in the extremely heavy soil, and their seed did not sprout.[31] Other leaders were equally concerned about their plight. In a letter from Köppental to the Trakt, Jacob Funk mirrored Janzen's anxiety. After recounting the dismal prospects for the crop and the miseries of the families of Siebert Goertz and Georg Reuffels in Tashkent, Funk expressed his thanks to God for the health of his wife and five children. He requested prayers and letters for Janzen's son, Heinrich, who was quite ill with an infected leg.[32]

Church Activities

As conditions worsened and the poor grew poorer during the summer of 1883, many settlers depended more and more on their deep faith in God to carry them through this difficult time. Millennialism waned through the colony, but a new fervor took its place. The teachings of Claas Epp had been shown repeatedly to be contradictory to the spirit of the Bible. The moderating force of their leaders, Abraham Peters, Jacob Janzen, and Jacob Funk, as well as their impoverished condition persuaded the majority to abandon eschatological preoccupations in favor of a concern for the here and now.

In this new revival of faith, the Kuban people began exerting a growing influence. Those from Molotschna and the Trakt who were connected with what they called the old Mennonite Church, or Kirchliche Mennonites, listened with interest to the teachings of the Mennonite Brethren from Kuban. Though they had composed the smallest party in the immigration, they were destined to have the greatest impact on the religious life of Aulie Ata. They convinced many of their brethren that strict adherence to the Bible and belief in immersion as the only mode of baptism would build a more dedicated Christian community. Sprinkling as a form of baptism, though generally practiced, they rejected as lacking in biblical foundation. In the final analysis, this theological dispute meant that two separate congregations were developing. As this separation progressed, they wisely made sure that no enmity would be shown to those who disagreed theologically. The Mennonite Brethren built a church at Nikolaipol and decided to admit even those not immersed into their fellowship if the doctrine of immersion was too hard for them to accept.[33] Köppental had a Mennonite (Kirchliche) Church; it later adopted immersion as a rule but did not strictly enforce it.[34] Mennonites from the four villages had a choice of where to go to church on Sunday.

As time went on, the strictness of the Mennonite Brethren Church became less rigorous, and there was a decline in emphasis upon discipline by biblical exhortation. In fact, some M.B. members became concerned about the growing laxity in their community. After convincing others in the Kirchliche Church, they formed a new congregation called simply the Alliance Church (*Allianz-Gemeinde*) which was to lead the whole community back to practicing the faith according to the example of the early Christians. This third church, with its emphasis on the "inner life," became the new model for religious devotion in Aulie Ata.

The more liberal Kirchliche Mennonite Church, overreacting to the new movement, voted stricter rules which made immersion man-

The church at Köppental in Aulie Ata. The old man is Wilhelm Penner's father-in-law and the girls are Cornelius Wall's daughters.

datory for new converts and restricted the Lord's Supper to believers and excluded the "unconverted." But even with these more explicit rulings they never actually demanded immersion for those coming to their fellowship from the other churches.

The Alliance Church continued its emphasis on the inner man. They also associated freely with the other two churches because they believed the competition strengthened all three. In later years, the Alliance Church merged with the Mennonite Brethren, leaving two fairly strong churches in the settlement.[35]

One manifestation of the impact of the new religiosity is that as early as August 1883, though still living in dire poverty, the people seemed happy in their faith. Their joy was expressed in a large baptismal service held by the Talas River. Among those baptized were young Siebert and Abraham Goertz, recently returned from a stay in Tashkent, and Peter Dalke, the future father-in-law of Goertz. The scene has been described in this way:

> The entire settlement came to this baptismal service at the big river and looked on. And this started such a movement and a

fire of the Spirit that immediately one after another came to be baptized, and the [Mennonite] Brethren Church grew through God's Word; it increased without great preachers.[36]

The revival of faith expressed itself also in a new missionary zeal to win their "heathen" Kirghiz neighbors to Christianity.[37] Although the Mennonites did not have official government permission, neither were they impeded in their efforts, so they decided to attempt religious evangelism. One barrier, however, was the Kirghiz language.[38] The young people were the first to attempt to become conversant with Kirghiz religion. They noted early that these Muslims referred to God as "Kudai" in their dialect, rather than using the more common "Allah." The Kirghiz emphasis on the one and only Kudai proved to be a larger barrier than language. These monotheistic natives could not accept the Mennonite belief in the Trinity. Instead they argued that Christians had three gods while they had only one.[39]

The trinitarian problem did not diminish the zeal of young men such as Johann Bartsch, however. Because of his earlier work with the Kirghiz while but a teenager, he was invited by the English Bible Society to start a Bible center in Tashkent. The main objective of this body was to put the Holy Scriptures of Christianity into all the languages of the Turkestan area and actively seek to win the natives to the Christian religion. Bartsch gained the permission of the government to evangelize among all the native peoples. Franz Bartsch, his younger brother, was hired to sell books and Bibles to the natives and discuss the meaning of Scripture with them. Becoming quite involved in teaching the natives, he gained for himself a profound understanding of many aspects of theology.[40]

The Question of Army Service

During this time of religious change, innovation, and missionary activity by men like the Bartsch brothers, one principle of their faith remained unaltered: a strong belief in nonresistance. Even though the settlers knew that the young men of Aulie Ata would be subject to forestry service when they came to the settlement, they prayed that they would not have to engage in an activity which so compromised their faith. As it turned out, their prayers were answered. A new and more liberal governor-general showed himself to be most accommodating to their convictions, and even sent representatives from Tashkent to insure that the Mennonites were happy at Aulie Ata.[41] By May 1884, only one young man, Tobias Daridow Schmidt, had been formally drafted, and even he was not required to serve because of lung trouble. Four others had been called to Tashkent over the two-year period, but none were required to serve; either their service number was too high or their family situation required them to remain at home.[42] Though on occasion impatient officials warned the Mennonites to meet their obligations in this regard or face deportation to Siberia, these threats never came to pass.[43] None of the original settlers of the Aulie Ata settlement ever served the state in any way, though new emigrants were occasionally drafted into the forestry service and a few even into the army.[44]

To be sure, the settlers planted trees in the state forests to replace those they cut down, but this could hardly be construed as "serving the state." Though the laws provided for compulsory forest service by the Mennonites, they were never enforced at Aulie Ata. The promise of 15 years free from obligation incorporated in their original contract was kept and even extended.[45] Whether other Mennonites recognized the movement to Aulie Ata as a work of God or not, these nonresistant settlers praised it as a blessing of God.[46]

In spite of the hardships of their early days, the settlement struck deep roots and remained. Over the years there were groups who returned to Tashkent, the Trakt, Molotschna, and the Kuban, or immigrated to America, but there was never a total exodus. Descendants of these original settlers can be found in Aulie Alta today.

13

THE KHIVAN REFUGE

Plans to Leave Serabulak

Because of their dedication to a theology of millennialism, the Mennonites in Serabulak would experience more trying circumstances than their brethren at Aulie Ata. Wandering from one hopeless situation into another, these courageous pioneers would endure ever-increasing hardships, and their quest for unity in Christ would end in a permanent and irrevocable division in their ranks. Every antici-pated refuge was to prove illusory and perilous. Such was to be the character of Khiva, too. Even before the arrival of Claas Epp, the entire fellowship of the Bride Community had come to a consensus that they must move away from both Russia and Bukhara. The big question, however, was: Would the khan of Khiva give them a firm offer? If so, they decided to accept it gladly. By the time the Epp train reached Serabulak, the group had come to a unity of purpose: that of seeking Christ in the khanate of Khiva.

Offer of the Khan of Khiva, July 1882

At last they obtained official sanction to go to Khiva. In June 1882, Heinrich Jantzen received a letter from General Dreech, a Russian official in Samarkand, in which the entire group was granted permission to travel through Bukhara in order to settle in the khan-ate of Khiva. Dreech explained also that the khan would most gladly give them land for a settlement in a most beautiful location along the Amu Darya. It was imperative, he urged, that a delegation be sent to investigate the possibilities.[1]

Deputation to Petro-Alexandrovsk

With less than a week of rest since his arrival, Epp counseled immediate action. On June 21, 1882, an elected deputation composed of Epp, Jantzen, and the articulate and optimistic teacher, Emil M. Riesen, were chosen to represent the group. With the full knowledge of Bukhara officials, they started a journey that would take them over 600 miles and last well over a month.

When Khiva had been conquered by the czar's troops ten years earlier, the Amu Darya was designated as the boundary between Russian territory on the north and the Khivan lands to the south. Though the khanate was a Russian protectorate, the khan still held nominal sovereignty along the south bank of the river, and it was he who had the right to grant the Mennonites the land they desired. Consequently, the delegation halted first at the Russian garrison at Petro-Alexandrovsk, where they obtained from the commander, General Grottenhelm, a safe-conduct pass to the khan's court at Khiva. This official also provided a Russian officer to escort the group before the khan.

Meeting with the Khan

The Uzbek Khan graciously greeted the Mennonites in his palace receiving room and told them they could have as much land as they could cultivate along the Amu Darya about 100 miles farther downstream. For four years he would not expect them to pay taxes or serve the government in any way. After that period, however, they must give one twentieth of their harvest and twelve days' labor a year to projects of the khanate. The four years of freedom from taxes particularly pleased the delegation. Then, as the discussion continued, the khan spoke of more serious matters: the Mennonites would be subject to Khiva's harsh penalties against robbery, murder, and rape, all of which carried the death penalty. Further, said the khan, they must promise never to raise the "unclean animal" — hogs! As the delegates suppressed their amusement, Epp assured the monarch not only that he would not have to worry about Mennonites being law-breakers — they were noted for being law-abiding subjects — but he promised also there would definitely be no raising of hogs. Epp's manner, deportment, and speech made a favorable impression of the khan. When the Mennonite leader boldly requested permission for many future migrations from the West in order to organize a "refuge" from the great tribulation in their settlement, the khan unhesitatingly granted his request, though clearly failing to comprehend the full meaning of Epp's proposal.[2]

Pleased with the encounter with the Khivan monarch, Epp wrote a letter on July 21, in which he compared this new plan to settle in Khiva to that journey of the children of Israel to the Promised Land. The earlier misfortunes of his followers, he averred, were not suffered because they had gone astray from God's will at all; they constituted but a period of trial and testing of their faith to the end. If they were faithful, they would deserve to rule with Christ for 1000 years. Government officials in Russia, Turkestan, and Bukhara were merely being manipulated and used by God so He could show His will to the Bride Community. They were but "tools" to open the place of refuge on the Amu Darya prior to the imminent advent of the Western Antichrist. He further believed that the fact of their being led to Khiva when all looked hopeless should still all criticism of the venture. He closed the letter: "Where facts speak, opinions are not necessary, where the Lord speaks, humans keep silent." Epp, for one, was convinced that the trip to Khiva would be their final trek.[3]

Deputation Returns to Serabulak, August 1882

Returning to Serabulak in early August, the delegation gave glowing reports about Khiva and the khan. Although they had not seen the land for settlement, they knew the door was open, all they had to do was to walk through into paradise. Waiting for them, they believed, was fertile land, religious freedom, immunity from conscription, and a place of refuge to wait for Christ.

Plans were put in motion to leave for the refuge on August 30. First, they would go by wagon to the dreaded Kara Kul Desert, then take camels to the Amu Darya, boats to Petro-Alexandrovsk, and on to the promised land. Immediately letters were sent to relatives and friends telling of their auspicious plans and explaining how to retreat to the place of refuge during the time of the great tribulation. They even worked up elaborate routes from Germany and Russia by wagon and boat, and those receiving these directions were to tell other Christians about the refuge. Anxiously, they looked forward to Mennonite friends and relatives joining them soon in Khiva. Some of those receiving letters did not yet believe, they knew, but they would in due time because the last days were drawing near.[4]

The Mennonites of Serabulak then turned their attention to more

Heinrich H. Wiebe in Turkestan — brother of Anna

immediate problems at home. Ten families still lingered at Ebenezer, harassed by Bukharan officials but persistent in their refusal to go with the rest of the group. Also, young Jacob Jantzen was still in

Tashkent, and the group did not want to leave him behind. Then, two miracles occurred. They were informed by a letter that Jantzen was now free and was planning to join them in their migration to Khiva.⁵ About the same time the ten delinquent families were brought back to Serabulak by Bukharan soldiers who were ordered to send them on to Khiva with the rest. The ten families explained that they had stubbornly remained at Ebenezer only because they feared that Cornelius Quiring would be drafted if they touched Russian soil. Though encouraged by the news concerning Jantzen and the generous Khivan offer, they still had difficulty in arriving at a definite decision.⁶

For the ten families were not of one accord. Hermann Bartsch, one of the men of the group, stated firmly that he could agree neither with the Khiva plans nor the theology of Claas Epp. He and his family then abruptly left for Tashkent. Another man and his family said they could not undertake still another journey and decided to remain in Serabulak. The remaining eight families still regarded Epp "a wolf in sheep's clothing," but were urged by friends and relatives to moderate their attitudes lest they show themselves more radical and uncompromising than Epp himself. Meanwhile Epp made it plain to these recalcitrant brethren that they must ask forgiveness for their stubborn pride or God's judgment would come upon them. Here Epp was put into the unusual situation of trying to persuade a group to compromise and moderate their views because they had followed his teachings literally! Mennonites in other communities were amused at this strange turn of events and even more amazed when Epp succeeded in convincing them to moderate their attitudes. The B. Janzen family and the seven others finally decided to follow Epp to Khiva. They sincerely hoped, however, that this would definitely be their final journey and warned their leader that he had better be right this time.⁷

The Johann Drake Affair

While these events were transpiring, Jacob Toews was busily collecting money to support the entire group en route to Khiva. Toews was to act as a central receiving agent, and the people were to help each other through him rather than on an individual basis.

However, these diligent preparations were temporarily interrupted by an unusual turn of events. Johann Drake, a lanky young German who had fled his homeland to evade the draft, had come from the

Trakt with Epp and had moved in with the Jacob Toews family at Serabulak. The first Sunday of his stay, Toews found the man missing Then he discovered his best stud horse and several thousand rubles were also gone. The locked desk drawer of his living room had been forced open and the money belonging to the entire group taken. Several angry Mennonites hurried to Katakurgan where they were told Drake had been seen heading for Tashkent. In Katakurgan, they had a special prayer meeting and asked God to show Drake what he had done to their plans. After the prayer session, they decided not to follow him to Tashkent, but let God deal with him.

A week later, a letter came to Toews from the repentant Drake asking forgiveness. In his reply, Toews promised that if the young man would return and explain the reason for his wicked action, he would be forgiven. Upon Drake's return, he explained the reason for his absconding before a solemn meeting at Toews' home. He told of being refused by a girl he was courting and of joining the Epp train in his despondency. On the journey to Serabulak, he learned of the death of his mother in Germany, and his unhappiness and homesickness became too much to bear. When he learned of the funds Toews held in trust, he stole the money and ran away without thinking of the consequences. After selling Toews' horse in Tashkent, he rented a room for the night and went to buy a railway ticket for Germany. Here, a mystifying incident occurred. A stranger at the station called him by name and asked where he was going. Then the stranger brazenly called him a thief and asked him to return to Serabulak. Drake ran to his room wondering whether he had encountered an angel or a devil. He began contemplating suicide, but instead prayed to God for pardon for his crime. Then he wrote Toews. Toews and the others, even though they knew the story included unusual embellishments, were impressed with Drake's apparent sincerity and granted him their forgiveness. Perhaps Drake's confession would have undergone closer scrutiny if other events had not claimed their attention.[8]

After the Drake affair, the attention of the group turned to the journey itself. The delegation to Khiva had explored the Bukharan terrain, and considered it quite impassable for horse and wagon and even dangerous to their lives if they happened to stray from a caravan trail. Consequently, Heinrich Jantzen wrote General Dreech for advice as to the best route across that barren land. Dreech replied with the offer of an escort of soldiers to accompany them through Bukhara to the Amu Darya, where they would meet boats and float downsteam. The general also agreed to obtain permission from the khan of Bukhara.

Wagons Depart from Serabulak, August 1882

With these preparations finally completed, the unified wagon train, composed of not only the main faction but also the dissidents from Ebenezer and the draftees, departed for their final refuge on August 30, 1882. More than 60 families — about 150 people, some 50 wagons, 80 horses, 10 carts and about 140 camels began the trip.[9]

After stopping in Katakurgan for supplies, the camels were loaded with everything they could not get into the wagons. They then proceeded to the Bukharan border, which they crossed on September 1, and continued to Shirinchatin, a small Sart village, where they were met by an escort of 50 uniformed soldiers whose duty would be to assist them through Bukharan territory. These soldiers helped repair bridges and roads along the route, arranged for food to sustain everyone across the desert, and saw to it that the party paid only reasonable prices for their supplies.[10] A uniformed bek led the troop of men, and his elegant horse, dress, and equipment much impressed the Mennonites.[11]

Tearing down fences in their path and crossing cultivated fields, the escort helped the group cross the dangerous Zaravshan River and its tributaries several times. The steep banks, rocky bed, deep holes, and quicksand caused delay even with their help. One camel disappeared beneath the quicksand with a load of goods, but surfaced again and reached shore; a wagon went over a steep incline and almost turned over. The driver, Johann Jantzen, was especially terrified because Michael Klaassen lay ill with typhus inside. Later this same wagon and one other sank into quicksand up to their boxes and had to be dug out.[12]

The Kara Kul Desert

Finally, on September 11, after over 150 miles of travel, the wagon train camped at the village of Kara Kul, on the edge of the desert of the same name. Even with the escort, the journey from Katakurgan had been extremely difficult; wheels and axles broke time and time again. Remaining in Kara Kul a week, they prepared for the three-day desert crossing. Unfortunately, however, a young girl, Maria Albrecht, died, and their plans for departure were interrupted. The funeral was a particularly gloomy occasion because the Mennonites saw the death as a bad omen. The soliders showed themselves to be very understanding at the sorrow of the Mennonites and told the curious natives not to bother them during this two-day period.

After this brief period of mourning the Mennonites unpacked their wagons, took them apart, and loaded them piece by piece onto camels. This had to be done because the deep sand dunes of the Kara Kul Desert would never support the heavy, cumbersome wagons. Kirghiz and Turkomen inhabitants of Kara Kul graciously helped load the camels. In the midst of the bedlam of packing, the snorting of camels, and the haste of preparation, the women and children began to become fearful. To reassure them a device was invented which would comfortably and safely carry the women and children. On either side of the one-humped dromedaries, bed-frame boxes were slung. These were then covered with linen to protect the occupant from the sun. These criblike affairs were 5 x 2 1/2 feet and were balanced on each side of the camel and tied together by ropes. Johann Jantzen loaded food supplies and a goat on one side and his wife and three children on the other and achieved perfect balance. His large horse could even pass under the contraptions, they were so high off the ground. On another camel, the ailing Michael Klaassen was placed on one side and his mother and sister on the other. All this provided quite a sight to the native population, as each camel driver led groups of 10-12 camels with their strange loads. About 30 Mennonite men on horseback were to follow behind the strange procession.[13]

The experience of the two nights in the desert were unforgettable. On the evening of September 17, they passed old ruins on the desert and turned into the sand dunes, some of which were as much as 180 feet high. The party traveled at night, stopping at midnight for a two-hour rest, and navigated cautiously along a narrow caravan trail that usually followed the crest of the dunes. It was planned that the horses should follow the camel tracks to keep their footing. These nights passed silently except for an occasional cry of a camel or a driver, but were far brighter than usual. As the bed-frame boxes swayed back and forth along the crest of sand dunes overlooking clifflike inclines, a large comet, later called the Great Comet of 1882, whose tail reached halfway across the sky, shone very brightly. It was so bright, in fact, that one could read the songbooks and they sang songs such as "Our Journey Leads Through the Wilderness." On this brief interlude a child was born, and one mother, Mrs. Graeve, became very ill. Looking back in later years the participants in this strange journey were grateful that no sandstorm or rainstorm had occured to complicate their passage.[14]

Emerging from the region of deep sand, the group stopped, carefully rebuilt their wagons, and rolled along toward the Amu Darya. They knew they were approaching the river when the horses smelled the water and raised their heads, and the wagon drivers stood up to see the trees along the river in the distance. It was September 20 when they reached Ildshik, a village on the Amu Darya. From here the swift river flowed toward Khiva and finally emptied into the Aral Sea.

Kujaks, Horses and Sorrow

Resting in Ildshik, they dismissed the camel caravan and hired large flat boats, or *kujaks,* 140 feet long. A 12-inch wall of reeds covered with pitch kept the water out of these shallow craft as the party's possessions were loaded and packed on board. In all, eight boats were rented for $105.00 each. Partly because of the high cost of renting these boats, and also because of the fear they inspired in the horses, more than 50 men decided to ride along the riverbank to their destination.[15]

Both groups began their parallel journeys on September 24, hoping to reach Khiva in less than two weeks. Occasionally the kujaks would strike a sandbar, and the owners had to push the heavily laden boats with long poles to free them. Sometimes they met empty boats on their way upstream, drawn by men who walked slowly along the bank. The Mennonites were glad to be going downstream, even though strong winds slowed their progress at times. Even this relatively easy journey claimed its victims, as Mrs. Graeve, a beloved wife and mother of five children, died on one of the boats. She was buried on the bank of the Amu Darya under a small clump of apricot trees. Stopping for the night, some slept on deck while others found a spot on shore; fires had to be kept going all night because tigers and other predators inhabited the area.

The men riding overland had to worry more about bandits than tigers. As they were following the mail road, they were told that bandits in the hills had recently killed a postal employee and stolen his mail. Indeed, Jacob Jantzen encountered a band of brigands, but fortunately escaped unharmed. Having unknowingly dropped a saddle bag late in the night, he had to ride back along the trail alone to pick it up. He then came upon two riders who had rifles slung over their shoulders, revolvers on the belts, cartridges across their chests, and long swords. Riding straight toward them, he saw the saddle bag on the ground and picked it up, just as one of the riders asked, "Where are the others?" Jantzen answered, "Behind the hill," though they were, of course, miles away. They probably knew he was lying, but they let him ride away unharmed.[16]

Arrival in Petro-Alexandrovsk

The two separate parties reached Petro-Alexandrovsk on October 1, some 200 miles from their embarkation point at Ildshik. The horsemen camped near the wall of the garrison while the remainder of the party bivouacked on the river a few miles from the town. On Sunday, October 4, a few of the horsemen walked to the other camp to take part in worship services and to see how the river journey had been.[17] It had not been easy. One woman in the party wrote friends on the Trakt that she had completed the trip only with the help of God. The camel-back journey and the crowded boats were the most trying conditions she had experienced in more than two years of traveling.

Soon after arriving in this Russian garrison town, a rumor was passed around that the khan of Khiva had changed his mind about admitting the Mennonites. But they sent word of their arrival to the khan, and General Grottenhelm personally rode to their camp to encourage them and advise them to buy plenty of supplies for their new homes, such as windows, doors, hinges, and nails. On October 5, both parties broke camp to continue about 100 miles downstream. The boats landed near the Turkomen village of Kipchak four days later and were told their destination was only three hours away. Notifying the horsemen who were nearby, they pushed out into the stream for the last time.

Arrival in Lausan, October 1882

On October 9, the groups joined at their new settlement on the Khiva side of the Amu Darya. After unloading the boats and unpacking the horses, the riverbank was full of boxes, trunks, wagon wheels, axles, and a variety of items including small children running and playing among the supplies. After resting for a brief time, they began looking over the site. They found themselves in a low-lying, insect-infested marshy area, where brush and tall reeds were growing and the occasional sound of wild animals, such as hogs, jackals, and tigers could be heard. This "open door" they had so expectantly looked forward to presented almost insurmountable obstacles to the discouraged band.[18]

The first Saturday night was spent in the tall reeds of the marshy flats adjacent to the river. The next day, after observing Sunday with a thanksgiving service, the men surveyed the land as to the best location to build temporary quarters. The marsh was bordered by a low plateau with hills in the distance, but this higher ground was stony. The lower lands were sandy and could be irrigated during times of high water using small dams and canals which had been built by government engineers before their arrival. Because of seemingly better conditions, they decided to build on the flats. Early on Monday morning, they began assembling the wagons in their settlement, constructing dugouts, each with a window and a door, and digging wells. Later, a dugout church, with one end projecting from a small hill, was constructed. An extra room was also added to this hillside chapel for a school. Some of the young men were put to work clearing the area of reeds. So tall were the reeds that the settlers could only see over them by standing on their horses. Other Mennonites began measuring garden areas on either side of a small canal that got its water from the river. Still other workmen went to Turkomen neighbors and purchased wood, reeds, mats, groceries, and fuel. After these initial projects, the Mennonites began calling their fledging settlement Lausan, after the local Turkoman name for the irrigation canal and hill beyond. They did not care what their refuge was called, just so long as they could at last find peace and stability.[19]

Lausan, however, did not bring immediate peace to the weary Mennonites. December floodwaters flowed into a number of the dugouts, forcing many families to move to higher ground. Claas Epp and about 20 families moved to "the hill," while ten more located within an enclosed courtyard purchased from the natives. Soon five more families constructed their own courtyard.[20] Each separate group became a close-knit community, built its own canals and gardens, and purchased pumps for irrigation. Epp urged his close friends to build another small church on the hill.[21] But in the process of new construction a more serious problem arose with the government.

A scene from the fledgling settlement at Lausan, Khiva, in 1883.

Governmental Indecision

Uncertainty as to their position still persisted owing to the precarious position of the Protectorate of Khiva in Russian imperial policy. In fact, the khan soon summoned representatives of the settlement to his palace. Making a quick trip to Khiva, Hermann Jantzen and Wilhelm Penner returned with a report that the khan did not believe that Russia would permit their stay. Then on February 27, an official of the khan came from Khiva and informed them they must move in twelve days! The order, he told them, was not from the khan but from Petro-Alexandrovsk. The next day, Hermann Jantzen, Claas Epp, and Wilhelm Penner hastily conferred with General Grotten-helm. The general, always gracious to his German friends, explained that Governor-General Chernayev had expressed his concern about their occupying territory along the still undefined border between Russia and Khiva. The governor-general offered no elaboration of this problem, and Grottenhelm explained he could do nothing to guarantee them permanent occupancy. Instead, he advised them to either wait and deal with the governor-general personally since he was soon expected at Petro-Alexandrovsk, or go and live with their brethren at the Aulie Ata settlement. The deputation told Grottenhelm that under no circumstances would they ever move to Aulie Ata; they preferred to wait in Petro-Alexandrovsk for Chernayev. The governor-general was expected daily, so a nervous Grottenhelm rode out to greet him, but learned he had been delayed in Tashkent. During Grottenhelm's absence his personal chamberlain frankly told Epp that Russian annexation of Khiva was imminent, but that he felt their four-year contract would be honored. Epp responded that the Lord would not have led them there if they were not supposed to stay. The chamberlain agreed that the Russian government would probably let them stay at their "place of refuge."[22]

When Chernayev did not arrive after several days, Grottenhelm ordered the khan to allow them to stay until April 1, and the men went home. Finally, a meeting with the governor-general was held on March 23, with Jacob Toews, Hermann Jantzen, and Emil Riesen representing the colonists. All of their anxiety had been for nothing. After brief amenities, Chernayev was asked about the future of the Mennonite settlement. He told them he did not object to their staying, inquiring merely, "Will it be good for you?" The delegation affirmed their desire to stay, and the matter was closed.[23]

Johann Drake's Insanity

This governmental indecision was not the only problem facing the leadership of the Lausan community. One incident particularly disturbed the whole group. One Sunday night a group of girls saw "the outsider" Johann Drake jumping, laughing, and clapping his hands in a field near the hillside church. Though they mentioned this to some of the men at church, the entire congregation was horrified when Drake walked into the church, marched up to the podium, and began singing the Prussian national anthem. At first no one knew how to respond to his strange irreverence. After a tense silence, one of the men walked up to Drake and asked him to leave. Drake then began struggling, and it took several men to carry the husky, six-foot Drake from the building. Later, after completing services, they saw him standing quietly on the crest of the hill. When several men went to investigate, they found him leaning on a staff, a small book in his mouth. It looked as if he were trying to swallow the book. One of the brethren stepped forward and roughly jerked the book from Drake's mouth, causing it to bleed. After emotions subsided, Claas Epp asked if he was really trying to devour the book. Speaking in a very incoherent manner, Drake replied the Holy Spirit had told him that he had been chosen to swallow this small Bible and then go preach the contents. Some time passed before he stopped his babbling and he became very quiet. The men surmised that Drake had become mentally deranged over the recent death of his father added to the previous sorrows of his mother's death and the broken engagement with the girl he loved. Drake was cared for tenderly and became an object of pity in the community.[24]

Making a Living

The Mennonites tried to banish these problems through hard work. They spent the month of April 1883, in plowing, improving irrigation works, digging new canals, and obtaining the necessary fertilizer. Their crops of potatoes, beans, onions, carrots, cabbage, melons, maize, barley, peas, and clover demanded intensive irrigation. The Amu Darya was not especially high that spring, and all crops required special care and concern. Then, the fear of all farmers of the region came in the form of a black cloud on the horizon — grasshoppers! The majority of the pests passed them by, but here and there they left a blackened field. After this plague, wild hogs came to finish off anything missed by the grasshoppers and ate everything they could find. Hence, the expected harvest was very small for some; others harvested nothing.[25]

Epp's Religious Work

In the midst of this disastrous destruction of their crops, Claas Epp went happily about his religious duties despite the hardships of his flock. He was deeply involved and put all his energy in promoting a community assembly hall, where he hoped all the people from both small churches could unite in religious instruction and preparation for the great tribulation. The problems his people were having now, taught Epp, were nothing compared to the final trials of the last days.

To accomplish the task of building his unifying hall, he ordered every able-bodied man to work two days a week on the project. Many of the men complained that they were having a hard time even making a living and bridled at the extra labor. Epp urged them to work because he said the Lord wanted the assembly hall ready the first of August. In fact, Epp said, it must be ready by August 7, 1883, in order to celebrate a festive occasion. The celebration Epp anticipated was a baptismal service. To him, this service was more important that anything the community was doing.

Portents of Future Troubles

Once again, Epp's impulse to unify turned into another cause for growing divisiveness. Seven of the 12 young people to be baptized had already been baptized by J. K. Penner in Serabulak, but Epp pronounced the baptisms void because Penner had strayed from the truth, and the youngsters had not had a true conversion experience. Several of the brethren, however, believed that the seven young people should not be rebaptized. This very controversial baptism became a point of contention among the settlers and brought even more disunity.[26] These were days of bitter feelings at Lausan, and the Mennonites were soon to face added perils and anxieties that culminated in a deepening sense of fear.

14

REFUGE BECOMES A TRAP

The insecurity of life in the Lausan settlement was compounded by the growing hostility of their Turkoman neighbors. These natives became resentful of the Mennonites, and their jealousy was increased by the khan's perceptible predilection to favor them. This festering resentment turned into such an open animosity that it eventually brought the refuge settlement to an end.

Trouble with Turkoman Natives

While ostensibly friendly during the daylight hours, these Turkomans expressed their hostility through almost nightly raids on the Mennonite farms. Numbering about 300,000 in the entire desert and steppe region between the Syr Darya and the Caspian Sea, they lived in small clan villages.[1] The Turkomans indulged in blood feuds against other clans and "invaders" and were noted for their marauding habits. While contemporaries credit them with great skill in making rugs and mud bricks, others emphasize their penchant for cruelty, lying, stealing, and murderous raids.[2] Though most of the Turkomans near Lausan made their living in settled pastoral or small agricultural pursuits, they had still not completely cast off their old character of nomadic marauders.

The first of many confrontations between the Turkomans and their Mennonite neighbors occurred on March 24, 1883. One family living on "the hill" reported that someone had come in the night and stolen a horse. The owner blamed the Turkomans living nearby, but when accused, they hotly contested the charge. They did not like being blamed, they argued, for something another clan did.

After this initial incident many horses were stolen from the fields of the people of "the hill." At first the thieves had proceeded stealthily, but upon finding no opposition, they resorted to more brazen methods. Unlocked stables were broken into, and when the farmers locked their stables, the marauders began breaking the locks to get at the horses. These depredations continued until within a short time about fifty horses and more than thirty cows had been stolen. One horse was unchained from a wagon standing beside the owner's house and spirited away. As time went on, the Turkomans became even bolder. Horses were taken in the daytime; some even rode the horses past the homes of the Mennonites, dismounted, walked into their homes, stole clothing or other items, went back outside, and rode away. So serious was the situation that Johannes Jantzen moved his family from the hill to one of the walled courtyards in the flats to seek greater security.

Mennonite determination to remain true to their tenets of nonresistance simply emboldened the Turkoman bandits to acts of greater violence.[3] No longer satisfied with merely stealing horses, they began entering homes by force. Their usual tactic was to break windows by shooting into them and screaming for the families to come out. They would then break down the door, drive the people out, break chairs and tables to start a fire, and search the house for money or clothing. Many homes were then vandalized: bedding was cut up and clocks or other useful articles were destroyed. Inevitably, this humiliating treatment led to physical injury. When two Mennonite men tried to stop a band of housebreakers, they were stabbed with sabers. Hearing the commotion, neighbors ran to help and confronted three Turkomans on horseback with sabers and knives raised. Charging forward, the Mennonites beat the robbers' horses with sticks until they broke and ran with the riders. Even this mild form of resistance was too much for many of the elders to accept.

But the young men of the settlement found the continuing depredations intolerable and wanted to fight back — at least for purposes of self-defense. They had been told that the reason the Turkomans had become bolder was that they knew Christianity taught: "And if any man will . . . take away thy coat, let him have thy cloak also." It seemed only right, to their way of thinking, that the Mennonites would only be following their Scriptures if they complied with their neighbors' demands for their property. To further justify their marauding, they let it be known that the devil the Mennonites feared had commanded them to steal and even murder if they resisted. If the Turkomans were not shown the error of their way, the young men insisted, they would cheerfully destroy the entire colony. [4] They demanded weapons for self-defense.

But the leaders of the community were not willing to go that far. Instead, they merely granted permission for the young men to form a nightly guard, to arm themselves with canes, clubs, and sticks, and to use them in a defensive way. Later, when the Turkomans attacked a house, seven young men stood in front of it to block the way, holding their makeshift weapons. The robbers demanded that they move, but the night watch adamantly refused. The result was that all seven defenders were wounded. Another young Mennonite hiding on a roof became so agitated that he yelled at a Turkoman, who wheeled around, fired his rifle, and hit the young man in the head with buckshot. Another group of guards tried to draw these same bandits away from their homes by riding some distance away. They were intercepted by a large band of riders who stole their horses. [5] These diversionary tactics simply did not work.

Murder of Heinrich Abrahms

Unchecked in their brigandry, the Turkoman raiders at last committed a truly serious crime. One day some of the natives from the tent village near "the hill" had jokingly offered to buy Heinrich Abrahms' pretty young wife, Elizabeth. This was a bad omen indeed. For the next night, a band of Turkomans crept into the Abrahms home at the far end of the village to steal Mrs. Abrahms. The pregnant wife woke up first after she heard some noise and saw lights in the living room. Abrahms himself then jumped out of bed, and hurried to the door to frighten the robbers away. But they shot him on the spot and repeatedly stabbed his body. Meanwhile his wife hurriedly slipped out of the bedroom window to take refuge in a neighbor's home across the street. Glancing back, she saw a man she recognized from the tent village with a light in one hand and a sword in the other, stealthily entering the Abrahms bedroom. Terrified, she hid under the neighbor's bed and could only whisper, "Be quiet, they are coming."

When the men of the village arrived at the Abrahms home, the robbers had gone. Abrahms was lying in a pool of blood with 20 to

30 stab wounds and a gunshot in the head. Numerous household items were missing, and the men at first feared that the Turkomans had kidnapped Mrs. Abrahms.

After satisfying themselves as to her safety, they formed a search party of all the men from the flat to track down the cowardly murderers. As they were riding around the hill, they surprised the bandits in the process of dividing the Abrahms possessions. Though unarmed, Peter Unruh angrily called, "You thieves and murderers. What are you doing?" Instantly, about 50 men surrounded him and his companions. Unruh was ordered to kneel and pray to his God because they were going to shoot him for having the audacity to call them thieves and murderers. To this, Unruh responded, "Who are you and why did you mercilessly kill that young man?"

"Because," one answered, "he did not want to let us have what we wanted." They raised their guns, and the Mennonites began begging them not to shoot Unruh. At that moment, the poor demented outcast, Johann Drake, suddenly stepped out of the group, raised Unruh to his feet, and placed his arms around him.

Looking directly at Unruh he said, "Brother, I will die for you." Then he confronted the Turkomans and boldly said, "Take me in place of this man. For there is no one who will miss me or cry for me, since my parents are both dead. I am alone, and I am willing to die for this man; for he has a wife and small children who care."

A Turkoman spokesman replied, "This we cannot do, because not only does our religion not allow it, but it is against our conscience; go away and let us quickly kill this man who called us thieves and murderers." Drake did not even flinch at these words but kept his arms around Unruh. The bandits began murmuring among themselves, lowered their guns, and said, "We grant you both your freedom and your lives." Then they mounted their horses and rode away to the profound relief of the defenseless Mennonites. None of those present had ever experienced anything like this incident and would never forget it.[6]

When local Turkoman authorities were notified about the murder, they merely suggested that the Mennonites should build their houses closer together, build walls around them, and buy guns for protection. Russian officials in Petro-Alexandrovsk said they could not help the settlement because of its distance from their garrison; and, after all, Lausan was on Khivan soil. By now, a number of Mennonite families wanted to leave Lausan because of this seemingly indifferent atti-

tude by the officials, but the fear of crossing the desert where more
Turkomans lived soon dissuaded them. Many others who were not yet
ready to leave found that their basic belief in nonresistance was being
put to the supreme test.

When the news of the murder reached the Russian General Grottenhelm, he suggested that the khan be notified immediately. When
the Mennonites reported the incident to the khan he immediately
ordered an investigation of the murder and also the robberies. Promising the Mennonites restitution for stolen property, he explained
that he was a staunch Uzbek who did not like Turkomans anyway,
and he promptly initiated steps to shut off the Turkoman water supply
in the Lausan area to bring them under submission. In fact, with
the khan's help, within a few months several of the robbers were captured and sent to Khiva for trial.

In showing their concern for the problems of the Mennonites, both
Grottenhelm and the khan hired Mennonites for work in Petro-Alexandrovsk, Khiva, and at Urgench, another city of the Amu Darya.
Mennonite carpenters and wood-carvers began laying a large wooden
floor for Grottenhelm, while others made glass mosaics and a wooden
floor like the one belonging to the czar in St. Petersburg for the khan's
Jewish wife in a new building under construction at Khiva. These extra jobs, however, did not satisfy the majority of the people.

Hiring of Cossack Guards

The majority were far more concerned about continued Turkoman
banditry than they were about the additional income these jobs
would bring. The settlers debated the issue of self-defense at length,
and at last arrived at an uneasy compromise: the majority decided
to hire two cossack night watchmen to protect the settlement. Though
the minority argued that this was a repudiation of the very basis of
their belief in nonresistance, they could not dissuade their distraught
and fearful brethren. The cossacks were to be paid 12 rubles, or about
six dollars a month for their trouble. They were excellent marksmen
with rifles, and the word of their nightly presence and warlike
prowess was well publicized. A few nights after they began work, several Turkomans tried to raid a Mennonite walled compound. The
cossacks simply fired over their heads and they retreated. The presence of the night watchmen resulted in a definite drop in the rate
of robbery and assaults.

A relative calm returned to the upper and lower villages. But it did not last. The minority still argued that it was against God's will to use force, and He would bring judgment upon them. Their antagonists, however, were grateful for the protection, because it was learned that the arrested bandits had recently been released from Khiva and had sworn revenge. Individuals of both opinions were unhappy at Lausan because of the dissension in the settlement, and several openly maintained that Lausan was no longer the place of refuge; the entire group should move to a new land.[8]

Fantasy of Claas Epp

Their problems were further compounded because the group had lost faith in their erstwhile prophet, Claas Epp, during this period of controversy and general confusion. He lost much support when he loftily maintained that he was a "special witness" and could not be bothered with the temporal problems of the community. Worldly concerns no longer were important, he said, because the kingdom of God was near. Because of his complete indifference to their immediate problem, the majority faction rejected him as fanatical and irrelevant. Epp maintained only a small group of faithful followers who remained by his side. They believed Epp was right, that the end was near, and the more practical ministers were being used by the devil.

Those ministers, Jacob Toews, J. K. Penner, and Johann Jantzen, convinced that following Epp was an irrational course against the best interests of the community, began to attack his theology. They openly admitted they had been duped by Epp for a long time and said the so-called "refuge" was a farce and a figment of Epp's imagination. Penner, who had for some time believed that Epp was not a competent biblical interpreter, now frankly labeled him unreasonable and irresponsible. With Jantzen and Toews agreeing with him, it seemed Epp would be completely discredited.[9]

In fact, these were not the only leaders critical of Epp. A former Lutheran minister turned Mennonite who was in Lausan began advocating immersion as the only acceptable mode of baptism. Although Epp completely disavowed this method and spoke against the man, three families joined him in his crusade and defiantly held a baptismal service in the Amu Darya. They then began meeting together, used the Baptist hymnal, *Voice of Faith,* and attacked Epp for his authoritarianism. Although this group contributed to the general discredit

**The palace of the khan of Khiva, who hired Mennonites as carpenters
and wood-carvers and to make glass mosaics for a new building.**

of Epp, the majority of the Mennonites felt they were preoccupied
with minor criticisms and neglecting the larger plight of the community. The four Baptist-minded families moved to Khiva when they
saw they could no longer live happily either with Epp or his opponents.[10]

Invitation by the Khan

By spring, 1884, others began contemplating a move to the city
of Khiva. The khan encouraged such a move because, in his opinion,
it was difficult to "protect" the Mennonites at Lausan. He even
suggested that he had a "big garden" near Khiva that would suit them
well. Emil Riesen was sent to negotiate with the khan, and he came
back telling of a beautiful ten-acre garden just eight miles southwest of
Khiva. The garden, belonging to one of the khan's kinsmen, was an
ideal site, and he had promised those who settled there many special
privileges — more in fact, than his own people enjoyed. Not only did
the khan promise land but also $2000 in reparation for their hardships

among the Turkomans, if they would come. The Mennonites who did not want to leave Khiva were overjoyed by this news. Abruptly the 39 families who agreed with Epp began preparing to leave Lausan and make their home in the safer "big garden."[11]

On April 16, 1884, Epp, Riesen, Wilhelm Penner, Jacob Jantzen, Michael Klaassen, and 34 other families left by boat, carts, and wagons. They took everything they could use in a new settlement: lumber, doors, and furniture. So abrupt was their departure that families did not have a chance to reconcile differences and many simply separated without further discussion. For example, Johann Jantzen's son cast his lot with Epp because his good friends, Michael Klasssen and Jonas Quiring, were going to Khiva. Even J. K. Penner's brother Wilhelm chose to stay with Epp in the Khivan refuge.[12]

Founding of Ak Metchet

After a week of traveling, this faction began their new settlement. Their "big garden" was surrounded by high walls, had huge gates and a courtyard. Within this walled compound they tried to forget the past hardships and dissension. With little land to farm, the men became carpenters on a new building of the khan, and the women did a good business as seamstresses and made small boxes which were widely sold as containers for personal belongings. Outside their wall they raised vegetables, melons, and some rice. Their first project within the walls was to build a church, personally financed by Epp, and a school and residence for teacher Wilhem Penner. From the beginning the church was the only building in the community painted white, and the friendly natives began referring to the Mennonite village garden as "Ak Metchet" or the "White Mosque" in the Uzbek language. The Mennonites, anxious to adapt to their new surroundings, began using the same term for the settlement.[13]

Ak Metchet was totally controlled and dominated by Claas Epp. The local natives never bothered the Mennonites, and left to himself, Epp's popularity once again began growing. He preached with a new vigor that Ak Metchet was the real refuge and that Christ would return there in early 1889. In fact, under Epp's watchful eye the Mennonites began to construct apartments for the great influx of refugees they expected would soon begin arriving. Epp's little flock rallied behind their leader because of his effective preaching.

Epp's preaching not only captivated his congregation, but his

Ak Metchet, Khiva, in 1884, a Mennonite village totally controlled and dominated by Claas Epp.

poetry became popular too. It was even read on the Trakt, where Claas Hamm, the son of Epp's former opponent, became so completely enthralled with this religious verse that he began writing similar poetry and signing it "Claas Epp." When Hamm visited Ak Metchet, Epp graciously received him as a disciple even though many on the Trakt viewed his poetry as a cacophony of radical ideas. [14]

In Ak Metchet also Epp's preaching and poetry found its detractors. One of the first men to come into open conflict was Jonas Quiring. Although it is not known what caused the break between these former allies, Epp excommunicated Quiring from the Bride Community as the "dragon" mentioned in Revelation. The disenchanted Quiring decided to take his family to America. The day before they left, Epp audaciously led a celebration that was for "believers" only, and his former supporter and his family were not invited. In fact, this disregard of the Quiring family is but an example of how Epp increasingly justified choosing new religious holidays to suit his own personal convictions. Later he attacked known religious holidays, such as Christmas, because, he argued, they had worldly rather than biblical origins.[15] It did not cross his mind that neither his attitudes toward dissident brethren nor his new celebrations were very biblical. The majority of Epp's followers, however, blindly accepted his whims, and he continued his harsh treatment of those who disagreed with his leadership.

Another critic of Epp had been a staunch supporter whose opposition evolved gradually. Community teacher Wilhelm Penner became the focus of attention and controversy over a practical problem. Penner's home, which was attached to the school, used more fuel than any other in the village. One member of the community who had the duty of going into the desert to search for fuel complained to Epp that teacher Penner was ungrateful for his fuel and never did any manual labor to help himself. Epp therefore announced that the Lord had told him that teachers were not privileged people and that Penner must henceforth gather his own fuel. Penner was personally offended by this turn of events not because he had to use study time to gather fuel but because Epp had said the Lord told him. Thus he began questioning in his own mind other commandments which the Lord had delivered through Epp's tongue.[16] Penner did not speak out against Epp at this time but waited patiently as other events strengthened his questioning spirit.

As time went on, Epp's increasing authoritarianism and prophetic pretensions began to alienate more followers. In one sermon, Epp preached that Christ had suffered for human beings for their souls' salvation; now Epp was being called upon by God to give salvation to their bodies when they were resurrected. Therefore, Epp believed, he had to go through spiritual suffering and trials so he would be worthy. One woman in the congregation that day could not agree with this teaching and she stood up and verbally disagreed. Pausing for a moment, Epp said he did not appreciate being "stabbed in the back" by one of his followers. Even the long-suffering Penner still could not attack Epp's authority. One reason for Penner's reticence was that in the midst of all these problems Epp gained in popularity when he gave an outstanding funeral oration that impressed all the people of Ak Metchet. For all his eccentricity, Epp's ability as a leader could not be questioned at this time, even by Penner.[17]

Epp's Trip to the World Empires

In 1886, Epp proclaimed that the Lord told him he would soon have to leave Ak Metchet. He began teaching that he was going with the Prophet Elijah for a face-to-face confrontation with the Antichrist in the West. He was to travel first to Transcaspia to hold several meetings with sympathizers and then confront the great "world empires." With Epp absent for several weeks, his followers began wondering what was happening outside their refuge. Abruptly Epp returned, however, and began to proclaim Ak Metchet as the "way" of refuge from the Antichrist and that the remaining three years before the inauguration of the millennium would be important ones. Later it was learned that during Epp's trip west he had been advised by several ministers to stop his revelatory preaching, but Epp did not take their suggestion.

As the predicted second coming of Christ came closer, Epp regained a deeper respect as he announced the very date, March 8, 1889, not earlier, not later, as the great day. The Lord, he said, had revealed this to him in His glory. With the millennium approaching, some of the people wondered why refugees from the Occident were not arriving to take up residence during the tribulation, but they were so preoccupied with their own preparations that they decided not to worry about details.

March 8, 1889

The great day came. Epp explained that the Lord had decided he would be the first to be caught up and then the rest would follow. A church altar table was carried outside as a "throne" for Epp, and when the community assembled Epp gave a prayer and seated himself on his throne.[18] All day the standing assembly, dressed in white robes, waited for the Lord in an attitude of fasting and prayer. At nightfall Epp told the group that the Lord had tarried; they were to return later. Although they assembled three times that day, the resurrection day came and went in bitter disappointment.[19]

Epp Explains Failure

Epp, however, would not be discouraged by the tarrying of the Lord. He explained to Penner and P. Dyck that the Lord had decided to leave him with his community, and that was why Christ had not come. Besides, he pointed out, his clock, which had revealed to him the date by pointing with its hands to the eight and nine, had caused the mistake. Actually, he excitedly explained, the clock was hanging on the wall lopsided; had it been straight it would have pointed to nine and one, indicating the second coming would occur in 1891. This explanation aroused Epp so much that he called the whole community to see the "miracle." And he even persuaded many that they could look forward once again to a great day two years hence.[20]

This humiliating fiasco prompted some disenchanted Ak Metchet families to leave for America, Aulie Ata, or a small Russian settlement near Tashkent named Konstantinovka in honor of General von Kaufmann.[21] Many of those remaining stopped attending Epp's worship services.[22] When in 1891 the postponed second coming still did not materialize, Epp's completely irrational attitude caused the population of Ak Metchet to dwindle even more. Although discouraged, the patient Penner even then did not repudiate Epp's leadership though he was living in abject poverty since Epp had reduced his salary to $7.50 a month.[23] Something more serious would have to occur to force this loyal disciple to break with Epp.

Such a situation arose when Penner's wife persuaded her husband to take her to visit her parents in Aulie Ata. Epp granted the Penner family permission to leave, but before they left he preached on "Spiritual Suicide" in such a way that Penner knew he meant they were wrong for wanting to mix with Aulie Ata "sinners." When Penner tried to reason with Epp, he would only say that the Penner family trip was a "test" of their faith. Upon their return to Ak Metchet, Penner and his wife found certain alarming changes in the settlement. First, Epp had devised a "day of judgment" when he said he would reveal to all in the Bride Community what the Lord had against them. Second, two brethren were appointed to care for the temporal needs of the Epp family so that Epp himself would not have to work. Finally, the Penners learned that Epp had reached the conclusion that he was a biblical "prince" and therefore above ordained community preachers.[24]

A Special Communion

Soon after these proclamations Epp became ill, could not atttend services, and requested that Penner bring communion to his sickbed. When Penner arrived at the Epp home, he told Epp that he did not want to present communion because he was tired and did not

feel worthy to present it that day. Epp then surprised Penner by saying, "You shall not give it, only bring it over. There is a new
Lord's Supper being instituted. I cannot take from a human hand or
share with the community except I give it." Shocked by Epp's
audacity, Penner told Epp that he would have nothing to do with blas-
phemy and that it was entirely Epp's responsibility. This caused the
break between these friends of many years. Epp started a rumor that
Penner had denied God as his heavenly Father while in Aulie Ata,
and Penner's denial of that rumor only caused further friction between
the men.[25]

Conflict with Penner

Epp further alienated Penner and others by teaching that because of the approaching new age, many of his former prophecies had
become invalid and that he was now the son of Christ as Christ was
the Son of God. Epp was essentially saying that there were now four
members of the Godhead — Father, sons, and Holy Ghost! In fact, all
future baptisms were to be done in the name of the quadruple godhead
rather than the Trinity! The meek and mild Penner exploded in a
fury. He knew many in the flock were naive enough to believe Epp,
and so he took the offensive against his teachings. Courageously, Penner and two newly elected ministers, Schmidt and Kopper, began a
concerted assault on Epp's leadership.

Epp as the Son of Christ

Epp responded to their criticisms with the vigor of a general
whose army was under siege. He prohibited Penner from teaching in
"his" building, excommunicated the dissidents, and made an all-out
effort to convince the people that their leader was a completely new
man, "Elijah of the New Testament, Melchizedek of the New Earth,
formerly Claas Epp." At this point Penner and many others left Epp's
community. But Epp still had a flock of ten to fifteen families who
stubbornly relied on his preaching and poetry. As the nineteenth
century ended, this small group of Mennonites staunchly held to
their millennial convictions in Ak Metchet.

15

MIGRATION TO AMERICA

Those Left in Lausan

The Lausan Mennonites who had chosen not to settle at Ak Metchet in 1884 had taken a course far different from their more radical brethren. Realizing the survival of the millennial refuge at Lausan was no longer possible because the departure of 39 families so depleted their ranks, the remaining one third of the inhabitants chose to leave Khiva for America, a migration they hoped would be their last.[1]

These pioneers had come to believe that it was the Lord's will for them to travel westward, a definite reversal of opinion from their previous conviction that a move in that direction would have meant a confrontations with the Antichrist. The continuing danger from the Turkoman bandits was but a secondary consideration; by 1884 most were convinced that their earlier convictions concerning the second coming of Christ were in error. They were now prepared to discard a belief they had once seriously held to be a central teaching of Christianity. Concomitantly they were reevaluating another hallowed tenet — that of nonresistance. Their hiring of cossack guards as protectors seemed to suggest that many were no longer sure that God would take care of them. It was these two religious uncertainties rather than the hardships — crop failures, grasshopper plagues, the depredations of wild hogs, fear of bandits, and the increasing radicalism of Epp — which provided the main motivation for their American migration.

Change of Mind: Not the Lord's Will

During their Lausan stay, even the uncertainty about future Khivan or Russian army service had not troubled them as much as millennialism. As far as they were now concerned, the Lausan settlement had been a disastrous experiment; it proved to them that the millennial refuge was but a fantasy. They also saw that their staunch belief in nonresistance could be easily abandoned if pressure were sufficiently intense. Perhaps, they thought, in America they could temper their millennial position and regain the belief in nonresistance they had once maintained. Furthermore, their leaders — men like Jacob Toews, J. K. Penner, and Johann Jantzen — at last came to the conclusion that the God-forsaken marsh at Lausan was far from being a sanctuary. When they could stand it no longer, these leaders made it known to all the people that they believed it would be "Soul Suicide" (to use Epp's sermon title) to remain in the settlement.

Appeal to America for Aid

Realizing that a parting of the ways was inevitable, these men had been corresponding with Heinrich Zimmerman of Beatrice, Nebraska, and Peter Claassen of Newton, Kansas, for some time. Since these American Mennonites promised that they would receive financial aid to come to America, it seemed to them that the Lord was leading them westward. In fact, many American Mennonite brethren had registered a willingness to help. Many began opening their pocketbooks as well as their hearts to their Central Asia brethren. During 1883 alone, 6533 rubles, or well over $3200, had been contributed by private individuals to aid Mennonites in Central Asia. Many of these relatives and friends had warned them earlier against going to Central Asia, but when they saw the plight of brethren in need they responded faithfully nonetheless.[2]

Help from Distant Plains

This seeking of assistance from America was a natural recourse because of the many Russian Mennonites who had settled there during the major migration a decade earlier. Many were relatives, and they had corresponded conscientiously throughout the intervening years. Some of these letters had found their way into newspapers read by the Mennonite communities. One such paper, *Der Christliche*

Bundesbote, published by David Schmidt in Halstead, Kansas, took pride in informing its readership of happenings in other parts of the world. David Georz, its editor, periodically wrote editorials and even put in notices concerning gifts to Central Asian Mennonites. The importance of the publicity newspapers gave these needy people is inestimable. Through these friends who communicated by way of newsprint, it was soon learned that more than 20 of the Lausan families were planning to come to America. They would travel by wagon along the western side of the Aral Sea to Orenburg, obtain passports, go by train to Bremen, Germany, and take a Lloyd Lines Steamship to New York. From there a train would carry them to the American plains states. Encouraging letters from America were received in Lausan during March and early April 1884.

Owing to all this informal encouragement and a growing interest among all Mennonite communities about the plans of the Central Asian refugees, several organizations were formed in order to aid them systematically. Of these groups the "Board of Guardians" of Newton, Kansas, and the "Aid Committee for the Needy in Khiva" of Beatrice, Nebraska, were the most active. Soon an effort was made to combine the efforts of these two important organizations. They had tended to draw into their scope the smaller aid associations, and it was believed that a single all-out effort could save all the brethren in Central Asia.[3]

At the instigation of Peter Claassen of Newton, a group of influential men who had been individually sending help to Central Asia came together on April 4, 1884, at the home of Bernard Regier to discuss the most rapid means of expediting aid to the coming refugees. As the meeting began, a well-known Mennonite immigrant, Christian Krehbiel, was named chairman and David Goerz was elected secretary. Claassen presented documents and letters from Nebraska Mennonites telling of their desire to have a joint meeting to discuss mutual concerns. Claassen was promptly chosen to represent the Newton group in Nebraska. In the meantime, an emergency subcommittee was formed to handle immediate requests for help. Each member of the committee was given specific responsibilities, such as contacting newspaper help, actively seeking contributions and support from other American groups, and also sending word to Prussian Mennonites. Goerz was appointed to inquire with steamship companies and railroads about special rates. He was even given the option to negotiate contracts. Estimating that it would take anywhere from $8000 to $10,000 to bring the refugees to the United States, the men discussed ways of obtaining means of procuring low-interest loans that could be easily secured. Closing the meeting, they chose the "American Mennonite Aid Committee" as their name and sent a telegram to Khiva and a letter to six families in Aulie Ata telling them of their ambitious plans.[4] Following the meeting, Claassen left for Nebraska.

Six days later, L. E. Zimmerman called several leaders together for a special meeting at his home in Beatrice, Nebraska, where Claassen outlined the hopes and plans of their Kansas brethren. The Nebraskans expressed their willingness to cooperate, urging only that it was imperative to help the Lausan refugees first because of their great need and their dangerous situation among the Turkomans. Previously, on April 2, this group had committed themselves to an all-out effort for Lausan when they sent a telegram to the noted J. F. Funk, editor of the *Herold der Wahrheit*, a Mennonite paper, in Elkhart, Indiana, entitled a "Call for Help," which had received wide distribution. Feeling they were already involved in an active campaign, they did not feel they should dissipate their limited resources through a commitment to help Central Asia. They wondered, moreover, whether joint effort would hinder the progress already made toward helping the Lausan people.[5] As the meeting continued, however, Peter Jansen, an important Nebraska Mennonite, was given a liaison assignment similar to that of Goerz. Plans were also made to send money to an intermediary named Johann Bergmann at Lysanderhöh, in the Trakt, in order to help the Lausanites travel from Orenburg to Germany.[6]

Returning from Nebraska, Claassen called a meeting at his home on April 18, in which he informed his brethren of the actions of the "Aid Committee for the Needy Brethren in Khiva" at Beatrice. Somewhat peevishly, the Kansas committee charged that the Nebraska group was interested only in helping the Khivan refugees because of their numerous relatives in the group. The Kansans went on record as opposed to helping only the Lausan settlers and stubbornly declared that they desired to aid all Mennonites in Central Asia who wanted to come to America.[7] With this charge, Goerz was sent back to Nebraska to try to work out some coordinated plan with Jansen.[8]

Meanwhile, the Lausantes were busily preparing to leave. From both Kansas and Nebraska they had received much encouragement and assurances of continued support, and 23 families resolved to undertake the long journey to America.[9] This was indeed a difficult time for the America-bound group because the majority party with diametrically opposed convictions were anticipating a much shorter move to Ak Metchet and were trying continually to convince those tottering on the brink of indecision to come with them to a "new" refuge.

Journey from Lausan, April 1884

On Easter Sunday, 1884, the America-bound Mennonites, having received Russian permission to cross their territory, held their final communion service in Khiva. Although the decision had been made after much controversy and turmoil, it was still difficult to leave their homes again after less than two years' residence. But the newly constructed mud-brick houses and barns were sold to the natives, and the cossack watchmen were paid in full. A week later, on April 17, a day after their dissident brethren departed for Ak Metchet, 23 stalwart families left for America, over 12,000 miles away. As the small wagon train, composed of 130 people, 17 wagons, and 30 horses, left the village of Lausan, they could see their Turkoman neighbors fighting over the belongings they had been forced to leave behind.[10]

Having sent most of the women, children, the infirm, and the baggage ahead by riverboat, the men and a few women drove westward on a road which led through thick reeds and underbrush. The primitive road and even worse bridges caused repeated delay for the cumbersome wagons. Having covered less than ten miles the first day, they camped in a circle, as they had on many other occasions, slept amid the reeds under a clear sky, and posted six men to stand guard. Few slept that first night, however, since they feared at any moment an onslaught of vengeful Turkomans. But that onslaught never came.

Arriving a week later at Kungrad, near the mouth of the Amu Darya, they met the boats that had arrived earlier. Although this place was but a dirty little town with simple mud-brick houses and trash conspicuous on its streets, they found a lively marketplace where they rented camels to carry their household goods across another formidable desert.[11] At Kungrad, they received two telegrams that had been forwarded from Kansas and Nebraska. This renewed the courage of the group to push onward, for they knew that the prayers and money of kinsmen stood behind their efforts. Calculating the distance from Kungrad to Orenburg at well over 650 miles, they planned

Henry H. Wiebe and his first wife, Maria Jantzen, with their son John H. Wiebe, about 1890.

on traveling about two miles per hour and arriving at their destination in 300 hours. They subsequently discovered the distances to be much farther, but they would make it in less time than they had planned.[12]

With this long distance facing them it was imperative that they hire a guide with special qualifications: knowing the quickest route and where water was available as well as being a capable leader of camel drivers. They found such a man in a Tartar named Kardijigit, who was immediately hired. With him leading the way the wagons and the heavily loaded camels set out on May 1, toward the city of Karakamish (Temirskoye Ukreplinie in the Russian language) far to the north of Aral Sea.

After three days they reached Aral Sea and proceeded along its western shore below the Ust-Urt Mountains farther to the west. This would be a new experience for all of them; on their passage into Central Asia they had seen only the eastern side of the Aral. Approaching this area, which Kardijigit told them had never been crossed by a wagon train, they had to detour through muddy alfalfa fields. The Abraham Jantzen wagon slowed the line down when it sank in deep mud. After it was pulled out they bore closer to the seashore on a caravan road that was fairly level but totally devoid of supplies of fresh water.

In order to reach the plateau that rose some 600 feet above the sea, the group encountered their most difficult day of travel in four years of wandering. Foregoing their usual noontime rest, the men laboriously pushed the heavy wagons up the steep incline, as the women and children walked behind. Rocks had to be placed behind the wheels at almost every step in order to prevent the wagons from rolling backward into the sea. At the end of four hours of tedious, backbreaking labor they had succeeded in moving only 600 feet nearer to their destination.[13] After a most welcome respite at a cold spring atop the plateau, they renewed their weary journey.[14]

For two weeks the trail carried the wanderers between the rugged cliffs of the Ust-Urt and the vast Aral Sea.[15] Then, after fording the bed of the Chegan River, they entered the bleak wasteland to the North. Kardijigit skillfully led the caravan across country so barren of forage that had their trek occurred in summer, it would have been impossible to find adequate grazing for the horses. Familiarity with shortcut trails and the location of grass and water was within the competence of their knowledgeable guide, however, and when the

Mennonites later looked back on their journey, they were full of praise for Kardijigit's services. He could easily have betrayed the defenseless wanderers to nomadic bandits, but he took pride in doing his duty.[16]

As always, the children suffered most from the privations and dangers of the journey. One little boy fell beneath the wheels of a wagon, which crushed his chest. But after his broken ribs were set and oil and lard applied to his injuries, the little fellow enjoyed a miraculous recovery. Other children were not so fortunate. Of the two babies born in the desert, one died after a few weeks.[17]

As the trip passed the halfway mark they began seeing Kirghiz tent villages along the road. How happy they were to see people, for they had not seen native inhabitants for several weeks. As they passed by, the friendly nomads came to the wagons to talk and bring fermented camel's milk, or *kumys*, as a hospitable gesture to the weary Mennonites.

Almost 500 miles from Kungrad, with much of the distance through deep shifting sand, they reached Karakamish just before Pentecost Sunday. In this half-native, half-Russian town they observed the days of the religious holiday. From Karakamish, J. K. Penner and Jacob Toews went ahead to begin arranging passports in Orenburg. In order to make it to that city as fast as possible, Widow Klaassen loaned them her easily maneuverable one-horse buggy. After the wagon train passed Ak Tube on June 1, they found good roads to Ilgtzaya Tashchita. Here they were all invited to see a salt mine in which stood a solid wall of clear white salt 80 feet high. They were much impressed by the phenomenon of nature.[18]

Finally, after some eight weeks of traveling, they reached Orenburg on June 8. Their trip of over 820 miles lasted 53 days, with 32 spent in driving and 21 resting.[19] Camping along the Ural River in a grove of trees, they remembered the area as their previous halting place on the road to Turkestan years earlier.[20] Continued rain and wind made the stay a muddy one, however, since they could not obtain housing in Orenburg.[21] Moreover, the officials in the city were slow to act upon their requests for passports owing to the death of the govenor-general of Orenburg, the customary period of mourning, and the search for a new govenor. Three separate times they telegraphed St. Petersburg for assistance, but no help came. They remained stranded in Orenburg for more than two months.[22]

With their brethren unwillingly delayed in Orenburg, the worried

Mennonites in the United States began a petitioning campaign. A passionate appeal for help first went to Governor James W. Dawes of Nebraska and then even to United States Secretary of State Frelinghuysen. It is not known if these petitions had any impact, but state and federal officials were at least aware of the plight of the Mennonites in Orenburg.[23]

Awaiting passports, the Orenburg refugees were not idle. Some went to visit relatives at Saratov; others went all the way to Molotschna and Kuban to see if their passport problems could be resolved by the authorities there. Still others received guests at their riverbank campground. The Klaassens and Penners were lucky enough to rent an apartment in the city where they could look for interim work. Some of the young men found work loading and unloading freight at the railroad station. The leaders disposed of their wagons and faithful horses by selling most of them to Kirghiz natives; Frederick Dirks and some friends, impatient with merely waiting in Orenburg, drove to Samara to sell their horses for a higher price.[24]

These men were still absent on August 10, when a number of the requested passports at last arrived at Orenburg. It was therefore decided that the group be divided into two parties, the first departing immediately while the remainder awaited additional passports and the return of the Dirks contingent from Samara. The first party boarded the train forthwith and set out on their long journey to Germany and then to America.

Arriving in Bremen on September 1, 1884, the emigrants were issued identification cards and directed aboard the *Ems*, the second largest passenger ship of the North German Lloyd Line. Of its more than 1000 passengers, the Mennonites comprised the not inconsiderable minority of 78, including 15 families under 11 different names.[25] They were of course dazzled by the immensity of the vessel and fascinated by the sight of the sea. They delighted in the simultaneous views of the French and English coasts as they passed through the Channel toward the open Atlantic. But though they made good speed, the voyage was a stormy one, and seasickness plagued the passengers considerably. The Mennonites prayed for solid ground to walk on, and they were quite ready to disembark when the *Ems* docked at New York on September 9.[26]

Heinrich Zimmerman and Gerhard Wiebe of Nebraska and David Goerz of Kansas were there to meet them. The greetings were warm and joyous. In fact, Johann Jantzen and Zimmerman had been

Heinrich and Anna Toews in later life in Idaho.

fellow ministers in Germany years earlier; after a heart-to-heart talk with his old friend, Jantzen decided to switch his train ticket from Halstead, Kansas, to Beatrice, Nebraska. In all, nine families decided to go to Nebraska while six elected to stake their future on Kansas. Those besides Jantzen who took their families to Nebraska were Heinrich Jantzen, J. K. Penner, Cornelius Unruh, widow Marie Klaassen, Gerhard Fast, Heinrich Albrecht, Johann Martens, Heinrich Wegeli, and the spinster, Anna Penner. Those who chose Kansas, 30 people in all, were Peter Unruh, Tobias Dirks, Abraham Dirks, Bernard Wiebe, Heinrich Graeves, and Cornelius Wiebe.[27]

The day after arrival, they took a river steamboat to Castlegarden, New York, where they met immigration officials. From there 48 of the immigrants boarded a separate rail coach which took them to Beatrice, arriving some three years and twelve days after they had left the Trakt. Later the Kansas group traveled by train to Newton. Thus ended a journey which had taken many of the older ones from Prussia to Russia, Turkestan, Bukhara, Khiva, and now America.[28]

Concern was now focused on the group left behind in Russia. It was learned on September 24 that the rest of this company had received their passports and had started for Bremen. Among the 39 members of this party were the families of Abraham Jantzen, Jacob Toews, Heinrich Toews, Benjamin Dirks, Friederich Aron Dirks, Heinrich Albrecht, Hermann Bartsch, Philipp Bier, the Ensz and Pauls families, and Mrs. Elizabeth Abrahms, the widow of the murdered Heinrich Abrahms, and her young child. After a nine-day voyage from Bremen, they arrived in New York aboard the *Fulda*.[29]

But even then the recurrent tragedy which had dogged their steps from the beginning had not yet run its course. While visiting relatives in Saratov, little fourteen-month-old Maria Toews, daughter of Anna and Heinrich Toews, had been exposed to smallpox. On board ship she became violently ill and was placed in quarantine with her mother by her side. The day the *Fulda* arrived in New York the baby died and was buried on Ellis Island.[30]

So far, the American Mennonite Aid Committee had brought a total of 117 refugees to America. It now undertook an elaborate accounting of receipts to show American Mennonites how their contributions of more than $6000 had been used. To transport the first group from the Russo-German border to its final destination had cost the aid committee approximately $2000, while the second party required about $1000 in support. Besides other funds spent for inciden-

Gustav Janzen, born in Turkestan, with a cello he made himself.

tals, there were still almost $2000 left in their treasury to help future refugees.[31]

Further Trips

Most of these would come from the Aulie Ata settlement. Originally, only six of these families had requested aid to come to America, but by the beginning of 1885, it was learned that the number had increased to 15 families, or 79 people in all. As early as August 11, the American Mennonite Aid Committee had sent some 2500 rubles ($1280) to help these people reach the railhead at Orenburg, and they were subsequently given $2810 for the completion of their journey.[32] Among those at Aulie Ata, who sailed from Bremen to New York in August 1885, were the Eck, Esau, Funk, Janzen, Koop, Kornelsen, Reimer, Riffel, Schmidt, Schultz, Wedel, and Wiens families.[33] With the arrival of three more families, this group dispersed to their various destinations in Kansas, Nebraska, the Dakotas, and Minnesota. They constituted the last of the large immigrant parties, and the original aid committees were officially dissolved. Their remaining funds were distributed to the Indians and to Mennonite missionaries.[34]

Though the last of the great migrations was over, separate family groups continued to repeat the emigration experience until well into the twentieth century. For each had its unique story to tell. In 1892, for example, the families of Jacob Jantzen, Peter Quiring, and Jacob and John Becker left Ak Metchet for America. Jacob Becker had been married to Marie Epp, the only daughter of Claas Epp, but she had died and he married Ernestine Pauls. Jantzen married Becker's sister, Susanna, and had two children while in Ak Metchet, Lena and Johann. John Becker married Marie Dick in 1889, after the second coming of Christ did not occur, with Wilhelm Penner officiating at the wedding. These young couples drove their wagons to Petro-Alexandrovsk, took the steamer *Czar Alexander* to Astrachan on the Caspian Sea, and a German steamer up the Volga to see relatives in Sartov. When they reached Seelman, Germany, in July 1892, a cholera epidemic forced them to stay there until January 1893. Then they found out that they would have to return to Russia to get official passports. In the dead of winter, they boarded large sleds for Saratov. From here they went to Moscow, where they obtained their passports, and went by train to Smolensk, Eidkuhnen, and to Bremen. In Bremen, they boarded the vessel *Aller* and after a nine-day voyage reached New York. After this trying and complicated trip, they arrived at Brainard, Kansas, in March 1893. The John Beckers later moved to Aberdeen, Idaho, while Jantzen and Jacob Becker moved to Beatrice, Nebraska and then to Marion, South Dakota. After the opening of the Cherokee Strip in Oklahoma, on September 16, 1893, Jantzen's first cousin, also named Jacob Jantzen, chose to move further south to Bessie, Oklahoma, and became pastor of the Herald Mennonite Church. These two men named Jacob Jantzen have sometimes had their names mistakenly used in some sources.[35]

Another example of a later group that came to America is the Siebert Görz family, which left Aulie Ata in August 1893. With their one-month-old daughter, Katarina, they went by railway to the Caspian Sea. After reaching the sea, the young girl died and was buried in the town of Baku. After this tragedy, for a respite, they stayed two months in their old home in the Kuban. Then in November, after a two-week wait in Bremen, they completed a stormy, seven-day voyage to New York. They later arrived in Inman, Kansas, shortly before Christmas, 1893, after a four-month trip.[36]

Leaving many brethren behind in Central Asia, other remnants of the Great Trek continued to migrate to the United States until the late 20s and early 30s when the Soviets would no longer permit them to leave Central Asia.[37] Good farmers were needed to help develop cooperative farms, and since Mennonites had been there for some 50 years, they were chosen to take part in the experiment. Those coming to America found a new life in a strange new land, but they would always remember Turkestan and their brethren who had stayed behind.

16

CONCLUSION

The major Mennonite migrations from Central Asia to America which began in the mid-1880s did not bring all Turkestan Mennonites to a New World refuge. In fact, many Mennonites chose to stay in Ak Metchet and the villages of Aulie Ata. In Ak Metchet, Claas Epp continued his teachings into the second decade of the twentieth century. Soon after the turn of the century, Epp began preaching that a "New Ak Metchet" would come down from heaven in the near future, a parallel of the New Jerusalem in the Book of Revelation. Some remaining followers believed Epp had gone too far in his predictions and one by one more families left his fold. A disappointed old man who stood alone many times in his life, Epp died on January 19, 1913, at 75 years of age, just five days after the death of his beloved wife, Elizabeth. This self-styled prophet of Central Asia succumbed to stomach cancer, thus ending a colorful era of erratic leadership among Mennonites.[1]

The Fate of Central Asia Colonies

Epp's death did not end millennial belief in Ak Metchet, however. This model brotherhood actually made few changes in its theological attitudes but set aside some of its more extreme tenets for the time being in order to attend to pressing tasks on newly acquired farms. Instead of emphasizing millennialism they concentrated on learning to fertilize and irrigate the sandy Central Asian soil.[2] For several decades they lived relatively undisturbed and unmolested, hardly affected by either the ravages of World War I or the subsequent change to a Soviet regime. In 1925, when the Soviets were seeking to improve all of Central Asia economically, the government issued a decree guaranteeing the spiritual and economic autonomy of all Ak Metchet Mennonites.[3] Even though the surrounding population was forced to join collective farms, the Mennonites were allowed to retain their traditional way of life of family farming. Being secure economically, their attention turned to a spiritual growth which they believed had been neglected for over a decade. Their new millennial studies promoted the belief that Claas Epp soon would return to earth with Christ.[4] But this economic and spiritual security was destined to be shattered.

In 1935 the second five-year plan of the Soviets directly led to the demise of the utopian dreams of Ak Metchet Mennonites. Early in that year the mayor of Ak Metchet was ordered by Soviet authorities at Khiva to reorganize the settlement into a collective farm. After the mayor met with the members of the settlement he reported to the officials that they did not want to be collectivized because they believed in personal freedom and wanted the right to control their own affairs. Besides, they argued, they had been guaranteed these rights earlier by governmental decree.[5] Soon several Soviet officials appeared in Ak Metchet to hold a town meeting of their own. At this meeting the mayor once more announced to the people what the officials wanted and again there were no signs of positive response in the audience. That night the mayor was arrested and jailed. The following night the officials called another meeting, saw to it that a new mayor was elected, and made the same demand of the population. The Mennonites again voted against collectivization. That night the new mayor disappeared and with him the elder of the congregation. This same procedure was repeated nightly until ten hostages had been arrested.[6] Still the people refused to comply, and the exasperated officials began seeking new alternative measures to jar them from their stubborn complacency.

Soon it was announced that the ten persons recently arrested were to be tried publicly as counterrevolutionaries. When the prisoners returned to Ak Metchet for trial they were pale and thin and surrounded by a heavily armed guard. The next day the trial began at three o'clock in the afternoon and lasted far into the night. The testimony by these hostages was impressively defiant: with a Bible in hand, each of them unashamedly stated that the severest punishment would not make them waver from their belief that collectivism was wrong for them and not God's will. After their lengthy testimony the verdict came swiftly: death by firing squad for each of them, and their families were to be exiled to Siberia!

On the following day government trucks appeared to take the families to be exiled. A quiet crowd slowly enveloped the area around the trucks. Then, softly at first, a chant began demanding that all or none be taken: "all or none, all or none" rang through the streets of Ak Metchet. As the momentum of the chant increased some began to prostrate themselves before the wheels of the trucks; others piled on top of them forming a human barricade against this injustice. The truck drivers, shocked by Mennonite dedication to each other and their courageous display of civil disobedience, left the trucks where they stood and walked back to Khiva for further orders.[7] After several days many trucks came to Ak Metchet — this time to take the entire colony to an unknown destination.

Each family was permitted to take as many belongings as they could carry. Surprisingly, they submitted to this new Soviet move very obediently even though they were leaving a village that had been their home for more than half a century. As the trucks drove away from the village, tears flowed freely, but to bolster their faith they sang hymns to show they had no fear. The trucks took them to the Amu Darya port of Novo-Urgench where they boarded boats, and after a long river journey, they took a train to Samarkand. From there trucks transported them about 100 miles southeastward into the desert for resettlement. To their surprise they found themselves in the area their ancestors had wanted to settle over fifty years earlier — Shari-i-Sabs.[8]

Thus Mennonite Ak Metchet was no more, and its brave people were once again pioneers in a new region that their forefathers had sought before them.[9] Their former village was settled by Uzbeks. In 1947 a visitor reported that although one could still see remnants of Mennonite influence, Muslim culture now dominated the area.[10]

The Aulie Ata Mennonites did not experience such a dramatic turn of fate as their Ak Metchet brethren. In fact, little is known about those Mennonites who remained behind in the villages of Aulie Ata. We do know, however, to what extent they remained true to their anti-militaristic beliefs. None of the original settlers were involved in military service, but as the years passed, the young men in newly arrived Mennonite families could be found in state forests and working on trains of the medical corps and in hospitals during World War I. In the first decades of the twentieth century these people apparently abandoned the millennialist doctrine that originally inspired their trek to Central Aisa and slowly acculturated to Soviet society.

Today it is estimated that approximately 100,000 people living in Siberia and Central Asia have a German Mennonite ethnic background. Of this number about 5000 live in areas settled by Great Trek Mennonites, but not all of these people are practicing Mennonites because of their assimilation into the Russian culture. Those who do openly practice their Mennonite faith generally worship in Russian Baptist Churches as, for example, in Moscow and Alma Ata. Very little contact exists today between Russian Mennonites and their counterparts in the United States other than through correspondence. Many Canadian Mennonites have had not only a steady stream of letters but also exchange visits with their Russian coreligionists because visas for Canadian visitors can be obtained more easily than those for the United States.[11]

Fates of Survivors in America

The fate of the survivors of the Great Trek who safely made it to America is a story in itself and not within the scope of this work. Suffice to say that following their initial migration of 1884 to Newton, Kansas, and Beatrice, Nebraska, veterans of the Central Asia trek spread widely over the North American continent. Many of the descendants of the original group were assimilated and concentrated in Mennonite communities in the states of Kansas, Nebraska, Oklahoma, and the provinces of Saskatchewan and Manitoba. These Central Asian Mennonites joined large and successful colonies in Harvey, Marion, and McPherson counties in Kansas, settled in and near Beatrice, Nebraska, and established farms around Bessie, Oklahoma. Since then, many new communities have been established by people going out from these "parent" colonies. Consequently, the small bands of Central Asian Mennonites have influence in Mennonite circles that exceeds their numerical strength. In fact, of the 350,000 Mennonites living in North America today, a substantial minority are descendants of the Central Asian pioneers.

Unique Significance of the Great Trek

The significance of the Great Trek, however, does not reside primarily in the subsequent fate of its participants in Central Asia or America but in the light it casts upon the unique nature of

Mennonite society and religious convictions. In Central Asia, this group of sincere Christians endured great sacrifices for their convictions and the truth as they saw it. These truths and convictions, they believed, could not be comprehended within the materialistic context of the world around them. They were completely otherworldly in outlook. If this had not been the case, the dangers, hardships, and turmoil would have ended their pilgrimage far sooner than they did. Keeping in mind this otherworldly emphasis in their lives, one can identify three minor and two major aspects of this stirring episode which explain its ultimate failure.

The first minor aspect is the fact that the Mennonites were rooted in the soil; they believed that God had made them to be an agrarian people. Not only did they believe this out of faith, they also thoroughly enjoyed the cultivation of good land as a source of livelihood. But Central Asia was a poor choice for the realization of this goal. Time and time again they found the region sterile and unproductive. The very heart of their agrarian way of life was continually threatened no matter where they wandered.

Second, in seeking a place where they could live unrestricted in a closed community, they also wanted independence in the areas of education, religion, politics, and economics. Gradually but decisively, they began to realize that they would never gain a satisfactory degree of autonomy in any of these important areas. Wherever they were, whether in Turkestan, Bukhara, or Khiva, they were restricted in one or more of these areas. In fact, the education of their children became even more inadequate and their faith diluted, politicians used them for personal gain, and the life savings of most of the participants were exhausted in the struggle to survive.

Third, an element that so capriciously worked against them was the fact that they always considered themselves to be German foreigners. Unfortunate for them was the fact that Germany was coming to be regarded as Russian's principle enemy in the 1880s. This hostility and enmity between the Mennonites and their environment deepended as the years progressed.

But more important than any of the above, the basic failure of the Great Trek venture may be explained as a product of the very two reasons for attempting the movement in the first place: millennialism and nonresistance. Since millennialism by its very nature was a controversial theological issue, it tended to be divisive rather than unifying. Many opportunities arose for radicalism and fanaticism to divide their ranks even before the first wagon train left home. This divisiveness deepened progressively as the pioneering Mennonites reached each new stage of their trek.

Reacting to these divisions, two extremes clearly emerged: one descended further into radicalism; the other denied the validity of any millennial goal. The more radical experiment at Ak Metchet sought a complete withdrawal from a sinful world. It was a chosen place of refuge that would assure its followers of heavenly bliss. The Aulie Ata community, on the other hand, rebelled against this attitude because they believed it had destroyed the unity and solidarity of the faithful. Those coming to America from Lausan agreed with this latter position and added fuel to the fires of alienation from their more radical brethren at Ak Metchet. The only result could be disunity.

The doctrine of nonresistance was also to emerge as a bone of contention. Seeking a refuge from Russian militarism, they soon discovered they could not elude a militaristic state completely. Not even at Aulie Ata, Bukhara, or Khiva were they completely immune from state service requirements. It was in Lausan, moreover, that they learned in the face of Turkomen raids that they too were not above resorting to the necessity of self-defense or violence. The cherished Mennonite doctrine of nonresistance was put to the supreme test. As they ardently disagreed concerning millennialism, so also did they divide over this issue. The spectrum of options offered, from complete nonresistance to armed self-defense, presented them with another dilemma. Under the circumstances, they decided to go their separate ways and withdraw from the dilemma rather than decide on a total course of action. Both divergent groups believed they could escape these dilemmas by seeking the peace and tranquility of a new promised land. The tragic adventure of the Central Asian trek is a period of Mennonite history that cannot soon be forgotten, nor can it be ignored.

Notes

Chapter 1

1. The problem of migration in Mennonite history, although repeatedly studied, is an extremely complex issue. See B. H. Unruh, *Die niederländisch-niederdeutschen Hintergründe der mennonitischen Ostwanderungen im 16., 18., und 19. Jahrhundert* (Karlsruhe: priv. pub., 1955), pp. 188-195; H. Quiring, "Die Auswanderung der Mennoniten aus Preussen, 1788-1870," *Auslandsdeutsche Volksforschung*, Vol. II (1938), pp. 50-60; D. G. Rempel, "The Mennonite Migration to New Russia (1787-1870)," *MQR*, Vol. IX, No. 2 (April, 1935), pp. 71-84.

2. Some of the standard works on Mennonite history are John Horsch, *Mennonites in Europe* (Scottdale, Pennsylvania: Mennonite Publishing House, 1950); C. Henry Smith, *The Story of the Mennonites* (4th ed., rev. by Cornelius Krahn, North Newton, Kansas: Mennonite Publication Office, 1957); Stephen Hirzel, *Heimliche Kirche* (Hamburg: Friederich Wittig Verlag, n.p.); Edmond Diebold, *Folge dem Licht* (Zurich: Gotthelf Verlag, 1945), and J. C. Wenger, *Glimpses of Mennonite History and Doctrine* (Scottdale, Mennonite Publishing House, 1947.)

3. Franz Bartsch, *Unser Auszug nach Mittelasien* (Vol. V in Historische Schriftenreihe des Echo-Verlags) (North Kildonan, Manitoba, 1948), pp. 1-6.

4. Aaron Klaus, *Unsere Kolonien: Studien und Materialien zur Geschichte und Statistik der ausländischen Kolonisation in Russland*, trans. by J. Töws (Odessa: Odessaer Zeitung, 1887), p. 163; John B. Toews, "The Social Structure of the Russian Mennonites," *Mennonite Life*, Vol. XXVI, No. 3 (July, 1971), pp. 133-137.

5. Franz Haxthausen, *Studien über die innern Zustände, das Volksleben und insbesondere die ländlichen Einrichtungen Russlands* (2 vols., London: priv. pub., 1847, 1952), I, pp. 420-432. Also see D. H. Epp, *Johann Cornies* (Berdyansk: priv. pub., 1909), pp. 25-100; and Walter Kuhn, "Cultural Achievements of the Chortitza Mennonites," *Mennonite Life*, Vol. III (July, 1948), p. 35.

6. G. E. Reimer and G. R. Gaeddert, *Exiled by the Czar: Cornelius Jansen and the Great Mennonite Migration, 1874* (North Newton: Mennonite Publication Office, 1956), pp. 43-65.

7. Wenger, *Glimpses of Mennonite History*, p. 97; Johannes Janzen, "The Mennonite Colony in Turkestan," *MQR*, Vol. IV, No. 4 (October, 1930), p. 282.

8. Bartsch, *Unser Auszug*, pp. 6, 8-9, 18-19; Jansen, "The Mennonite Colony in Turkestan," p. 282; Jacob Jantzen, "Memories of Our Journey to Asia" (mimeographed account, trans. by Mrs. Margaret Horn with an Introduction by Harold H. Jantzen, Cordell, Oklahoma, 1958, 32 pp., MHLA), p. 4; Karl Stumpp, "Deutsche Siedlungen in Mittelasien und im Amürgebiet," *Heimätbuch der Deutschen aus Russland* (1964), 15; and Wenger, *Glimpses of Mennonite History*, p. 98.

9. Stumpp, *HB* (1964), p. 14. For one of the best summations of this journey in English see Douglas Hale, "From Central Asia to America," *Mennonite Life*, Vol. XXV, No. 3 (July, 1970), pp. 133-138.

10. C. H. Smith, *The Coming of the Russian Mennonites: An Episode in the Settling of the Last Frontier*, 1874-1884 (Berne, Indiana: Mennonite Book Concern, 1927), p. 129.

11. James C. Juhnke, *A People of Two Kingdoms* (Newton: Faith and Life Press, 1975), p. 9.

12. See for example: C. H. Smith, *The Story of the Russian Mennonites*, p. 4; and Cornelius J. Dyck, ed., *An Introduction to Mennonite History* (Scottdale, Pennsylvania: Herald Press, 1967), p. 29. Anabaptists were considered the radicals of the left by conservative Catholics. "Anabaptist" is a Greek term meaning "rebaptizer" and was used in Latin Christendom after the fourth century. These rebaptizers did not use the term themselves because it was one of derision. During the Reformation the term was used indiscriminately to apply to all left-wing radicals. Even then the Anabaptists did *not use the German form (Wiedertäufer)* or the Dutch term (Wederdooper); most simply called themselves "Brethren."

13. See Harold S. Bender, "Conrad Grebel as a Zwinglian, 1522-23," *MQR*, Vol. XV, No. 2 (April, 1941), pp. 67-82.

14. M. Simeon Friederich Rues, *Aufrichtigen Nachrichten von den gegenwärtigen Zuständen der Mennoniten, oder Taufgesinnten, wie auch Collegianten, oder Reisbürger* (Jena: n.p., 1743), pp. 25-27. Most contemporary Mennonite-Anabaptist historiography tends to emphasize theology rather than its radical social implications in the context of the sixteenth century. For a stimulating dissenting view see Lowell H. Zuck. "Anabaptism: Abortive Counter-Revolt Within the Reformation," *Church History*, Vol. XXVI (September, 1957), pp. 211-226. John H. Yoder emphasizes Zwingli's fears of the social effects of Anabaptism in "Anabaptist Origins in Switzerland," in Dyck (ed.), *An Introduction to Mennonite History*, pp. 30, 33. A recent and challenging Marxist interpretation of the Anabaptists is found in Gerhard Brendler, *Das Täuferreich zu Münster, 1534-35* (Berlin: Deutscher Verlag der Wissenschaften, 1966), pp. 11-70.

15. Romans 12:1-2 and Luke 6:27-28 were frequent Scripture references.

16. A. Brons, *Ursprung, Entwickelung und Schicksale der Taufgesinnten oder Mennoniten* (Norden: Druck von Diedr. Soltan, 1884), p. 88. Also see C. H. Smith, *Story of the Mennonites*, p. 106.

17. Juhnke, *Two Kingdoms*, p. 9.

18. A good description of the Münster uprisings and an evaluation of the literature is in Cornelius Krahn, "Münster Anabaptists," *ME*, III, pp. 777-782. *Mennonite Life* and *MQR* issues of the last decade have also devoted an increasing amount of attention to Münster. Leading Münster scholars such as Stayer, Hillerbrand, Gretsch, and Franz wrote concerning Münster in the *MQR* between 1963 and 1970. Walter Klaassen, Hans-Jürgen Goertz, and Krahn contributed writings on Münster during this same period. In addition, books by Krahn and John Oyer deal with the Münster issue in some measure. See Krahn, *Dutch Anabaptism: Origin, Spread, Life and Thought (1450-1600)* (The Hague: Martinus Nyhoff, 1968) and John S. Oyer, *Lutheran Reformers Against Anabaptism* (The Hague: Martinus Nyhoff, 1964).

19. James H. Waltner, *This We Believe* (Newton, Kansas: Faith and Life Press, 1968), p. 135. For the Schleitheim Confession see Robert Friedmann, "The Schleitheim

Confession (1527) and Other Doctrinal Writings of the Swiss Brethren in a Hitherto Unknown Edition," *MQR*, Vol. XVI, No. 2 (April, 1942), pp. 82-98. The most recent edition of the confession can be found in John H. Yoder, *The Legacy of Michael Sattler* (Scottdale, Pennsylvania: Herald Press, 1973). Juhnke, *Two Kingdoms*, p. 10.

20. Juhnke, *Two Kingdoms*, pp. 10-11.

21. Juhnke, *Two Kingdoms*, p. 11.

22. A stimulating and perceptive essay on this topic is by Robert Friedmann, "The Doctrine of the Two Worlds," in *The Recovery of the Anabaptist Vision*, ed. by Guy F. Hershberger (Scottdale: Herald Press, 1957), pp. 105-118. Friedmann contrasts Anabaptist "kingdom theology" derived from the Gospels, the dualism of God's kingdom and Satan's kingdom, with the Reformers' "salvation theology," derived from the Pauline epistles, and emphasizes a dualism of spirit and flesh. Hans J. Hillerbrand, "The Anabaptist View of the State," *MQR*, Vol. XXXII, (April, 1958), pp. 83-110. Juhnke, *Two Kingdoms*, p. 10.

23. Harold S. Bender, "Church and State in Mennonite History," *MQR*, Vol. XIII (April, 1939), pp. 83-103.

Chapter 2

1. Ernst Crous, *Wie die Mennoniten in die deutsche Volksgemeinschaft hineinwuchsen* (Sonderabdruck aus dem 4. Jahrgang der Mennonitischen Geschichtsblätter) (Karlsruhe: priv. pub., 1939), p. 13.

2. Ernst Crous, "The Mennonites in Germany Since the Thirty Years War," *MQR*, XXV, No. 4 (October, 1951), p. 236.

3. *Ibid.*

4. William I. Schreiber, *The Fate of the Prussian Mennonites* (Göttingen: The Göttingen Research Committee, 1955), p. 18.

5. Horst Quiring, "Die Auswanderung aus Preussen 1788-1870," *Mennonite Life*, VI, No. 2 (April, 1951), pp. 37-40.

6. Wolfgang G. Fieguth, "The Rise and Decline of the Principle of Non-Resistance Among the Mennonites in Prussia" (term paper, Bethel College, North Newton, Kansas, 1948), p. 36.

7. W. Mannhardt, *Die Wehrfreiheit der alt-preussischen Mennoniten* (Marienburg: im Selbstverlage der alt-preussichen Mennonitengemeinden, 1863), p. 126.

8. Adolph Ehrt, *Das Mennonitentum in Russland* (Berlin: Julius Beltz, 1932), p. 24.

9. M. D. Harder, "The Origin, Philosophy, and Development of Education Among the Mennonites" (doctoral dissertation, University of Southern California, 1949), p. 84.

10. *Polnoe Sobranie Zakonov, Rossiiskoi Imperii*, 55 Vols. (St. Petersburg: Government Printing, 1830-55), XVIII, No. 12949, Art. 265; Franz Isaac, *Die Molotschnaer Men-*

noniten (Halbstadt, Taurien: H. J. Baum, 1908), pp. 1-7.

11. E. K. Francis, *In Search of Utopia* (Glencoe, Illinois: Free Press, 1955), pp. 16-17. For Mennonite principles of non-resistance in Prussia see: W. Mannhardt, *Die Wehrfreiheit der alt-preussischen Mennoniten*, and Emil Händiges, "Historisches Memorandum zur Wehrlosigkeit der Mennoniten," *DB*, January 17, 1941, p. 5.

12. Walter Kuhn, "Cultural Achievements of the Chortitza Mennonites," *Mennonite Life*, III (July, 1948), 35; Isaac, *Die Molotschnaer Mennoniten*, pp. 5-7. These homesteads were to be of good, arable, productive land (*undobnie*) and each family received 65 dessiatines, or 175.5 acres.

13. D. G. Rempel, "The Mennonite Colonies in New Russia," (doctoral dissertation, Stanford University, 1933), pp. 103-108.

14. Anatole G. Mazour, *Russia: Tzarist and Communist* (Princeton: D. von Nostrand Co., 1962), p. 294; Kuhn, "Cultural Achievements," p. 37. There is disagreement among scholars as to the exact number of Mennonites immigrating from Prussia to Russia at this time. Cornelius Krahn, "Some Social Attitudes of the Mennonites of Russia," *MQR*, IX (July, 1935), p. 169, places the number at 8,000 families, whereas Orie Miller states there were 9,000 families in "The Present Mennonite Migration," *MQR*, I (April, 1927), p. 8. Perhaps the exact number will never be known.

15. *Polnoe Sobranie Zakonov*, XXXVI, Nos. 27, 912 and 27,954.

16. Krahn, "Some Social Attitudes of the Mennonites of Russia," p. 175.

17. *Ibid.*, 171.

18. Francis, *In Search of Utopia*, p. 21.

19. Cornelius Krahn, "Mennonite Community Life in Russia," *MQR*, XVI (July, 1942), p. 175.

20. Aaron Klaus, *Unsere Kolonien*, pp. 163-164.

21. J. W. Fretz and H. S. Bender, "Mutual Aid," *ME*, III, p. 798.

22. C. J. Dyck (ed.), *An Introduction to Mennonite History*, p. 143.

23. D. H. Epp, *Die Chortitzer Mennoniten* (Odessa: A. Schultze, 1889), p. 143.

24. Rempel, "Mennonite Colonies in New Russia," p. 81.

25. P. M. Friesen, *Die Alt-Evangelische Mennonitische Bruderschaft in Russland, 1789-1910* (Halbstadt, Taurien: Raduga, 1911), pp. 152, 153.

26. Rempel, "Mennonite Colonies in New Russia," p. 84.

27. *Polnoe Sobranie Zakonov*, XXVI, No. 25, p. 752a.

28. Quiring, *Auslandsdeutsche Volksforschung*, pp. 21-22; C. C. Regier, "The Mennonites of Russia" (MS MHLA), pp. 50-60.

Chapter 3

1. Bernard Pares, *A History of Russia* (New York: Alfred A. Knopf, 1960), p. 365; Anatole G. Mazour, *Russia: Past and Present* (Princeton: D. van Nostrand and Co., 1951), p. 163.

2. Mazour, *Russia*, pp. 758-759.

3. Peter Braun, "The Educational System of the Mennonite Colonies in South Russia," *MQR*, III (July, 1929), pp. 171-177.

4. Kuhn, "Cultural Achievements of the Chortitza Mennonites," p. 38.

5. C. H. Smith, *The Story of the Mennonites*, p. 440.

6. Ehrt, *Das Mennonitentum in Russland*, p. 66; Leonhard Froese, "Das Pädago gische Kultursystem der Mennonitischen Siedlungsgruppen in Russland" (doctoral dissertation, Göttingen, 1949).

7. Walter Kirchner, *An Outline History of Russia* (New York: Barnes and Noble, Inc., 1950), pp. 147-149; "Emigration of the Russian Mennonites," *Herald of Truth*, X (September, 1873), p. 153; C. H. Smith, *The Story of the Mennonites*, pp. 442-443.

8. Helen B. Shipley, "The Migration of the Mennonites from Russia, 1879-1880, Their Settlement in Kansas" (Master's thesis, University of Minnesota, 1954), pp. 22-25.

9. J. J. Hildebrandt, *Chronologische Zeittafel* (Winnipeg: J. J. Hildebrandt, 1945), p. 234.

10. George Leibbrandt, "The Emigration of the German Mennonites from Russia to the United States and Canada in 1873-1880," *MQR*, VI (October, 1932), pp. 209-210; Cornelius Jansen, ed., *Sammulung von Notizen über Amerika* (Danzig: Paul Thieme, 1872); for a biography of Jansen and his role in migration see G. E. Reimer and G. R. Gaeddert, *Exiled by the Czar*.

11. Peter Jansen, *Memoirs of Peter Jansen, the Record of a Busy Life: An Autobiography* (Beatrice, Nebraska: privately published, 1921), pp. 29-30. See also the fine work *Exiled by the Czar*.

12. Peter Wiens, "Letter from Russia," *Herald of Truth*, XI (June, 1874), p. 105.

13. Leibbrandt, "The Emigration of the German Mennonites," *MQR*, VI, p. 224; John D. Unruh, Jr., "Mennonites to Nebraska, 1873-1878" (Master's thesis, University of Kansas, 1959), pp. 33-56.

14. See Cornelius Krahn, ed., *From the Steppes to the Prairies* (Newton, Kansas: Mennonite Publication Office, 1949).

15. See Ernst Correll, ed., "The Congressional Debates on the Mennonite Immigration from Russia, 1873-1874," *MQR*, XX, No. 2 (July, 1946), pp. 48-60.

16. M. A. Carleton, "Hard Wheats Winning Their Way," in bulletin of *United States Department of Agriculture, 1914*.

17. *Ibid.* A fuller account of the history of hard winter wheat is included in *United States Department of Agriculture Bulletin No. 1074* (Washington: G.P.O., 1922) and *Classification of American Wheat Varieties* (Washington: G.P.O., 1922). See also an interesting discussion about Mennonites in William B. Bracke, *Wheat Country* (New York: Sloan and Pierce, 1950), pp. 85-98.

18. W. L. Morton, *Manitoba: A History* (Toronto: University of Toronto, 1957), pp. 160-161; Leibbrandt, "The Emigration of the German Mennonites," *MQR*, VII, pp. 7-11; Gertrude S. Young, "A Record Concerning Mennonite Immigration, 1873," *American Historical Review*, XXIX, No. 3 (April, 1924), pp. 518-522; Cornelius Jansen, "The Mennonites," Mt. Pleasant, Iowa, *Free Press* (January 13, 1876); C. B. Schmidt, "Reminiscences of Kansas Immigration Work," *The Mennonite*, XXXVI (September 28, 1911), pp. 2, 4, 9; Christian Krehbiel, "An Earnest Call: Immediate Help Needed," *Herald of Truth*, XI (February, 1874), p. 21.

19. Krahn, "Russia," *ME*, IV, 381-393. A more extensive treatment of this alternative service and the Russian laws governing it will be given in a later chapter.

20. C. B. Schmidt, "Reminiscences of Kansas Immigration Work," p. 2.

21. *Ibid.*, XXXI (October 5, 1911), p. 2.

22. C. H. Smith, *The Story of the Mennonites*, pp. 455-456; Cornelius Jansen, "The Mennonites"; Krahn, "Russian Nationalism and the Mennonites," MQR, XXII, No. 4 (December 9, 1948), p. 4; P. M. Friesen, *Die Alt-Evangelische Mennonitische Brüderschaft in Russland.*

Chapter 4

1. Ira D. Landis, *Eschatology and the Faith of Our Fathers* (Lititz, Pa.: published by the author, 1946), p. 55.

2. Revelation 20:2-10. Translation from the original Greek by the author.

3. 1 Corinthians 15:24 ff.

4. Revelation 12:17; 13.

5. Revelation 19:11.

6. Revelation 19:20; Rev. 20.

7. Revelation 20:2-7.

8. *DB* (November 5, 1947), pp. 3-4.

9. *Ibid.* See also Marjorie Reeves, *The Influence of Prophecy in the Later Middle Ages* (New York: Oxford Press, 1969).

10. *Ibid.*

11. Cornelius Krahn, *Menno Simons (1496-1561): Ein Beitrag zur Geschichte und Theologie der Taufgesinnten* (Karlsruhe: Heinrich Schneider, 1950), p. 112.

12. J. C. Wenger, "Chiliasm," *ME*, I, p. 557.

13. *Ibid.*, p. 558.

14. Christian Neff and Elizabeth Bender, "Jung-Stilling," *ME*, III, pp. 127-128, Edward Manger, "Jung-Stilling," *Allgemeine Deutsche Biographie*, 37 vols., XIV (Leipzig: Liliencron, 1875-1912), pp. 697-704.

15. Tatjana Lanko, "Jung-Stilling und Russland" (doctoral dissertation, Marburg, Germany, 1954), pp. 1-66; Stilling, *Der graue Mann*, 5 vols. (Nürnberg: Rowsche Buchandlung, 1795-1812).

16. Christian Neff, "Jung-Stilling," *ML*, ed. by Christian Hege and Christian Neff (3 vols., Frankfort am Main, Weierhof, and Karlsruhe: Heinrich Schneider, 1913-1937), II, p. 446; see also H. R. G. Günther, *Jung-Stilling* (Münich: Federmann, 1948).

17. Johann Stecher, *Jung-Stilling als Schriftsteller* (Berlin: Scheible, 1913), p. 183; Christian Neff et al., "Arnold, Gottfried," *ML*, II, pp. 85-90. Arnold based his writings upon original sources that were hostile to Anabaptists as well as statements from Anabaptists themselves.

18. Like Jung-Stilling, the Swiss Pietist Lavater was also in friendly contact with the Mennonites and in 1774 visited them in the Palatinate. See Christian Neff, "Lavater," *ML*, II, p. 625.

19. Ernst H. Correll, *Das Schweizerische Täufermennonitentum* (Tübingen: Mohr, 1925), p. 122.

20. Neff, "Möllinger," *ML*, III, 132 ff; Correll, *Das Schweizerische Täufermennonitentum*, p. 126; Neff, "Jung-Stilling," *ML*, II, p. 447.

21. Christian Neff, "Jung-Stilling über Menno Simons," *Christlicher Gemeinde-Kalender* (Kaiserslautern: Losch, 1937), pp. 49-53.

22. J. W. Goethe, *Dichtung und Wahrheit* in *Sämmtliche Werke*, 20 vols., IX (Berlin: P. Reclam, 1775), pp. 40-50.

23. Johann Heinrich Jung-Stilling, *Heinrich Jung-Stillings Jugend* (Berlin: P. Reclam, 1780); *Idem, Heinrich Stillings Wanderschaft* (Berlin and Leipzig: P. Reclam, 1778), pp. 47-70; *Mennonitische Blätter*, XXXIX (1892), 139; *ML*, II, p. 684. A letter from Jung-Stilling to Becker is published in the *Mennonitische Jugendwarte*, XVIII (1901), p. 34.

24. Neff, "Jung-Stilling," *ML*, II, 447. J. H. Jung-Stilling, *Sämmtliche Werke* (II vols., Stuttgart: J. Scheibles Buchhandlung, 1841), V, p. 310.

25. J. H. Jung-Stilling, *Das Heimweh* (Marburg: Akademischen Buchhandlung, 1794), V, p. 425.

26. J. H. Jung-Stilling, *Sämmtliche Werke*, IV, p. 665.

27. *Ibid.*, V, p. 406.

28. Lanko, "Jung-Stilling und Russland," p. 66; Robert Friedmann, *Mennonite*

Piety Through the Centuries (Goshen, Indiana: The Mennonite Historical Society, 1949). p. 71.

29. Karl Traub, *Jung-Stilling* (Cassel: Oncken, 1920), p. 20. Jung-Stilling's hymn, "Vater, Deines Geistes Wehen" was adopted into the hymnal of the South German Mennonites in 1910.

30. *Ibid.*; also Günther, *Jung-Stilling.*

31. Jung-Stilling, *Sämmtliche Werke*, IV, p. 311.

32. Lanko, "Jung-Stilling und Russland," pp. 66, 68.

33. P. Friesen, *Die Alt-Evangelische Mennonitishe Brüderschaft in Russland* (1789-1910), p. 570; Martin Klaassen, Geschichte der Wehrlosen tafgesinnten Gemeinden (Köppental, Trakt, Russia: Privately published by Köoppental-Orloff Mennonite Church, 1873).

34. Kurt Kauenhoven, "Die Sippe Epp," pamphlet in MHLA; Neff, A. Braun and H. G. Mannhardt, "'Epp," *ML*, I, pp. 596-597; G. Reimer, "Epp," *ME*, II, pp. 233-238.

35. Kauenhoven, *Mitteilungen*, Letters of B. Epp, MHLA, pp. 87-88.

36. Krahn, "Trakt Mennonite Settlement," *ME*, IV, pp. 743-744.

37. David H. Epp and Krahn, "Hahnsau," *ME*, II, p. 629; *Am Trakt*, pp. 7-10 and *ML*, II, p. 233; Margaret Horn, *Abrahms Horn*, p. 2.

38. Krahn, "Köppental," *ME*, III, pp. 225-226.

39. Jacob Klaassen, "Memories and Notations," MHLA, p. 2.

40. *Ibid.*

41. Krahn, "Trakt Mennonite Church," *ME*, IV, pp. 742-743; Krahn, "Johann Wall," *ME*, IV, pp. 878-879; Krahn, "Orloff," *ME*, IV, pp. 83-84; Bartsch, *Unser Auszug*, p. 25.

42. Klaassen, "Memories and Notations," p. 2.

43. Krahn, "Johann Wall," *ME*, pp. 878-879.

44. H. G. Mannhardt, "Fürstenwerder," *ME*, II, p. 427; Franz Bartsch, "Claas Epp, Jr.," *ME*, II, p. 234; Krahn, "To Meet the Lord in Asia," *Mennonite Weekly Review* (March 18, 1948), p. 4.

45. Bartsch, *Unser Auszug*, pp. 6-9.

46. Eventually twelve children were born to the Epps but only two survived. Bartsch, "Claas Epp, Jr.," p. 234; Naomi Reimer, "Family Tree of My Great-Great-Great-Grandfather, Cornelius Jantzen" (research paper, Bethel College, 1962); "Epp Manuscript," MHLA, n.p., n.d.

47. *DB* (November 12, 1947), pp. 4-5.

46. Eventually twelve children were born to the Epps but only two survived. Bartsch, "Claas Epp, Jr.," p. 234; Naomi Reimer, "Family Tree of My Great-Great-Great-Grandfather, Cornelius Jantzen" (research paper, Bethel College, 1962); "Epp Manuscript," MHLA, n.p., n.d.

47. *DB* (November 12, 1947), pp. 4-5.

48. Revelation 3:8-10; *ML*, I, p. 596.

49. Revelation 12:4; *ML*, I, p. 596.

50. Anna Toews, "Diary," p. 6; Bartsch, *Unser Auszug*, pp. 78-81. Also see Jung-Stilling's *Leben*.

51. Bartsch, *Unser Auszug*, pp. 18-23.

52. Claas Epp, *Die entsiegelte Weissagung des Propheten Daniel und die Deutung der Offenbarung Jesu Christi* (Alt-Tschau bei Neusalz: Friedrich August Rubiner, 1878), pp. 1-88.

53. *Ibid.*, p. 5.

54. *Ibid.*, p. 85.

55. *Ibid.*, p. 85.

56. *Ibid.*, 3rd ed., 1898.

Chapter 5

1. See map on page 79.

2. W. P. Coates and Zelda Coates, *Soviets in Central Asia* (London: Lawrence and Wishart, Ltd., 1951), pp. 16-21.

3. The lack of a mountain barrier in the north has exposed the region to many invasions.

4. Lack of outlets to the open seas has always hindered access of Turkestan's peoples to other lands.

5. Richard A. Pierce, *Russian Central Asia, 1867-1917*, (Berkeley: University of California Press, 1960), pp. 6-13; Coates, *Soviets in Central Asia*, pp. 21-22.

6. George B. Cressey, *Asia's Lands and Peoples* (New York: Harper, 1940), pp. 343-350.

7. *Ibid.*

8. Pastureland comprises less than 44 percent of the total area, while deserts cover 54 percent. This leaves about 4 million acres as possibly arable when properly irrigated. See Coates, *Soviets in Central Asia*, p. 22.

9. G. N. Curzon, *Russia in Central Asia in 1889 and the Anglo-Russian Question* (London: Longmans Green and Co., 1889), pp. 71-73; A. M. Kononov, *Sovetskaia Geografia* (Moscow: Gosigdatgeolit, 1960) p. 410.

12. Jantzen, "Memories of Our Journey to Middle Asia," p. 15.

13. Frye, *The History of Bukhara*, p. 3. The Persian historian Juvaini wrote in 1260, long after the Mongols had sacked Bukhara, that "Bukhar" in the language of the Magians means "center of learning" or that it could be a word for places of worship.

14. *Ibid.*, p. 654.

15. *Architectural Monuments of Middle Asia*, pp. 31-37.

16. Seventy percent of all cotton fiber used in Russia during the late nineteenth century came from Turkestan. See M. M. Smirin, *Weltgeschichte* (4 vols., Berlin: Deutscher Verlag der Wissenschaften, 1964), IV, pp. 649-653.

17. *Ibid.*, pp. 652-653.

18. *Ibid.*, pp. 648-651.

19. Michael Rykin, *Russia in Central Asia* (New York:Collier Books, 1963), p. 15.

20. By the late nineteenth century (1888) Russia controlled 2,100,000 square miles in Europe and over 6,450,000 in Asia. The population grew from 14 million in 1725 to over 120 million under the hegemony of imperial Russia by 1888. See: Curzon, *Russia in Central Asia*, p. 259; Coates, *Soviets in Central Asia;* pp. 43-45.

21. Geoffrey Wheeler, *The Modern History of Soviet Central Asia* (London: Weidenfeld and Nicolson, 1964), pp. 49, 59, 64.

22. During the American Civil War, when rebel cotton could not reach Eastern Europe, cotton goods from Turkestan to Russia increased fivefold. Coates, *Soviets in Central Asia*, p. 42; Allworth, *Central Asia*, p. 131.

23. Coates, *Soviets in Central Asia*, p. 17; *Turkestanskii Krai: Sbornik materialov dlia istorii ego zavoevaniis* (Tashkent: Izdanie Shtaba turkkestanseago voennago Ikruga, 1914), XIX, No. 1, p. 210; Franz von Schwarz, *Turkestan: die Wege der indo-germanischen Volker* (Freiburg im Breisgau: Freiburg University Press, 1900), p. 47. Schwarz tells of Russian General Chernayeff taking Tashkent on June 15, 1865, with 1,501 men and 12 old cannons. The inhabitants numbered 90,000 and had 15,000 to 30,000 troops.

24. Arminius Vambrey, *Western Culture in Eastern Lands* (London: John Murray, 1906), pp. 15, 47.

25. Frederick G. Burnaby, *Ride to Khiva: Travels and Adventures in Central Asia* (London: Cassell, Petter and Galpin, 1877), p. 96.

26. Wheeler, *Soviet Central Asia*, pp. 95-96.

27. *Ibid.*, p. 65; Mazour, *Russia; Tzarist and Communist*, p. 295; Coates, *Soviets in Central Asia*, p. 49. For a good brief history of czars and khans and their wars see: William Mandel, *The Soviet Far East and Central Asia* (New York: Dial Press, Inc., 1944), pp. 97-118.

28. Serge A. Zenkovsky, "Kulturkampf in Pre-Revolutionary Central Asia," *The American Slavic and East European Review*, XIV (1955), pp. 17-18.

29. *Polozenie ob upravlenii Turkestanskogo Kraia* (Petersburg, Government Printing, 1892), Articles 73 through 115 on local jurisdiction, Articles 211 through 255 on Muslim judges. See also Schuyler, *Turkistan*, pp. 160-170, on the early period of Russian control of Central Asia.

30. *Polnoi zakonov rossiis koi imperii*, XXXII, p. 1156; Pierce, *Russian Central Asia*, p. 26.

31. *Kotkrytiiu pamiatnika: General Adjiutant K. P. fon Kaufmann kak ustroitel Turkestanskago Kraia*, 1867-1882 (Tashkent: n.p., 1915); Pierce, *Russian Central Asia*, p. 5; Mazour, *Russia; Tzarist and Communist*, p. 294; Coates, *Soviets in Central Asia*, p. 46.

32. N.P. Ostroumov, "K'istorii narodnago obrazovaniia v'turkestanskom kraie," *Konstantin Petrovich von Kaufmann, ustroitel turkestanskays Kraia. Lichnya vospominaniia* (Tashkent: n.p., 1889), pp. 44, 107; Vambrey, *Western Culture*, pp. 39-42.

33. It must be noted here that the policies of Kaufmann and the very creation of the guberniia of Turkestan were opposed in the Russian High Command. General Kryzhanovskii, then governor-general of Orenburg, was opposed to the area being set up because it was far from the center of the empire, destroying, he believed, the unity of command of the steppes. The strong personality of Kaufmann, however, won out in the conflict, and opposition soon waned. See Eugene Schuyler, *Turkistan: Notes of a Journey in Russian Turkistan, Kokand, Bukhara, and Kuldja* (2 vols., New York: Schribner and Armstrong Co., 1876), p. 204. This American traveler gives a very interesting account of General Kaufmann's attitude toward the khanates on pp. 274-312.

34. Pierce, *Russian Central Asia*, p. 26; Coates, *Soviets in Central Asia*, p. 52; Mazour, *Russia: Tzarist and Communist*, p. 294.

35. A. I. Dobrosmyslov, *Tashkent v. proshlom i nastoiashchem. Istoricheskii ocherk* (Tashkent; n.p., 1911-1912), p. 61.

36. Vambrey, *Western Culture*, pp. 49-55; Coates, *Soviets in Central Asia*, pp. 47-49; Allworth, *Central Asia*, pp. 143-145.

37. Coates, *Soviets in Central Asia*, p. 52; Seymour Becker, *Russia's Protectorates in Central Asia: Bukhara and Khiva*, 1865-1924 (Cambridge: Harvard University Press, 1968), pp. 92-93.

38. Wheeler, *Soviet Central Asia*, pp. 69-72; Vambrey, *Western Culture*, p. 59.

39. Curzon, *Russia in Central Asia*, p. 136.

40. See Fred R. Belk, "Turkestan: Russian Mennonite Promised Land," *Studies in Islam* (January-April, 1973), pp. 58-79.

Chapter 6

1. Cornelius Krahn, "Forestry Service — A Mennonite Alternative Service in Russia," *Mennonite Weekly Review* (January 12, 1949), p. 7.

2. *DB* (August, 1879), p. 62.

3. *Ibid.*, p. 63.

4. *Ibid.*

5. *ZH* (April, 1880), p. 53.

6. *Ibid.* This appeal No. 3519 dated May 3, 1879, made its way to the Secretary of State for Receiving Appeals and then was presented to the Secretary of the Interior, who ruled that by previous order by the czar (April 8, 1875) the Mennonites had already been privileged. After conferring with the Secretary of War he felt the appeal should not be granted because Turkestan natives would soon be drafted. The czar probably never saw this appeal.

7. Jacob Klaassen, "Asienreise," pp. 1-2.

8. *ZH* (April 7, 1880), p. 53.

9. *Ibid.*

10. *Ibid.*

11. *Ibid.*

12. Jacob Toews, "A Brief Sketch," p. 12.

13. *ZH* (September 7, 1880), p. 133.

14. *Ibid.*; Toews, "Sketch," p. 14; *ZH* (April 7, 1880), p. 53; Anna Toews, "Diary" (MS, Aberdeen, Idaho, 1943). Original in possession of Mr. and Mrs. Ernst Claassen, Whitewater, Kansas, p. 8.

15, *ZH* (September 7, 1880), pp. 133-134.

16. *ZH* (April 7, 1880), p. 54; *GB* (July, 1880), p. 55; Jantzen, "Memories," p. 4; Johannes Bartsch, ed., *Geschichte der Gemeinde* (Elkhart, Indiana; Mennonite Publishing House, 1898), pp. 136-137; Toews, "Sketch," p. 15; *ZH* (September 7, 1880), p. 133; Klaassen, "Asienreise," pp. 1-2; Jacob Klaassen, "Memories of a Journey" (40-page MS in MHLA), pp. 1-2; Carl R. Jantzen, "A Brief Sketch of my Ancestors" (research paper Bethel College, 1952), p. 4.

17. *Ibid.*

18. *ZH* (September 7, 1880), pp. 133-134.

19. *Ibid.*, p. 134. They had also received much criticism from their own people concerning the trek to Turkestan because they were using God's Word to justify it. See *Der Mennonitische Friedensbote* (October 1, 1881), p. 150.

20. *ZH* (April 7, 1880), p. 54.

21. Wenger, "Chiliasm," *ME*, I, p. 559.

22. *ZH* (April 7, 1880), pp. 54-55.

23. *Ibid.* Ideas in this paragraph were in an article entitled "Declaration of the Mennonite Brothers in Russia to go to Turkestan." This also appeared in a more detailed form in *GB* (September, 1880), pp. 66-68, as: "Declaration of Special Rights

of Those Mennonite Brothers in Russia Who Desire to Migrate to Turkestan; as explained before high and low, written or verbally, against the other Mennonite communites."

24. *Ibid.*

25. Helen Goertz, *Family History of Siebert Goertz and John Harms and Their Descendants* (Newton, Kansas: privately published, 1965), pp. 120-121.

26. *ZH* (September 7, 1880), 134; *Am Trakt: Eine mennonitische Kolonie in mittleren Wolgagebiet*, Vol. VI of Historische Schriftenreihe des Echo-Verlags (North Kildonan, Manitoba, 1948), p. 18.

27. *Ibid.*

28. Wall later parted with Epp's teachings and settled in Aulie Ata; Toews later became minister of a Mennonite church in Newton, Kansas; Bartsch, after years in Turkestan, returned to the Trakt to become a teacher and write a book about the trek; Klaassen died on the trip to Bukhara, but a son, Michael, later became a minister in Bessie, Oklahoma; J. K. Penner later became a teacher and minister in Beatrice, Nebraska, while his brother remained faithful to Epp for years; Jantzen became one of the outstanding wagon masters of the trek. Martin Klaassen's book was written in 1873 and is entitled *Geschichte der Wehrlosen Taufgesinnten Gemeinden*. See Walter Klaassen, "A Belated Reivew: Martin Klaassen's 'Geschichte Der Wehrlosen Tauf-Gesinnten Gemeinden,' Published in 1873" *MQR*, XLIX (January, 1975), 43 ff.

29. *ZH* (September 7, 1880), pp. 3-4.

30. Johannes Janzen, "The Mennonite Colony in Turkestan," *MQR*, IV, No. 4 (October, 1930), 282; Stumpp, *HB* (1964), p. 15.

31. Bartsch, *Unser Auszug*, p. 21.

Chapter 7

1. Klaassen, "Memories of a Journey" (MS in MHLA, 40 pp., n.p., n.d.), p. 2.

2. *ZH* (September 7, 1880), p. 133.

3. Dates are according to the Julian calendar in the Mennonite writings of this period. To convert to the Gregorian calendar in use in the West, add twelve days.

4. Bartsch, *Unser Auszug*, p. 24; *Am Trakt*, p. 18.

5. *Ibid.* The numbers used here are taken from the account of Franz Bartsch, who was a member of this wagon train. Other sources disagree as to the actual number. Hermann Bartsch, Franz's brother, who was also on the trip, stated that 21 wagons and 11 families were in the group; *DB* (November 12, 1947), p. 5, mentioned 18 wagons and 10 families; Hermann Jantzen in "Ihr sollt meine Zeugen sein" (MS, n.p., n.d., in possession of John Wiebe, Whitewater, Kansas) agreed with *DB*; and *GB* (October, 1880), p. 76, states that 11 families and 21 wagons took part.

6. Bartsch, *Unser Auszug*, pp. 26-27; Krahn, "A Mennonite Refuge in Central

Asia," *Mennonite Weekly Review* (April 29, 1948), p. 8; Jantzen, "Ihr sollt meine Zeugen sein." The village of Hahnsau was sold to a Mr. Muller of Wahrenburg. Perhaps this is one reason why Claas Epp turned back. Muller later sold all the land of the village to the Russian government, making a great profit. See Carl R. Jantzen, "A Brief Sketch of My Ancestors," p. 5.

7. BM.

8. Klaassen, "Memories of a Journey," p. 11.

9. Arlin G. Claassen, "A Study of the Mennonites in Russia" (research paper, Bethel College, 1959), p. 5.

10. BM; Jantzen, "Memories," pp. 5-6.

11. Bartsch, *Unser Auszug*, pp. 24-25; 35-38; Jantzen, "Memories," pp. 4-7; Stumpp, *HB* (1964), p. 15. The Bartsch Map erroneously dates the departure October 15, 1880.

12. Bartsch, *Unser Auszug*, p. 38; *GB* (July, 1881), pp. 51-53; *MR* (February 1, 1882), p. 2.

13. *GB* (October, 1880), p. 77.

14. Discrepancies as to the actual numbers involved in the second journey are as follows: Jacob Toews, "Short Sketch," p. 15 (23 wagons); Bartsch, *Unser Auszug*, p. 44 (12 families); Klaassen, "Memories," p. 3 (12 families and 29 wagons); BM (13 families and 34 wagons); Cornelius Krahn, *Mennonite Weekly Review* (April 29, 1948), p. 8 (13 families and 28 wagons); Carl Jantzen, "A Brief Sketch," p. 7 (12 families and 32 wagons); and *DB* (November 12, 1947), p. 5 (13 families). The above differences are not unusual as one studies source materials of this movement to Turkestan. One newspaper account, *CBB* (February 15, 1882), p. 30, even has the group leaving from another town — Lysanderhöh.

15. *GB* (October, 1880), p. 76; Klaassen, "Asienreise," p. 2; Toews, "A Short Sketch," p. 15.

16. Klaassen, "Memories," p. 2; Klaassen, "Asienreise," p. 2. There are many discrepancies in these two MSS by the same author.

17. Klaassen, "Asienreise," pp. 2-5.

18. *GB* (October, 1880), p. 77.

19. Klaassen, "Asienreise," p. 9.

20. BM; *CBB* (February 15, 1882), p. 30.

21. Klaassen, "Memories of a Journey," p. 11.

22. Art Toews, "A Translation of 'About the Immigration of the Mennonites to Central Asia' by M. Klaassen" (research paper, Bethel College, February, 1957), p. 3.

23. Klaassen, "Asienreise," p. 17.

24. Klaassen, "Memories of a Journey," pp. 14-15.

25. *CBB* (February 15, 1882), p. 30.

26. *Ibid.*; Klaassen, "Memories of a Journey," p. 17.

Chapter 8

1. Eldon Smith, *A History and Record of the Schartner Family* (Newton, Kansas: Herald Book and Printing Co., 1952), p. 70; Mrs. Siebert Goertz, "Translation of Parts of Mother Goertz's Diary, 1929-1930: page 12 and Past the Middle of the Book" (MS in MHLA: n.p., n.d.), p. 3.

2. Helene Goertz, *Family History of Siebert Goertz and John Harms and Their Descendants* (Newton, Kansas: privately published, 1965), p. 120.

3. *Ibid.*, 119-121; Mrs. Siebert Goertz, "Translation," p. 3; Cornelius Krahn, "Taurida," *ME*, IV, p. 687; Siebert Goertz, "Mother Goertz's Diary of 1933" (MS in MHLA, n.p., n.d.).

4. Cornelius Krahn, "Abraham Peters," *ME*, IV, p. 152; Krahn, "Taurida," *ME*, IV, p. 687; Krahn, "Ukraine," *ME*, IV, p. 766; Helene Goertz, *Family History*, p. 120; Siebert Goertz, "Mother Goertz's Diary."

5. *GB* (October, 1880), p. 76-77.

6. *ZH* (July 7, 1880), p. 102.

7. Eldon Smith, *A History*, p. 70; Lorene Dick, "The Story of the Dirks Family" (research paper, Bethel College, January, 1959); Krahn, "Waldheim," *ME*, IV, p. 876.

8. Goertz, *Family History*, pp. 33-34; Mrs. Siebert Goertz, "Translation," p. 3; Jacob Reimer, "Article," *Hillsboro Vorwärts*, XXXVI, No. 52 (December 30, 1938), 3; the Bartsch map states that 54 wagons and 56 families made up the group.

9. Smith, *A History*, pp. 70-71.

10. Elizabeth Schultz, "Autobiography" (trans. Annie Keyes and entitled "What a Heritage," MS in possession of author, n.p., n.d.), p. 13.

11. Schultz, "Autobiography", p. 16.

12. Schultz, "Autobiography", pp. 16-17.

13. Jacob Reimer, "Article," p. 3. These supplies, 75 pud flour, 25 pud potatoes, and 95 pud rye flour, were considered a large order by the local merchants.

14. Schultz, "Autobiography," pp. 16-18.

15. Jacob Reimer, "Article," p. 3.

16. *Ibid.*, pp. 19-20; Jacob Reimer, "Article," p. 3.

17. *Ibid.*, pp. 20-21.

18. Cornelius Krahn, "Abraham Peters," *ME*, IV, p. 152; Bartsch, *Unser Auszug*, p. 40; "Peters," *ML*, III, p. 353; Janzen, "Colony," p. 283; Klaassen, "Asienreise," pp. 121-123; *History and Dates of Peter and Maria Abrahms*, pp. 4-6; BM; Goertz, "Family History," p. 34; Ruth Graber MS; and *ZH* (May 7, 1881), p. 69.

Chapter 9

1. Bartsch, *Unser Auszug*, p. 44.

2. *CBB* (February 15, 1882), p. 30.

3. For an understanding of contemporary Muslim life in Tashkent in dress, food, narcotics, drinks, games, customs, diseases, religious life, education, etc., see: Schuyler, *Turkistan*, I, pp. 118-172. In 1877, Tashkent had a population of 120,000 and came under gradual Russian influence in 1841-84; Coates, *Central Asia*, p. 17; and Cornelius Krahn, "Turkestan," *ME*, IV, p. 755.

4. Schultz, "Autobiography," p. 21.

5. *Ibid.*, p. 22; *ZH* (May 7, 1881), p. 69.

6. Dick, "The Story of the Dirks Family," p. 4; Eldon Smith, *A History*, p. 71; and Jacob Reimer, "Article."

7. *ZH* (May 7, 1881), p. 69.

8. Schultz, "Autobiography," p. 24.

9. *Ibid.*, Wheeler, *Modern History of Central Asia*, p. 95.

10. Ruth Graber MS; Art Toews, "A Translation," p. 4; Klaassen, "Asienreise," p. 21; *CBB* (February 14, 1882), p. 30.

11. *GB* (July, 1881), pp. 51-53.

12. Klaassen, "Asienreise," p. 24.

13. Klaassen, "Memories and Notations," p. 6.

14. Schultz, "Autobiography," pp. 21-22; *MR* (September 15, 1882), p. 2; *MR* (February 1, 1882), pp. 1-2. The Jacob Jantzens lost two sons, Jacob and Cornelius, and appreciated the ministry of Abraham Peters during their grief.

15. *MR* (February 1, 1882), p. 2.

16. Substantiating this probability are the names of people previously mentioned, sources that give much larger numbers, and the fact that most of the above names, maiden names, and places of birth show that these were generally Molotschna people living in Tashkent. Taking into consideration that about 280 people were in the Molotschna congregation and averaging the 22 families from the Trakt at about 10 members per family, and understanding that there were some very large families and some widows and single persons, we can conservatively place the Mennonites' population, prior to the departure of the Epp wagon train, at about 400 persons. Using the low figure of

50 deaths among the Tashkent group and about 15 more at Kaplan Bek, it means that about 15 percent of the Mennonite population died of typhoid. If the larger figure of 80 is used, then perhaps 20 percent of the Turkestan millennialists died.

17. *CBB* (February 15, 1882), p. 30; Jantzen, "Memories," p. 7; *ZH* (April 7, 1881), p. 2; Neff, "Alexander II," *ME* I, p. 44; Neff, "Alexander II," *ML*, I, p. 21.

18. Alexander Kornilov, *Modern Russian History* (New York: Alfred A. Knopf, 1952), p. 247.

19. Klaassen, "Asienreise," p. 23.

20. Jacob Toews, "Sketch," p. 16.

21. Kornilov, *Modern Russian History*, pp. 249, 261; Mazour, *Russia: Past and Present*, pp. 72-73; Curzon, *Russian Central Asia*, pp. 23-24; Wheeler, *Modern History of Russia*, p. 96.

22. Toews, "Sketch," p. 16; Curzon, *Russian Central Asia*, pp. 21-23. Curzon on his personal excursions found hostility toward Germans in Russia.

23. Schultz, "Autobiography," p. 23.

24. *CBB* (February 15, 1882), p. 30; Jantzen, "A Brief Sketch," p. 10. The year is 1881 and not 1882 as Jantzen incorrectly reports.

25. Schultz, "Autobiography," p. 23; Jantzen, "Memories," p. 7.

26. Jantzen, "Memories," p. 7; Janzen, "Colony," p. 83; *DB* (November 12, 1947), pp. 4-7; D. J. Schellenberg, "A Moses of Our Day — David Toews," *Mennonite Life*, V, No. 3 (July, 1950), pp. 6-9; *CBB* (February 15, 1882), p. 30; Stumpp, *HB*, (1959), p. 15.

27. Bartsch, *Unser Auszug*, p. 44.

28. *Ibid.*

29. Krahn, "Abraham Peters," p. 152; Bartsch, *Unser Auszug*, p. 40; "Peters," *ML*, III, p. 353; Stumpp, *HB* (1964), p. 15; Jansen, "Colony," p. 283.

30. Claassen, "A Study of the Mennonites in Russia," p. 8.

31. Krahn, "Peters," p. 152; *ZH* (September 21, 1881), p. 142; *CBB* (February 15, 1882), pp. 30-31; Stumpp, *HB* (1964), p. 15; *GB* (April, 1883), p. 28; Janzen, "Colony," p. 283; *ZH* (September 21, 1881), p. 142; *CBB* (February 15, 1882), pp. 30-31.

32. Claassen, "A Study of the Mennonites in Russia," p. 9.

33. *GB* (January, 1882), pp. 4-5; *ZH* (November 21, 1881), p. 174; *ZH* (December 7, 1881), p. 182.

34. *CBB* (June 15, 1883), pp. 93-94.

35. *ZH* (September 21, 1881), p. 142.

32. Claassen, "A Study of the Mennonites in Russia," p. 9.

33. *GB* (January, 1882), pp. 4-5; *ZH* (November 21, 1881), p. 174; *ZH* (December 7, 1881), p. 182.

34. *CBB* (June 15, 1883), pp. 93-94.

35. *ZH* (September 21, 1881), p. 142.

36. *GB* (August, 1881), p. 61; Bartsch, *Unser Auszug*, p. 81; *CBB* (September 15, 1882), p. 143.

37. Klaassen, "Asienreise," pp. 24-25; BM; *CBB* (February 15, 1882), p. 30; *CBB* (March 1, 1882), p. 38; Bartsch, *Unser Auszug*, p. 50; Eldon Smith, *History and Record*, p. 72.

Chapter 10

1. *ZH* (December 21, 1881), p. 191; *DB* (November 19, 1947), p. 5; *CBB* (February 15, 1882), p. 31.

2. Cornelius Krahn, "Bukhara," *ME*, I, p. 383; Curzon, *Russia in Central Asia*, p. 160, points out that by the treaty of 1873 with Russia, slavery was prohibited in the khanate, but in reality *de facto* slavery was not abolished until November 19, 1886.

3. *ZH* (December 21, 1881), p. 191.

4. Klaassen, "Memories of a Journey," p. 21; Jantzen, "Memories of a Journey," pp. 8-9.

5. *CBB* (March 1, 1882), p. 37; BM; for an excellent historical description of this city see the recently published *Samarkand* (Tashkent: Verlag Usbekistan, 1971), pp. 1-8.

6. *CBB* (March 1, 1882), p. 37; Jantzen, "Memories of a Journey," p. 9; Klaassen, "Memories of a Journey," pp. 22-23; Jacob Toews, "Sketch," pp. 17-24; Eldon Smith, *History and Record of the Schartner Family*, p. 72; Lorene Dick, "Story of the Dirks Family, p. 4; *CBB* January 15, 1882), p. 14.

7. Art Toews, "A Translation," pp. 6-7; *CBB* (January 15, 1882), pp. 13-14.

8. BM; *CBB* (June 15, 1883), p. 93; Klaassen, "Memories of a Journey," p. 24; *CBB* (December 1, 1882), p. 181.

9. *CBB* (January 15, 1882), p. 14.

10. *MR* (February 1, 1882), p. 2.

11. *CBB* (January 15, 1882), p. 14; *CBB* (March 1, 1882), p. 38; *MR* (February 1, 1882), p. 2.

12. *CBB* (December 1, 1882), p. 181.

13. *CBB* (March 15, 1882), p. 46.

18. Jantzen, "Memories of a Journey," pp. 10-11.

19. *Ibid.*

20. Anna Toews, "Diary" (MS in possession of Mr. and Mrs. Ernst Claassen, White-water, Kansas, 1943).

21. Smith, *Schartner Family*, p. 72.

22. *CBB* (December 1, 1882), p. 181.

23. *Ibid.*; Smith, *Schartner Family*, p. 72.

24. Dick, "Dirks Family," p. 5.

25. *CBB* (December 1, 1882), p. 182; Schultz, "Autobiography," pp. 25-40.

26. *Ibid.*

27. Art Toews, "A Translation," p. 7.

Chapter 11

1. Little is known about this fourth movement, but it is here presented and deserving of attention because of some unparalleled facts gleaned from obscure sources and the later importance of this faction in developing the Aulie Ata settlement.

2. *MR* (February 1, 1882), p. 2.

3. *GB* (April, 1883), p. 28.

4. *GB* (December, 1881), p. 92; BM; *MR* (January 15, 1882), p. 1.

5. *GB* (December, 1881), p. 92; BM; Carl R. Jantzen, "A Brief Sketch of My Ancestors," p. 9.

6. *GB* (December, 1881), p. 92.

7. *Ibid.*; BM.

8. BM.

9. *GB* (December, 1881), p. 92; Interview by writer with Mr. and Mrs. Ernst Claassen, Mr. and Mrs. John H. Wiebe, and Mrs. P. G. Harder on May 7, 1972, at Whitewater, Kansas.

10. *GB* (December, 1881), p. 92.

11. BM; Claassen, "A Study of the Mennonites in Russia," p. 10; "*History, Dates and Experiences of Peter and Maria Abrahms Horn*," p. 4; Jantzen, "A Brief Sketch of My Ancestors," p. 9.

12. "*History, Dates and Experiences*," p. 4; Reimer, "Family Tree of My Great-Great Grandfather," p. 2.

13. *CBB* (July 15, 1882), p. 11.

14. *CBB* (August 1, 1882), p. 120; BM; *CBB* (September 15, 1882), p. 143; *CBB* (January 15, 1882), p. 14; *CBB* (December 1, 1882), p. 182.

15. A. G. Claassen, "Russian Mennonites," p. 10; *CBB* (March 15, 1882), p. 45.

16. Bartsch, *Unser Auszug*, pp. 60-69; Art Toews, "A Translation," p. 7; *CBB* (July 15, 1882), p. 111; Carl R. Jantzen, "Story of My Ancestors," pp. 10-12.

Chapter 12

1. *MR* (February 1, 1882), p. 1.

2. *CBB* (January 15, 1882), p. 14; Jacob Reimer, "Article," p. 7.

3. *MR* (September 15, 1882), p. 2.

4. *Ibid.*

5. *CBB* (July 1, 1882), p. 103.

6. *CBB* (July 15, 1882), p. 132.

7. BM; Bartsch, *Unser Auszug*, pp. 46-47, 81.

8. Jacob Reimer, "Article," p. 7; *MR* (weekly, July 4, 1883), p. 2.

9. *CBB* (December 1, 1882), p. 181; C. Krahn, "Aulie Ata," *ME*, I, p. 190; Krahn, "The Mennonites of Russia Today," *Mennonite Life*, XXIV, No. 3 (July, 1969), 117.

10. *History, Dates and Experiences Peter and Maria Abraham Horn Family*, p. 4; BM.

11. *MR* (September 15, 1882), p. 2; Schellenberg, "A Modern Day Moses," p. 6.

12. Allworth, *Central Asia*, p. 120; Schuyler, *Turkistan*, Vol. I, passim.

13. *DB* (November 19, 1947), p. 7; Johannes Bartsch, *Geschichte der Gemeinde*, pp. 140-141; Stumpp, *HB* (1959), 17-18; BM; Siebert Goertz, "Mother Goertz's Diary for 1933."

14. Pierce, *Russians in Central Asia*, p. 8.

15. *CBB* (December 1, 1882), p. 181.

16. *Ibid;* Goertz, *Family History*, p. 34.

17. *MR* (weekly, December 19, 1883), pp. 1-2. One district chief suggested that the Mennonites register young men 15 and older so they could say they constituted 136 families instead of a mere 80 in order to qualify for more land. See MR (September 15, 1882), p. 2.

18. Janzen, "Colony," p. 284.

19. *Ibid.*, *MR* (semimonthly, March 15, 1883), p. 4.

20. *GB* (February, 1883), pp. 12-13.

21. *MR* (November 15, 1882), p. 1; *MR* (March 15, 1884), p. 4, lists the dead as the wife of David Reimer, formerly of Wernersdorf, Abraham Wiebe, son of Peter Wiebe, the son of Abraham Peters named Abraham, two sons of Cornelius Jantzen, who arrived ill from the Trakt, and a single man named Gustav Riesen, who died at Hermann Epp's home.

22. *MR* (weekly, December 19. 1883), pp. 1-2.

23. Jacob Reimer, "Article," p. 7.

24. *Ibid.;* Siebert Goertz, "Mother Goertz's Diary"; Mrs. Siebert Goertz, "Translation of a Diary," p. 3.

25. *MR* (semimonthly, June 1, 1883), p. 2; *MR* (semimonthly, October 1, 1883), p. 1. Five of the families in Tashkent were formerly from Kuban.

26. *MR* (semimonthly, June 1, 1883), p. 2. Benjamin Wedel's daughter died of smallpox.

27. *MR* (semimonthly, February 15, 1883), p. 3; *MR* (weekly, March 21, 1883), p.1.

28. Janzen, "Colony," pp. 285-286; *MR* (semimonthly, November 15, 1883), p. 2.

29. *MR* (semimonthly, October 1, 1883), p. 1. Of this 620 rubles ($310.00), a Mr. Schmidt was given 41 rubles and 25 kopecks, and Cornelius Eckert received 57 rubles and 75 kopecks. Cornelius Esau got 206 rubles from an Elder Gaeddert in Kansas, and 488 undesignated rubles came from Heinrich H. Richert of the Alexanderwohl Church of Newton, Kansas. In all, 2,086 rubles were donated to the group during the winter of 1882-83.

30. *Ibid.*

31. *Ibid.*

32. *MR* (weekly, October 31, 1883), p. 1.

33. *Friesen, Brüderschaft*, p. 482; Krahn, "Nikolaipol," *ME*, III, p. 882.

34. Krahn, "Romanovka Mennonite Church," *ME*, IV, p. 354.

35. Christian Neff, "Allianz Gemeinden," *ME*, I, p. 62; Neff, "Allianz Gemeinden," *ML*, I, p. 35; Friesen, *Brüderschaft*, p. 722.

36. Goertz, *Family History*, p. 31; Siebert Goertz, "Mother Goertz's Diary." Of those baptized that day, the daughter of Peter Dalke, Helena, married Siebert Goertz soon after the baptism and they both became staunch members of the Mennonite Brethren Church until their deaths years later in Kansas. One son of this union, Peter Siebert Goertz, born in 1886 in Aulie Ata, was one of the first in the family to join with the General Conference Mennonite Church when he became dean at Bethel Col-

lege, North Newton, Kansas, well over a quarter of a century later.

37. *MR* (semimonthly, March 15, 1883), p. 4.

38. Pierce, *Russians in Central Asia*, p. 10.

39. Klaassen, "Asienreise," pp. 22-24; *MR* (weekly, December 5, 1883), pp. 1-2; *MR* (weekly, July 4, 1883), p. 1.

40. *CBB* (September 15, 1885), pp. 141-142. In a letter in July 1883, to the newspaper *Der Christliche Bundesbote*, after expressing a heartfelt love for the natives, Bartsch showed a still lingering interest in millennial theories. Only in later years, as a teacher in Lysanderhöh, Trakt, would he mount a concerted attack on Claas Epp and radical millennialism.

41. *MR* (weekly, March 21, 1883), p. 2.

42. *MR* (semimonthly, February 15, 1883), p. 3. Apparently numbers were issued to the draftees, and only those with lower numbers were inducted.

43. *GB* (May, 1884), p. 39.

44. Janzen, "Colony," pp. 285-287.

45. *Ibid.*, *MR* (semimonthly, June 1, 1883), p. 2; Ruth Graber MS; *Polnoe Sobranie Zakronov Rossijskoj Imperii*.

46. Janzen, "Colony," p. 289.

Chapter 13

1. Arlin G. Claassen, "A Study of the Mennonites of Russia," p. 11.

2. *CBB* (December 1, 1882), p. 182; Cornelius Krahn and Cornelius Bergmann, "Khiva," *ME*, III, p. 173; Anna Toews, "Diary"; *GB* (February 1, 1883), pp. 12-13.

3. *GB* (November, 1882), pp. 83-84.

4. *CBB* (December 1, 1882), p. 182.

5. *Ibid.*

6. *Ibid.*; *CBB* (April 1, 1883), p. 2; BM.

7. *CBB* (April 1, 1883), p. 2; *GB* (February, 1883), p. 13.

8. Schultz, "Autobiography," pp. 38-41.

9. Jantzen, "Memories," pp. 14-16; Claassen, "A Study," p. 11: *BM*. Jantzen sets the numbers at 48 wagons, 81 horses, and 153 people. Hermann Bartsch says 63 wagons, 10 arbas, and 137 camels. Toews' records tell of 60 families.

10. Claassen, "A Study," p. 11; *CBB* (April 1, 1883), p. 54; Carl Jantzen, "My Ancestors," p. 12; Art Toews, "A Translation," p. 8.

6. *Ibid.; CBB* (April 1, 1883), p. 2; BM.

7. *CBB* (April 1, 1883), p. 2; *GB* (February, 1883), p. 13.

8. Schultz, "Autobiography," pp. 38-41.

9. Jantzen, "Memories," pp. 14-16; Claassen, "A Study," p. 11: *BM*. Jantzen sets the numbers at 48 wagons, 81 horses, and 153 people. Hermann Bartsch says 63 wagons, 10 arbas, and 137 camels. Toews' records tell of 60 families.

10. Claassen, "A Study," p. 11; *CBB* (April 1, 1883), p. 54; Carl Jantzen, "My Ancestors," p. 12; Art Toews, "A Translation," p. 8.

11. *CBB* (April 1, 1883), p. 54.

12. Klaassen, "Memories of a Journey," pp. 27-28.

13. Toews, "A Translation," p. 8; BM; *CBB* (April 1, 1883), p. 54; Carl Jantzen, "My Ancestors," p. 12; Klaassen, "Memories of a Journey," p. 15; Claassen, "A Study," p. 12; *GB* (February, 1883), p. 13.

14. BM; *CBB* (June 15, 1883), p. 3; Jantzen, "Memories," 16; Claassen, "A Study," p. 12; Toews, "A Translation," p. 9; *GB* (February, 1883), p. 13. The Great Comet of 1882 was perhaps the finest of the century. It was first sighted on September 3 from New Zealand and it shone brightly over Central Asia on September 16 and 17, just before transiting the sun and breaking into four smaller comets.

15. Klaassen, "Memories of a Journey," pp. 30-33; Jantzen, "My Ancestors," pp. 13-14; *GB* (February, 1883), p. 13; Toews, "Translation," p. 9; Jantzen, "Memories," pp. 16-20; Dick, "The Story," p. 6; *CBB* (April 1, 1883), p. 54.

16. *CBB* (June 15, 1883), p. 3; BM; Toews, "A Translation," pp. 9-10; *CBB* (April 1,1883), p. 54; Krahn, Interview with Cornelius Jantzen, April 22, 1945; *Der Bote* (November 19, 1947), p. 7; Jantzen "Memories," pp. 16-20; Klaassen, "Memories of a Journey," p. 29; Sharon Wiebe, "Russian Mennonite Migration, p. 6.

17. Carl Jantzen, "My Ancestors," pp. 13-14; BM; Dick, "Dirks Family," p. 6; *GB* (February 18, 1883), p. 13; Claassen, "A Study," pp. 12-13.

18. Schultz, "Autobiography," p. 30.

19. Sharon Wiebe, "Russian Mennonite Migration," p. 6; Claassen, "A Study," p. 13; Carl Jantzen, "My Ancestors," p. 14.

20. Carl Jantzen, "My Ancestors," p. 14; *CBB* (December 15, 1883), pp. 189-190.

21. *GB* (April, 1883), p. 31; *GB* (June, 1884), p. 44; Toews, "Translation," p. 10; Claassen, "A Study," p. 10; Jantzen, "Memories," pp. 22-23; Klaassen, "Asienreise," pp. 42-43.

22. Reimer, "Jantzen Family Tree," p. 3.

23. *GB* (July, 1883), p. 51; Carl Jantzen, "My Ancestors," p. 15; *CBB* (June, 1883), pp. 93-94; *GB* (November, 1883), p. 86.

2. Coates, *Soviets in Central Asia,* p. 51; Skrine and Ross, *The Heart of Asia,* p. 262; Curzon, *Russia in Central Asia,* pp. 72-73, 118-120. A proverb attributed to the Turkomen goes as follows: "He who puts his hand to his sword hilt has not need to ask for good reason."

3. Carl Jantzen, "My Ancestors," p. 15; *GB* (June, 1884), p. 44; "Asien" (MS in MHLA; n.p., n.d.,); Arlin Claassen, "A Study of the Mennonites in Russia," p. 13; *GB* (November, 1883), p. 86; *GB* (April, 1884), p. 27; Jacob Jantzen, "Memories," pp. 24-25; *CBB* (December 15, 1883), pp. 189-190.

4. "Asien"; *GB* (May, 1884), pp. 39, 44-45; *GB* (April, 1884), p. 28; Schultz, "Autobiography," pp. 57-58.

5. "Asien"; Claassen, "A Study," p. 13; *MR* (October 31, 1883), p. 1; *GB* (May, 1884), p. 39; *GB* (April, 1884), p. 28; Sharon Wiebe, "Russian Mennonite Migration," p. 7; *CBB* (December 15, 1883), p. 189.

6. *GB* (May, 1884), pp. 44-45; *MR* (weekly, October 31, 1883), p. 1; *GB* (November, 1883), p. 86; Schultz, "Autobiography," pp. 58-59; *CBB* (December 15, 1883), pp. 189-190.

7. *GB* (May, 1884), pp. 44-45; *GB* (November, 1883), p. 86; *GB* (April, 1884), p. 28; *GB* (July, 1884), p. 54; Schultz, "Autobiography," p. 58; "Rubles" (unpublished MS fragment in MHLA, n.p., n.d.).

8. Klaassen, "Asienreise," p. 44; Jantzen, "My Ancestors," p. 15; Schultz, "Autobiography," p. 60; Jantzen, "Memories," p. 26.

9. "Asien"; *GB* (May, 1884), p. 39; *CBB* (December 15, 1883), p. 190; *GB* (November, 1883), p. 86.

10. *GB* (April, 1884), p. 28.

11. Jantzen, "Memories," p. 26; *Mennonitische Blätter* (1884), pp. 64, 69; Smith, *Schartner Family History,* p. 96; Art Toews; "Translation," p. 11; Alexander Rempel, "Die Geschichte von Ak Metchet," *Der Bote* (November 5, 1947); *GB* (A 63; Cornelius Krahn, "Ak Metchet," *ME,* I, pp. 29-30.

12. *GB* (July, 1884), p. 54; *GB* (September, 1884), pp. 70-71; Schultz, "Autobiography," pp. 60-61.

13. Smith, *Schartner Family History,* p. 96; Stumpp, *HB* (1964), p. 15; Toews, "Translation," pp. 11-12; Kornelson, "Ak Metchet," *DB* (April 7, 1964), p. 10; Krahn, "Ak Metchet," *ME* I, p. 30.

14. "Letter from Johann Jantzen" (Plymouth, Jefferson Co., Nebraska, n.d., in MHLA); Schultz, "Autobiography," p. 61; Smith, *Schartner Family Records,* pp. 35-36; Ruth Graber MS; *DB* (November 19, 1947).

15. Bartsch, *Unser Auszug,* pp. 96-97.

16. *Ibid.,* pp. 98-99.

17. "Letter dated April 12, 1888, from Ak Metchet to the brothers and sisters"

"Translation," pp. 11-12; Kornelson, "Ak Metchet," *DB* (April 7, 1964), p. 10; Krahn, "Ak Metchet," *ME* I, p. 30.

14. "Letter from Johann Jantzen" (Plymouth, Jefferson Co., Nebraska, n.d., in MHLA); Schultz, "Autobiography," p. 61; Smith, *Schartner Family Records*, pp. 35-36; Ruth Graber MS; *DB* (November 19, 1947).

15. Bartsch, *Unser Auszug*, pp. 96-97.

16. *Ibid.*, pp. 98-99.

17. "Letter dated April 12, 1888, from Ak Metchet to the brothers and sisters" (in possession of Mr. and Mrs. Ernst Claassen, Whitewater, Kansas); "Letter dated April 18, 1888, from Ak Metchet from Jacob and Suzanna Jantzen" (in possession of Mr. and Mrs. Ernst Claassen).

18. Schultz, "Autobiography," p. 61; Ruth Graber MS.

19. "Undated letter from Central Asia" (in possession of Mr. and Mrs. Ernst Claassen, Whitewater, Kansas, n.p.).

20. *DB* (November 19, 1947), p. 7.

21. Stumpp, *HB* (1959), p. 18; Janzen, "Colony," p. 288; Stumpp, *HB* (1964), p. 15.

22. "Letter to Sister Wiebe from Ak Metchet, July 15, 1885, signed M.R." (in possession of Mr. and Mrs. Ernst Claassen).

23. Bartsch, *Unser Auszug*, p. 100.

24. *Ibid.*, pp. 100-101.

25. *Ibid.*

Chapter 15

1. For a fine discussion of the Russian imperial attitude toward Mennonite migration, see L. E. Strakhovsky, "Constitutional Aspects of the Imperial Russian Government Policy Toward National Minorities," *Journal of Modern History*, Vol. XIII, No. 4 (December, 1941), pp. 467-492. An excellent article on Western immigrants' incursion into Central Asia can be found in Stephen P. Dunn and Ethyl Dunn, "Soviet Regime and Native Culture in Central Asia and Kazakhstan: the Major Peoples," *Current Anthropology*, Vol. VII, No. 3 (June, 1967), pp 147-208.

2. "Beatrice" (two-page extract of a letter written by John Jantzen on June 19, 1884, now in MHLA, n.p.); "Letters" (eight-page MS in MHLA, n.p., n.d.); "Asien" (nine-page MS in MHLA, n.p., n.d.).

3. *CBB* (January 15, 1883), p. 13; *MR* (weekly, December 26, 1883), p. 3; *GB* (May, 1884), p. 39.

4. "Minutes of the Meeting for the Support of Needy Immigrants from Asia" (document in MHLA, n.p., n.d.).

9. "Rubles" (MS in MHLA, n.p., n.d.).

10. *GB* (September, 1884), pp. 70-71; Klaassen, "Memories of a Journey," p. 33, says there were 10 double teams and four single wagons; "Rubles"; BM says 24 families left; "Extracts from Letters Received at Beatrice, Nebraska" (MS in MHLA, n.p., n.d.).

11. Jantzen, "Memories," pp. 27-28; Klaassen, "Memories," p. 47.

12. *GB* (July, 1884), p. 54; BM.

13. Jantzen, "Memories," pp. 26-27; Klaassen, "Memories," pp. 33-35.

14. *Ibid.*

15. BM.

16. *Ibid.;* Jantzen, "Memories," p. 29; Klaassen, "Memories," pp. 35-36; Interview with John H. Wiebe by writer on May 7, 1972, in Whitewater, Kansas.

17. C. J. Jantzen, "My Ancestors," p. 17. Johann Jantzen, Jr., fell beneath the wagon, and Heinrich, son of Tobias Dirks, died as an infant.

18. BM.

19. *Ibid.*

20. Jantzen, "Memories," p. 30.

21. "Extracts from Letters at Beatrice, Nebraska."

22. *Ibid.*

23. "Petition Draft to Secretary of State of the United States" (document in MHLA, n.p., n.d.). There was fear for the brethren because it was known that there were such strong russophile attitudes that all foreigners were held in suspicion. For example, by 1888, there were only about 150 foreigners in Bukhara. Curzon, *Russia in Central Asia*, pp. 22-24, 33, 171.

24. *Herold der Wahrheit* (October 15, 1885); Lorene Dick, "Dirks Family" pp. 7-8; Klaassen, "Memories," pp. 38-39.

25. Duerksen and Schmidt, "Summaries of Passenger Lists of Mennonite Immigrants, 1873-1900" (MS in MHLA, n.p., April 5, 1967).

26. *Ibid.;* there were 6 Albrechts, 7 Dirkses, 6 Fasts, 5 Graeves, 14 Jantzens, 3 Klaassens, 5 Martenses, 7 Penners, 13 Unruhs, 7 Wegelis, and 5 Wiebes.

27. *CBB* (October 1, 1884), pp. 149-150; Cornelius Krahn, "J. K. Penner," *ME*, IV, p. 135; W. C. Andreas, "Highlights and Sidelights of Mennonites in Beatrice," *Mennonite Life*, I, No. 2 (July, 1964), p. 23; *Anniversary Booklet 1876-1951*, First Mennonite Church, Beatrice, Nebraska.

28. J. K. Penner, one of the most famous early arrivals, later called affectionately

"Onkel Lehrer" by students in a German school in Beatrice, reportedly requested that his diary of the Central Asia episode in his life be buried with him at his death. Several reports of this were given to this writer by descendants and friends of this great man. In the writer's possession is a letter from Mr. and Mrs. Ernst Claassen of Whitewater, Kansas, May 7, 1972, that verified these claims about the diary.

29. Klaassen, "Memories and Notations," pp. 39-40; Duerksen and Schmidt, "Passenger Lists," p. 35; *CBB* (October 1, 1884), p. 150; Shellenberg, "A Modern Day Moses," p. 6; John G. Rempel, "David Toews," *ME*, IV, p. 735; Lorene Dick, "Story of the Dirks Family," pp. 7-8.

30. Anna Toews, "Diary"; Interview with John H. Wiebe by writer on May 7, 1972.

31. *CBB* (March 15, 1885), p. 3.

32. *Ibid.; GB* (November, 1884), p. 87; Passenger lists; "Monies Sent to Johann Bergmann" (document in MHLA, n.p., n.d.); "Statement Concerning the Twelve Families in Aulie Ata" (document in MHLA, n.p., n.d.); "Committee Sessions on August 7, 1884" (document in MHLA, n.p., n.d.); *CBB* (October 1, 1884), p. 150; *CBB* (October 1, 1885), p. 5.

33. *Herold der Wahreit* (October 15, 1885). When the fifteen Aulie Ata families arrived on September 5, 1885, a Baptist missionary to New York, a Reverend Shriek wrote to the *Christlicher Bundesbote* about them. He told of meeting them at Castlegarden and giving the "dear children" small New Testaments and Baptist tracts. The mothers, he said, had small babies on their knees and though pale, one could tell their determination for freedom. After encouraging them, Shriek bade them Godspeed.

34. "Meeting of the American Mennonite Aid Committee, June 5, 1886 (document in MHLA, n.p.).

35. Arn, *The Herald Church*, passim; Smith, *Schartner Family History*, pp. 96-97; Also see Appendix about charter members of the Herald Church; Fred R. Belk, "The Final Refuge: Kansas and Nebraska Migration of Mennonites from Central Asia after 1884," *The Kansas Historical Quarterly*, Vol. XL, No. 3 (Autumn, 1974), p. 392.

36. Siebert Goertz, "Mother Goertz's Diary for 1933"; Goertz, *Family History*, p. 55.

37. By 1913, the year Claas Epp died, the number of Russian and non-Asian settlers in Turkestan numbered over two million or one fifth of the population. See *Lenin's Ideas*, pp. 14-15, and Wheeler, *Racial Problems*, p. 6. An honest appraisal of the colonization to Turkestan by Mennonites and other non-Asians, much like the colonization of America which drove the Indians back, shows the nomadic tribes were pushed farther into the desert. In fact, this process began the decline of the Kirghiz and by 1913 their population was down some 10 percent. The best available figures of this negative aspect of colonization in Turkestan can be seen in *Bolshaia Sovetskaia Entsiklopedia*, Vol. XXXII (Moscow, 1936), p. 377. Other scholars point out the large numbers of Germans that colonized Central Asia after the initial Mennonite influx. Max Baum, *Jahrbuch der Deutsch-Amerikanischen Historischen Gesellschaft von Illinois*, Vol. XXXI (Chicago: University of Chicago Press, 1931), pp. 5, 7; "The Size of the German Population in Kazakhstan and Central Asia," *Central Asian Review*, Vol. X (1959), pp. 372-373; Stumpp, *HB* (1964), p. 21. Dr. Stumpp in his more recent look at Germans in Central Asia placed the number at 120,000 with 450 villages. Baum and *Central Asian Review*

population was down some 10 percent. The best available figures of this negative aspect of colonization in Turkestan can be seen in *Bolshaia Sovetskaia Entsiklopedia,* Vol. XXXII (Moscow, 1936), p. 377. Other scholars point out the large numbers of Germans that colonized Central Asia after the initial Mennonite influx. Max Baum, *Jahrbuch der Deutsch-Amerikanischen Historischen Gesellschaft von Illinois,* Vol. XXXI (Chicago: University of Chicago Press, 1931), pp. 5, 7; "The Size of the German Population in Kazakhstan and Central Asia," *Central Asian Review,* Vol. X (1959), pp. 372-373; Stumpp, *HB* (1964), p. 21. Dr. Stumpp in his more recent look at Germans in Central Asia placed the number at 120,000 with 450 villages. Baum and *Central Asian Review* put the figure over 750,000. This apparent problem can be resolved, perhaps, by knowing that these scholars consider the states of Central Asia to have different boundaries.

Chapter 16

1. Bartsch, *Unser Auszug,* pp. 100-103; Schultz, "Autobiography," p. 61.

2. Stumpp, *HB* (1964), p. 15.

3. *DB* (November 26, 1947), p. 7.

4. Janzen, "Colony," p. 289.

5. *DB* (November 26, 1947), p. 7; Cornelius Krahn, "Faith of Our Fathers," *Mennonite Weekly Review* (June 3, 1948), p. 7.

6. *DB* (December 3, 1947), pp. 7-8.

7. *Ibid.*

8. *DB* (December 10, 1947), p. 7.

9. *Ibid.*

10. Krahn, "Faith of Our Fathers," p. 7; Alexander Rempel is the author of a series of articles appearing in *Der Bote* during 1947, "Auszüge aus der 'Geschichte von Ak-Metschet.'"

11. Interview with Cornelius Krahn by Fred Belk, January 16, 1973. The American Mennonite historian, Dr. Cornelius Krahn, has enjoyed a great deal of contact through relatives and tours he has conducted in the USSR. Krahn tells of worshiping in a Russian Baptist Church in Alma Ata in 1972 with Mennonites who have applied for a license for a church, suggesting that the restrictions on Mennonite worship are being relaxed.

APPENDIX A

Summary of Families Participating in the Greak Trek

I. First wagon train from Hahnsau to Kaplan Bek, July 3, 1880, to October 18, 1880.

Ten families participated, of which the following have been identified:

1. Bartsch, Franz
2. Froese, Franz
3. Froese, Franz J.
4. Horn, Peter
5. Penner, Wilhelm
6. Quiring, Jonas
7. Schmidt, Heinrich
8. Wiebe, Heinrich

II. Second wagon train from Medemtal to Kaplan Bek, August 13, 1880, to November 24, 1889.

Thirteen familites participated, of which the following have been identified:

1. Bartsch, Hermann
2. Jantzen, Hermann
3. Jantzen, Heinrich
4. Jantzen, Johannes
5. Klaassen, Johannes
6. Klaassen, Martin
7. Penner, J. K.
8. Penner, Cornelius W.
9. Peters, Dietrich
10. Quiring, Cornelius
11. Toews, Jacob
12. Wall, Cornelius

III. Third wagon train from Waldeheim, Molotschna, to Tashkent, August 1, 1880, to December 2, 1880.

Eighty families participated, of which the following have been identified:

1. Baergen, Johann
2. Braunen
3. Dirks
4. Duecken, Leonard
5. Esau, Cornelius
6. Esau, Gerhard
7. Goertz, Siebert
8. Graeve, Heinrich G.
9. Jantzen, Jacob
10. Janzen, Jacob
11. Koop, Isaac
12. Kroeker, Abraham
13. Pauls
14. Peters, Abraham
15. Unruh, Cornelius
16. Wedel, Cornelius
17. Wedel, Johann
18. Wedel, Tobias
19. Wiebe, Peter
20. Wiens, Dietrich
21. Wiens, Peter

IV. Fourth wagon train from the Trakt to Tashkent, August 1881 to October 1881.

Nine families participated, of which the following have been identified:

1. Funk, Jacob

V. Fifth wagon train from the Trakt to Serabulak, September 1, 1881, to June 1882.

Forty-seven families participated, of which the following have been identified:

1. Abrahms	5. Jantzen, Johann
2. Bartsch, Johann	6. Neumann
3. Drake, Johann	7. Riesen, Emil M.
4. Epp, Claas	8. Sterkel, Jacob

VI. Families settling at Aulie Ata that have been identified:

1. Abrahms	26. Koop, Isaak
2. Baergen, Johann	27. Kornelsen
3. Bartsch, Franz	28. Kroeker, Franz
4. Bartsch, Johann	29. Kroeker, Jacob
5. Dalke, Peter	30. Mandtler, Jacob
6. Eck, Peter	31. Neufeld, Johann
7. Eckert, Cornelius	32. Nickel, Gerhard
8. Epp, Heinrich	33. Nickel, Heinrich
9. Epp, Hermann	34. Pauls, Peter
10. Esau, Cornelius	35. Penner, Cornelius
11. Fieguth, Johannes	36. Peters, Heinrich
12. Funk, Cornelius	37. Peters, M.
13. Funk, Heinrich	38. Reimer, Cornelius
14. Funk, Jacob	39. Reimer, David
15. Goertz, Abraham	40. Reimer, Jacob
16. Goertz, Siebert	41. Reuffels, George
17. Harms	42. Riesen, Gustav
18. Hinz, Heinrich	43. Schmidt, David
19. Horn	44. Schultz, David
20. Horn, Peter	45. Toews, Peter
21. Horn, Peter F.	46. Wall, Cornelius
22. Jantzen, Cornelius	47. Wedel, Benhamine
23. Janzen, Heinrich	48. Wiebe, Bernard
24. Janzen, Jacob	49. Wiebe, Peter
25. Koop, Gerhard	50. Wiens

VII. Families settling at Lausan that have been identified:

1. Abrahms, Heinrich
2. Albrecht, Heinrich
3. Bartsch, Hermann
4. Becker, Jacob P.
5. Becker, Johann
6. Bier, Philipp
7. Dirks, Benjamin
8. Drake, Johann
9. Dyck, Peter
10. Ensz
11. Epp, Claas, Jr.
12. Epp, Claas, III
13. Esau
14. Fast, Gerhard
15. Fieguth, Johannes
16. Froese, Franz
17. Froese, Franz J.
18. Froese, Heinrich
19. Froese, Jacob
20. Graeves
21. Hamm
22. Jantzen, Abraham
23. Jantzen, Heinrich
24. Jantzen, Jacob
25. Jantzen, Johann
26. Janzen, B.
27. Klaassen, Jacob
28. Klaassen, Johannes A.
29. Klaassen, Michael
30. Klaassen, Mrs. Martin
31. Kopper
32. Martens, Johann
33. Pauls
34. Penner, J. K.
35. Penner, Wilhelm
36. Quiring, Cornelius
37. Quiring, Jonas
38. Quiring, Peter A.
39. Rauch, Martin
40. Riesen, Emil M.
41. Schmidt
42. Starkel, Jacob
43. Toews, Heinrich
44. Toews, Jacob
45. Unruh, Cornelius
46. Unruh, Peter
47. Wegeli, Heinrich
48. Wiebe, Cornelius

VIII. Families settling at Ak Metchet that have been identified:

1. Becker, Jacob P.
2. Becker, Johann
3. Dyck, P.
4. Epp, Claas, Jr.
5. Epp, Claas, III
6. Froese, Franz
7. Froese, Franz J.
8. Froese, Heinrich
9. Froese, Jacob
10. Hamm
11. Jantzen, Jacob
12. Kopper
13. Klaassen, Michael
14. Pauls
15. Penner, Wilhelm
16. Quiring, Peter A.
17. Quiring, Jonas
18. Rauch, Martin
19. Riesen, Emil M.
20. Schmidt

IX. Families migrating to the United States from Central Asia after 1884 that have been identified:

1. Abrahms, Mrs. H.
2. Albrecht, Heinrich
3. Bartsch, Hermann
4. Bier, Philipp
5. Dirks, Abraham
6. Dirks, Benjamin

7. Dirks, Frederick
8. Dirks, Tobias
9. Ensz
10. Esau
11. Fast, Gerhard
12. Fieguth, Johannes
13. Graeves
14. Jantzen, Abraham
15. Jantzen, Heinrich
16. Jantzen, Johannes
17. Klaassen, Jacob
18. Klaassen, Johannes A.
19. Klaassen, Mrs. Martin
20. Martens, Johann
21. Pauls
22. Penner, J. K.
23. Starkel, Jacob
24. Toews, Heinrich
25. Toews, Jacob
26. Unruh, Cornelius
27. Unruh, Peter
28. Wegeli, Heinrich
29. Wiebe, Berhnard
30. Wiebe, Cornelius

From Ak Metchet:
1. Becker, Jacob
2. Becker, Johann
3. Epp, Claas, III
4. Froese, Franz
5. Froese, Franz J.
6. Froese, Heinrich
7. Froese, Jacob
8. Jantzen, Jacob
9. Klaassen, Michael
10. Quiring, Jonas
11. Quiring, Peter A.
12. Schmidt

From Aulie Ata:
1. Abrahms
2. Baergen, Johann
3. Eck, Peter
4. Esau, Cornelius
5. Fieguth, Johannes
6. Funk, Cornelius
7. Funk, Heinrich
8. Funk, Jacob
9. Goertz, Siebert
10. Harms
11. Horn, Heinrich
12. Horn, Peter
13. Horn, Peter F.
14. Janzen, Heinrich
15. Koop, Gerhard
16. Koop, Isaak
17. Kornelsen
18. Kroeker, Franz
19. Neufeld, Johann
20. Nickel, Gerhard
21. Nickel, Heinrich
22. Penner, Cornelius
23. Peters, Heinrich
24. Peters, M.
25. Reimer, Cornelius
26. Reuffels, George
27. Schmidt, David
28. Schultz, David
29. Toews, Peter
30. Wedel, Benjamin
31. Wiens, D.

APPENDIX B

Turkestan Mennonites As Charter Members of Herald Mennonite Church in Oklahoma

Name	Birthplace	Date from Turkestan	To United States	To Washita Co. Oklahoma
Male Members				
1. Franz Froese	Markushof, W. Prussia	1892 Ak Metchet	Newton, Kan.	1894
2. Franz J. Froese	Hohendorf, Trakt	1892 Ak Metchet	Newton, Kan.	1894
3. Heinrich Froese	Hohendorf, Trakt	1892 Ak Metchet	Newton, Kan.	1894
4. Jacob Froese	Hohendorf, Trakt	1892 Ak Metchet	Newton, Kan.	1894
5. Johannes Fieguth	West Prussia	1892 Aulie Ata	Newton, Kan.	1895
6. Peter Horn	Augustwalde, W. Prussia	1885 Aulie Ata	Newton, Kan.	1894
7. Peter F. Horn	Hahnsau, Trakt	1885 Aulie Ata	Newton, Kan.	1894
8. Heinrich Horn	Hahnsau, Trakt	1885 Aulie Ata	Newton, Kan.	1894
9. Jacob Jantzen	Hahnsau, Trakt	1885 Aulie Ata	Newton, Kan.	1895
10. Michael Klaassen	Köppental, Trakt	1884 Ak Metchet	Beatrice, Neb.	1894
11. Jacob Klaassen	Köppental, Trakt	1884 Ak Metchet	Beatrice, Neb.	1894
12. Johannes A. Klaassen	Köppental, Trakt	1884 Lausan	Beatrice, Neb.	1894
13. Gerhard Nickel	Hohendorf, Trakt	1885 Aulie Ata	Newton, Kan.	1894
14. Peter A. Quiring	Petershagen	1893 Ak Metchet	Beatrice, Neb.	1894
Female Members				
15. Mrs. Franz (Cornelia Schmid) Froese	Markushof, W. Prussia	1892 Ak Metchet	Newton, Kan.	1894
16. Miss Maria Froese	Hohendorf, Trakt	1892 Ak Metchet	Newton, Kan.	1894
17. Mrs. Johannes (Louise Toews) Fieguth	Orloff, Trakt	1884 Lausan	Newton, Kan.	1895

No.	Name	Origin	Emigration	Destination	Year
18.	Mrs. Peter J. (Justina Klaassen) Gaeddert	Köppental, Trakt	1884 Lausan	Beatrice, Neb.	1895
19.	Mrs. Peter (Maria Abrahms) Horn	Schulwiese, W. Prussia	1885 Aulie Ata	Newton, Kan.	1894
20.	Mrs. Heinrich (Anna Horn) Hinz	Hahnsau, Trakt	1885 Aulie Ata	Newton, Kan.	1894
21.	Miss Elizabeth Horn	Hahnsau, Trakt	1885 Aulie Ata	Newton, Kan.	1894
22.	Mrs. Jacob (Helena Klaassen) Jantzen	Hahnsau, Trakt	1884 Lausan	Beatrice, Neb.	1895
23.	Mrs. Michael (Margarethe Jantzen) Klaassen	Hahnsau, Trakt	1885 Ak Metchet	Beatrice, Neb.	1894
24.	Mrs. Jacob (Katharina Toews) Klaassen	Lysanderhöh, Trakt	1884 Lausan	Newton, Kan.	1895
25.	Mrs. Aron (Helena Esau) Klaassen	Broeskerfelde, W. Prussia	1895 Lausan	Beatrice, Neb.	1895
26.	Mrs. Martin (Maria Hamm) Klaassen	Orloff, Trakt	1884 Lausan	Beatrice, Neb.	1894
27.	Mrs. Cornelius (Elizabeth Nickel) Krause	Hohendorf, Trakt	1885 Aulie Ata	Newton, Kan.	1894
28.	Mrs. David H. (Catarina Froese) McMichel	Hohendorf, Trakt	1892 Ak Metchet	Newton, Kan.	1894
29.	Mrs. Heinrich (Helena Harms) Nickel	Torichthof, W. Prussia	1885 Aulie Ata	Newton, Kan.	1894
30.	Mrs. Peter A. (Renate Jantzen) Quiring	Hahnsau, Trakt	1893 Ak Metchet	Beatrice, Neb.	1894
31.	Mrs. Abraham (Maria Horn) Rieger	Hahnsau, Trakt	1885 Aulie Ata	Newton, Kan.	1895

Sources: Arn, *The Herald Mennonite Church*, Duerksen and Schmidt, *Passenger Lists*

SELECTED BIBLIOGRAPHY

I. Primary Source Material

A. Government Documents

Polnoe sobranie zakonov rossii, koi imperii. Sobranie vtoroe, 55 vols.; Sobranie tretie, 33 vols. St. Petersburg: Government Printing, 1825-1916.

B. Newspapers and Journals

Bernays, C. L. "Unter den Mennoniten in Kansas," *Der deutsche Pionär,* Vol. X, No. 3 (June, 1878), 147-150.

Bigelow, P. "Cossack as Cowboy, Soldier, and Citizen," *Harper's Magazine,* Vol. LXXXIX (November 1894), 921-936.

Borodine, N. "Ural Cossacks and Their Fisheries," *Popular Science,* Vol. XXXXIII (October, 1893), 767-769.

Christlicher Bundesbote. Berne, Indiana, 1879-85, 1937, 1943, 1946, 1947.

"A Document on the Mennonite Colony in Turkestan," MQR, Vol. IV, No. 4 (October, 1930), 303-305.

Der Bote, Vols. 24-25, Rosthern, Saskatchewan, 1946-47.

Der Mennonitische Friedensbote. 2 vols. Milford Square, Pennsylvania: Mennonite Press, 1880-81.

Mennonitische Rundschau. Vols. 3-4, Elkhart, Indiana, 1882-1883.

"Emigration of the Russian Mennonites," *Herald of Truth,* Vol. X (September, 1873).

Gemeindeblatt. Vols. 10-15, Sinsheim, Germany, 1879-1884.

Händiges, Emil. "Historisches Memorandum zur Wehrlosigkeit der Mennoniten," *Der Bote* (January 17, 1941), 5.

Hubbard, J. M. "Russia as a Civilizing Force in Asia," *Atlantic Monthly,* Vol. LXXV (February, 1895), 197-205.

Jansen, Cornelius. "The Mennonites," *Mt. Pleasant (Iowa) Free Press* (January 20, 1876).

Janzen, Johannes. "The Mennonite Colony in Turkestan," *MQR,* Vol. IV, No. 4 (October, 1930), 281-289.

Kauenhoven, Kurt. "Aus dem Leben westpreussischer Mennoniten in den Ansiedlungen Am Trakt im Wolgagebiet," *Mitteilungen des Sippenverbandes Danziger Mennoniten Familien,* Vol. VIII (1942), 87.

Klaassen, Jacob. "Asienreise," *Der Bote,* Vol. XVIII (1941).

Kornelsen, P. O. "Ak Metchet," *DB,* No. 15 (April 7, 1964), 10-12.

Krehbiel, Christian. "An Earnest Call: Immediate Help Needed," *Herald of Truth,* XI (February, 1874).

Lansdell, H. "Issik Kul and the Khirghese," *Living Age,* Vol. CLXXXXIII (June 11, 1892), 689-695.

Reimer, Jacob. "Article," *Hillsboro Vorwärts,* Vol. XXXVI, No. 52 (December 30, 1938), 3.

"Some Account of the Colonies of Mennonites in South Russia, Extracted from a MS of Travels in That Country, in the Year 1819," *The Friend,* Vol. III, No. 24 (March 27, 1830), 189-190, 194-196.

Wiens, Peter. "Letter from Russia," *Herald of Truth,* Vol. XI (June, 1874), 105.

Zur Heimat. Vols. 6-7, Halstead, Kansas, 1880-1881.

C. Published Primary Accounts

Bartsch, Franz. *Unser Auszug nach Mittelasien* (Vol. 5 of Historische Schriftenreihe des Echo-Verlags), North Kildonan, Manitoba, 1948.

Bartsch, Johannes, ed. *Geschichte der Gemeinde.* Elkhart: Mennonite Press, 1898.

Bonvalot, G. *En Asie Centrale: De Moscow en Bactriane.* Paris: Privately Published, 1885.

Bundesbote-Kalender. 62 vols. Berne, Indiana: Mennonite Book Concern, 1886-1947.

Burnaby, Frederick Gustavus. *A Ride to Khiva: Travels and Adventures in Central Asia.* London: Brandywine Books, 1885.

Cherkassi, Prince A. B. *A Narrative of the Russian Military Expedition to Khiva in 1717.* Translated from Russian by R. Mitchell. Moscow: Privately Published, 1873.

Christlicher Familien Kalender. Halstead, Kansas: Mennonite Press, 1884-85. 2 vols.

Dobson, George. *Russia's Railway Advance into Central Asia: Notes of a Journey from St. Petersburg to Samarkand.* London: Privately Published.

Friesen, P. M. *Die Alt Evangelische Mennonitische Bräderschaft in Russland.* Halbstadt; Taurien, 1911.

Goertz, Helene. *Family History of Siebert Goertz and John Harms.* Newton: Privately Published, 1965.

Graham, Stephen. *Through Russian Central Asia.* New York: Privately Published, 1916.

Haxthausen, Franz. *Studien über die innern Zustände, das Volksleben und insbesondere die ländlichen Einrichtungen Russland.* London: Privately Published, 1847-1852, 2 Vols.

Jansen, Peter. *Memoirs of Peter Jansen.* Beatrice, Nebraska: Privately Published, 1921.

Khanikoff, N. de. *Bokhara: Its Amir and Its People.* Translated from the Russian by the Baron C. A. de Bode. London: Privately Published, 1845.

Krist, Gustav. *Alone Through the Forbidden Land.* London: Faber and Faber Lts., n.d.

MacGahan, Januarius A. *Campaigning on the Oxus and the Fall of Khiva.* New York: Privately Published, 1874.

Marvin, Charles. *The Eye-Witness Account of the Disastrous Russian Campaign Against the Akal Tekke Turcomans, Describing the March Across the Burning Desert, the Storming of Dengeel Tepe, and the Disastrous Retreat to the Caspian.* London: Privately Published, 1880.

—————. *The Russians at Merv and Herat and Their Power of Invading India.* London: Privately Published, n.d.

Moser, H. *A Travers d'Asie Centrale: Impressions de voyage.* Paris: n.p., 1886.

—————. *Durch Centralasien.* Wiesbaden: Brockhaus, 1888.

O'Donovan, E. *The Merv Oasis: Travels and Adventures East of the Caspian, During the Years 1879, 1880, 1881 including Five Months Residence Among the Tekkes of Merv.* London: Privately Published, 1882-1883, 2 vols.

Perovski, General. *Narrative of the Russian Military Expedition to Khiva in 1839.* Translated from the Russian by J. Mitchell. Calcutta: Privately Published, 1867.

Petzholdt, A. *Turkestan auf Grundlage einer im Jahre 1871 unternommenen Bereisung des Landes geschildert.* Leipzig: n.p., 1874.

Roskoschny, H. von. *Das Asiatische Russland.* Leipzig: Privately Published, 1884.

Schuyler, Eugene. *Turkestan: Notes of a Journey in Russian Turkestan, Bukhara, and Kuldja.* New York: Schribner, Armstrong and Co., 1876, 2 vols.

Schwartz, Franz Xaver von. *Turkestan: die Wieger der indogermanischen Völker nach fünfzehnjährigem Aufenthalt in Turkestan.* Freiburg: Privately Published, 1900.

Soviet Uzbekistan. Tashkent: Foreign Tourism Board, 1969.

Strumm, Hugo. *Der russische Feldzug nach Chiva.* Berlin: Privately Published, 1875.

—————. *Russia in Central Asia: Historical Sketch of Russia's Progress in the East up to 1873, and of the Incidents which Led to the Campaign Against Khiva, with a Description of the Military Districts of the Caucasus, Orenburg, and Turkestan.*

Translated by J. W. Ozanne and H. Sachs. London: Privately Published, 1885.
Ujfalvy, C. D. de. *Expedition scientifique francaise en Russie, en Siberre et dans le Turkestan.* Paris: University, 1878-1880, 6 vols.
Villeroi, B. de. *A Trip Through Central Asia.* Calcutta: Privately Published, 1878.
Wachs, Major Otta. *Die politische und militärische Bedeutung des Kaukasus.* Berlin: Privately Published, 1889.
Willfort, Fritz. *Turkestanisches Tagebuch: Sech Jahre in Russisch-Zentralasien.* Vienna: Privately Published, 1930.
Wood, Major Herbert. *The Shores of Lake Aral.* London: n.p., 1876.

D. Unpublished Diaries, Letters, and Documents

"Affidavit from the State of Oklahoma Affirmed by Abraham S. Goertz in 1940." MHLA, n.p., n.d.
"Affidavit from the State of Oregon Affirmed by Katherine Dalke Wiebe in 1940." MHLA, n.p., n.d.
"An Appeal to All to Aid the Needy Mennonites in Asia who Would Like to Migrate to America." MHLA, n.p., n.d.
"Anniversary Booklet: 1876-1951." First Mennonite Church, Beatrice, Nebraska, 1951.
"Asien." MHLA, n.p., n.d.
"Autobiographies." MHLA, n.p., n.d., Microfilm 50.
Balzer, Agatha Hiebert. "Diary." MHLA, n.p., n.d., Microfilm 36.
Bartsch, Hermann. "Kurze Übersicht der Reise ins Turkestanische Gebiet übergesiedelten Mennoniten." MHLA, n.p., n.d.
————. "Map." MHLA, n.p., n.d.
Claassen, Arlin G. "A Study of the Mennonites in Russia." Unpublished research paper, Bethel College, North Newton, Kansas, 1959.
Claassen, Menno and Sara. "The Claassen Family, 1665-1958." Unpublished family history, Beatrice, Nebraska, n.d.
"Committee Sessions on August 7, 1884." MHLA, n.p., 1884.
Cooper, Lydia Eck, "The Andreas Decker Family Record," MHLA, n.p., n.d.
————. "David Unruh Family Record." MHLA, n.p., n.d.
————. "The Zacharias Eck Family Record." MHLA, n.p., 1959.
"Diaries, Correspondence, Family Records, Autobiographies." MHLA, n.p., n.d., Microfilm 51.
Dick, Lorene. "The Story of the Dirks Family." Unpublished research paper, Bethel College, North Newton, Kansas, 1959.
Dick, Lorene. "Interview of John T. Dirks," MHLA, n.p., December 28, 1958.
"Distress in Asia." MHLA, n.p., n.d.
Duerksen, Jacob A. and John F. Schmidt. "Summaries of Passenger Lists of Mennonite Immigrants to America 1873-1900." MHLA, n.p., April 5, 1967.
"Extracts from Letters Received at Beatrice, Nebraska." MHLA, n.p., n.d.
"Epp Manuscript," MHLA, n.p., n.d.
"Father Goertz' Family Tree." MHLA, n.p., n.d.
Friesen, A. "Emigration in Mennonite History." Unpublished MA thesis, University of Manitoba, 1960. MHLA, Microfilm 160.
Froese, Leonard. "Das Pädagogische Kultursystem Mennonitische Siedlungengruppen in Russland." Unpublished Doctoral Dissertation, George August University, Göttingen, 1949.
"From *Herold der Wahrheit,* October 15, 1885." MHLA, n.p., n.d.
Gaeddert, Dietrich. "Diaries, 1871-97." MHLA, n.p., n.d., Microfilm 54 and 54a.
Graeves, Heinrich. "Chronicle," MHLA, n.p., n.d.
Gard, Zenora, Velda Duerksen, and Agnes Warkentin. "David Richert, 1806-1878." MHLA, n.p., June 26, 1954.

Goertz, P. S. "Notes on Uncle Abraham Goertz." MHLA, n.p., May 25, 1939.

————. "Biographical Sketch." MHLA, n.p., n.d.

————. "Personal Data." MHLA, n.p., n.d.

Goertz, Mrs. Siebert. "Translation of Parts of Mother Goertz's Diary, 1929-1930; page 12 and past the middle of the book." MHLA, n.p., n.d.

Goertz, Siebert. "Mother Goertz's Diary for 1933." MHLA, n.p., n.d.

Graber, Ruth. "Grandmother Unruh (nee Schmidt)." MS in possession of writer, Iowa City, Iowa, n.d.

Harder, M.S. "The Origin, Philosophy, and Development of Education Among the Mennonites." Unpublished Doctoral Dissertation, University of Southern California, 1949.

Hiebert, Agnetha. "Diary." MHLA, n.p., n.d., Microfilm 57.

Hiebert, Clarence. "The Holdeman People: A Study of the Church of God in Christ, Mennonite, 1858-1969." Unpublished Doctoral Dissertation, Case Western Reserve University, 1971.

"History, Dates, and Experiences of Peter and Marie Abrahms Horn, Their Ancestors and Descendants." MHLA, n.p., n.d.

"Jantzen Handwritten Record." MHLA, n.p., n.d., Microfilm 129.

Jantzen, Carl R "A Brief Sketch of My Ancestors." Unpublished research paper, Bethel College, North Newton, Kansas, 1952.

Jantzen, Hermann. "Ihr Sollt Meine Zeugen Sein." Unpublished MS in possession of John H. Wiebe, Whitewater, Kansas, n.p., n.d.

Jantzen, Jacob. "Den 10. Juli 1939," Unpublished MS, MHLA, n.p., 1939.

————. "Memories of Our Journey to Asia." Translated by Mrs. Margaret Horn, introduction by Harold H. Jantzen. Unpublished mimeographed MS, Cordell, Oklahoma, 1958.

Jantzen, Johann. "Extract." MHLA, n.p., July 26, 1884.

Janzen, Jacob H. "Wanderndes Volk." MHLA, n.p., 1945.

Janzen, John. "Beatrice," MHLA, n.p., 1884.

Klaassen, D. R. "The Revelation of Eschatology." Unpublished research paper, Bethel College, North Newton, Kansas, 1959.

Klaassen, Jacob. "Asienreise: Grandfather's Description of the Trip to Central Asia, 1880." Translated by Henry T. Klaassen. Unpublished mimeographed MS, Laird, Saskatchewan, 1964. The original MS in possession of John D. Klaassen, Laird, Saskatchewan.

————. "Memories and Notations About My Life." Translated by Walter Klaassen. Unpublished mimeographed account, n.p., 1966. In possession of Mrs. L. D. Williams, Dell City, Oklahoma.

————. "Memories of a Journey." MHLA, n.p., n.d.

Klaassen, Kathryn, Elizabeth Adrian, and H. E. Janzen. "The Peter Janzen Family, 1789-1948." MHLA, n.p., 1948.

Krahn, Cornelius. "Adventures in Conviction: Russia, Canada, Mexico." Bound clippings from *Mennonite Weekly Review*. MHLA, n.p., n.d.

Krahn, Cornelius. "Interview of Cornelius Jantzen." MHLA, n.p., April 22, 1945.

Krahn, Cornelius. "Interview of Jacob Wiebe." MHLA, Beatrice, Nebraska, April 23, 1943.

Kroeker, M. E. "The Mennonites of Oklahoma to 1907." Unpublished MA Thesis, University of Oklahoma, 1954.

Letter, Ak Metchet to the Brothers and Sisters, April 12, 1888. In possession of Mr. and Mrs. Ernst Claassen, Whitewater, Kansas.

Letter, Anna Toews to H. H. Wiebe, Aberdeen, Idaho, September 1, 1915. In possession of Mr. and Mrs. Ernst Claassen, Whitewater, Kansas.

Letter, Cornelius Krahn to J. J. Dyck, North Newton, Kansas, June 21, 1945. MHLA.

Letter, Jacob Toews to Peter Klaassen, Katakurgan, Bukhara, September 4, 1881. MHLA.

Letter, Jacob Toews to David Froese, Katakurgan, Bukhara, January 22, 1882. MHLA.

Letter, Jacob and Suzzana Jantzen, Ak Metchet, Khiva, April 18, 1888. In possession of Mr. and Mrs. Ernst Claassen, Whitewater, Kansas.

Letter, J. J. Dyck to Cornelius Krahn, Laird, Saskatchewan, April 16, 1945. MHLA.

Letter, J. J. Dyck to Cornelius Krahn, Laird, Saskathchewan, April 30, 1946, MHLA.

Letter, J. J. Dyck to Cornelius Krahn, Laird, Saskatchewan, May 15, 1945. MHLA.

Letter, J. J. Dyck to Kaete, Laird, Saskatchewan, June 16, 1945. MHLA.

Letter, Johann Jantzen, Plymouth, Nebraska, December, n.d. MHLA.

Letter, M. R. to Sister Wiebe, Ak Metchet, Khiva, June 15, 1885. In possession of Mr. and Mrs. Ernst Claassen, Whitewater, Kansas.

"Letters." MHLA, n.p., n.d.

"Meeting of the American Mennonite Aid Committee, June 5, 1886." MHLA, n.p. 1886.

"Minutes of the Meeting for the Support of Needy Immigrants from Asia." MHLA, n.p., n.d.

"Minutes of the Meeting of the American Mennonite Aid Committee, April 18, 1884." MHLA, n.p., 1884.

"Minutes of the Meeting Held April 10, 1884," MHLA, n.p., 1884.

"Monies Sent to Johann Bergmann." MHLA, n.p., n.d.

"Obituary of Helena Dalke Goertz." MHLA, n.p., n.d.

"Obituary of Siebert Goertz." MHLA, n.p., n.d.

"Old Colony Mennonites, John P. Wall Diary, Family Book of Franz Sawatzky and Other Documents." MHLA, n.p., n.d., Microfilm 58.

Penner, J. H. "Memories of a Mennonite Immigrant Boy." MHLA, n.p., n.d.

"Petition Draft to Secretary of State of the United States." MHLA, n.p., n.d.

"Pictures of Am Trakt and Chiva." MHLA, n.p., n.d., Microfilm 82N.

Quiring, Mrs. Aron B. "The Family Tree of Daniel and Maria (Epp) Peters." MHLA, n.p., n.d.

Regier, C. C. "The Mennonites of Russia." MHLA, n.p., n.d.

Reimer, Naomi. "Family Tree of My Great-Great Grandfather, Cornelius Jantzen." Unpublished research paper, Bethel College, North Newton, Kansas, 1962.

Rempel, Alexander. "Auszüge aus der 'Geschichte von Ak-Metschet,' " *Der Bote*, 1947.

Rempel, D. G. "The Mennonite Colonies in New Russia." Unpublished Doctoral Dissertation, Stanford University, Palo Alto, California, 1933.

"Reports from Asia." MHLA, n.p., n.d.

"Russian Book, Diary of Theo. Nickel, Hein. Goertz Family History." MHLA, n.p., n.d., Microfilm 74.

"Rubles." MHLA, n.p., n.d.

"Russian Telegram Telling of Assassination of Czar Alexander II." MHLA, n.p., 1881.

Schultz, Elizabeth "Autobiography." Translated by Annie Keyes. Unpublished mimeographed MS in possession of author, n.p., n.d.

Shipley, Helen B. "The Migration of the Mennonites from Russia, 1879-1880. Their Settlement in Kansas." Unpublished MA Thesis, University of Minnesota, 1954.

Smith, Eldon, et al. "Schartner Family Reunion Records." MHLA, Freeman, South Dakota, 1970.

Stahl, H. "Kulakenkutter." MHLA, n.p., n.d.

"Statement Concerning the Twelve Familes in Aulie Ata." MHLA, n.p., n.d.

Swartzendruber, Elmer. "Eine Deputationsreise von Russland nach America, 1897." MHLA, n.p., n.d.

"The American Mennonite Aid Committee Meeting on May 9, 1884." MHLA, n.p., 1884.

Toews, Anna (nee Wiebe). "Diary." n.p., June, 1943. Original in possession of Mr. and

Toews, Art. "A Translation of 'About the Immigration of the Mennonites to Central Asia' by M. Klaassen." Unpublished research paper, Bethel College, North Newton, Kansas, February, 1957.

———. "A Short Sketch of My Life as It Reveals the Direction and Guidance of of a Wonderfuland Gracious God." Translated by Frank L. and Anna (Toews) Wenger. Aberdeen, Idaho, May, 1963.

"Undated Letter from Central Asia." In possession of Mr. and Mrs. Ernst Claassen, Whitewater, Kansas.

Unger, Heinrich. "Old Colony Mennonite Diary." MHLA, n.p., n.d., Microfilm 53.

Unruh, Tobias. "Diary of the Journey and Search for the Settlement Land in America, 1873." Translated by Viola Siemens and Verney Unruh. Original in possession of Mrs. P. Goertz, Newton, Kansas, n.p., n.d.

Wiebe, Sharon M. "Russian Mennonite Migration to Asia and America." Unpublished research paper, Bethel College, North Newton, Kansas, February, 1958.

E. Interviews by the Author

Cornelius Krahn, North Newton, Kansas. January 15, 1973.

Ernest and Justine Claassen, North Newton, Kansas. March 7, 1972.

Ernst and Justine Claassen, John H. Wiebe, and Mrs. P. G. Harder, Whitewater, Kansas. May 7, 1972.

Margaret Anne Epp, North Newton, Kansas. February 24-28, 1972.

II. Secondary Sources

A. Special Studies, Books

Albertus, I. *Die Englisch-Russische Frage and die deutsche Kolonial-Politik*. Innsbruck: Privately printed, 1885.

Am Trakt: Eine Mennonitische Kolonie im Mittleren Wolgagebiet (Vol. 6 of Historische Schrifenreihe des Echo-Verlags), North Kildonan, Manitoba, 1948.

Anonymous. *Khiva and Turkestan*. Translated from the Russian by Capt. H. Spalding. London: Privately printed, 1874.

Arn, John. *The Herald Mennonite Church*. North Newton, Kansas: Mennonite Press, 1969.

Architectural Monuments of Middle Asia: Bokhara, Samarkand. Leningrad: Aurora Publishers, 1969.

Barrett, R. J. *Russia's New Era*. London: Privately printed, 1908.

Baum, Max. *Jahrbuch der Deutsch-Amerikanischen Historischen Gesellschaft von Illinois*. Vol. 31. Chicago: University of Chicago Press, 1931.

Becker, Seymour. *Russia's Protectorates in Central Asia: Bukhara and Khiva, 1865-1924*. Cambridge, Massachusetts: Harvard University Press, 1968.

Behrends, Ernst. *Der Steppenhengst*. Ulm: Hohenstaufen, 1969.

Bender, Harold S. and C. Henry Smith, eds. *The Mennonite Encyclopedia*. Scottdale, Pennsylvania: Mennonite Publishing House, 1955-59, 4 vols.

Berve, Helmut. *Das Alexanderreich auf Prosopographischer Grundlage*. Munich: n.p., 1926, 2 vols.

Biddulph, C. E. *Four Months in Persia and a Visit to Transcaspia*. London: Privately published, 1892.

Bondar, S.D. *Sekta Mennonitov Rossiyi*. Petrograd: Smirnava, 1916.

Boulger, D. C. *Central Asian Portraits: The Celebrities of the Khanates and Neighboring States*, London: n.p., 1880.

————. *England and Russia in Central Asia.* London: n.p., 1879, 2 vols.

Carleton, M. A. "Hard Wheats Winning Their Way." *United States Department of Agriculture.* Washington: G.P.O., 1914.

Coates, W. P. and Zelda. *Soviets in Central Asia.* London: Lawrence and Wishart Lts., 1951.

Curzon, G. N. *Russia in Central Asia in 1889 and the Anglo-Russian Question.* London: Longmans, Green and Co., 1889.

Diebold, Edmond. *Folge dem Licht.* Zurich: Gotthelf Verlag, 1945.

Ehrt, Adof. *Die Mennoniten in Russland.* Berlin: Julius Beltz, 1932.

Eisenach, George, *Pietism and Russian Germans.* Berne: Berne Publishers, 1948.

Epp, D. H. *Die Chortitzer Mennoniten.* Odessa: n.p., 1889.

————. *Johann Cornies.* Berdyansk: n.p., 1909.

Epp, F. H. *Mennonite Exodus.* Altona, Manitoba: Mennonite Press, 1962.

Fretz, W. *Mennonite Colonization.* Akron, Pennsylvania: Mennonite Publishing House, 1944.

Frye, Richard N. *Bukhara: The Medieval Achievement.* Norman: University of Oklahoma Press, 1965.

————. *The History of Bukhara.* Cambridge, England: The Medieval Academy of America, 1954.

Hayit, Baymirza. *Turkestan im XX. Jahrhundert.* Darmstadt: n.p., 1956.

Hege, Christian, and Christian Neff. *Mennonitisches Lexikon.* Vols. I-IV, Frankfurt and Weierhof: 1913-1937.

Hellwald, F. von. *Die Russen in Centralasien: eine geographisch-historische Studie mit einer Uebersichtskarte.* Vienna: n.p., 1869.

Hershberger, Guy F., ed. *The Recovery of the Anabaptist Vision.* Scottdale, Pennsylvania: Herald Press, 1957.

Hildebrandt, J. J. *Chronologische Zeittafel.* Winnipeg: J. J. Hildebrandt, 1945.

Hirzel, Stephen. *Heimliche Kirche.* Hamburg: Friederich Wittig Verlag, n.d.

Hofer, D. M. *Die Hungersnot in Russland.* Chicago: K.M.B., 1924.

Holdsworth, Mary. *Turkestan in the Nineteenth Century.* Oxford: Central Asian Research Center, 1959.

Hudson, Alfred E. *Kazak Social Structure.* New Haven, Conn.: Yale University Publications in Anthropology, 1938.

Isaac, Franz. *Die Molotschnaer Mennoniten.* Halbstadt, Taurien: H. J. Braun, 1908.

Istoriia Kazakhskoi S.S.R. Vol. I. Alma Ata: n.p., 1957.

Jantzen, F. F. *Jantzen Family Record 1704-1952.* Paso Robles, Calif: Privately Published, 1952.

Juhnke, James C. *A People of Two Kingdoms.* Newton, Kansas: Faith and Life Press, 1975.

Junge, Reinhard. *Das Problem der Europäisierung orientalischer Wirtschaft dargestellt an den Verhältnissen der Sozialwirtschaft von Russisch-Turkestan.* Weimar: n.p., 1915.

Kazaksko-Rysskie. Alma Ata: Academy of Science, 1961.

Kazaksko-Rysskie. Alma Ata: Hayka, 1964.

Klaassen, Martin. *Geschichte der wehrlosen Taufgesinnten Germeinden.* Köppental-Orloff, Trakt: Mennonite Church, 1873.

Klaus, A. *Unsere Kolonien: Studien und Materialien zur Geschichte und Statistik der ausländischen Kolonisation in Russland.* Odessa: Odessaer Zeitung, 1887.

Kostenko, L. F. *Sredniaia Aziia i vodvorenie v. nei Russkoi grazhdanstvennosti.* St. Petersburg: n.p., 1871.

Krahn, Cornelius (ed.), *From the Steppes to the Prairies.* Newton: Mennonite Publication Office, 1949.

Kroeker, A. *Unsere Brüder in Not.* Striegau: Urban, 1930.

————. *Pfarrer Edüard Wüst,* Leipzig: H. G. Wallmann, 1903.

nisse. St. Petersburg: n.p., 1873.

Lindemann, K. *Von den deutschen Kolonisten in Russland: Ergebnisse einer Studienreise 1919-1921*. Stuttgart: n.p., 1924.

Lorimer, Frank. *The Population of the Soviet Union: History and Prospects*. Geneva: n.p., 1946.

Mannhardt, Wilhelm. *Die Wehrfreiheit der alt-preussischen Mennoniten*. Marienburg: n.p., 1863.

Mende, Gerhard von. *Studien zur Kolonization in der Soviet-union*. (Quellen und Studien, Albteilung Wirtschaft, No. XI.) n.p.: Ost-Europa Institute, 1933.

Mennonitisches Jahrbuch. 10 vols. Newton, Kansas: Mennonite Publishing, 1948-1957.

Mochalski, Herbert and E. Kogan, eds. *Sowiet-Siberien und Zentralasien heute*. Frankfurt am Main: Stimme-Verlag, 1967.

Morton, W. L. *Manitoba: A History*. Toronto: University of Toronto, 1957.

Mosques de Samarcande. St. Petersburg: Expedition pour la Confection des Papiers de 'Etat, 1905.

Olzscha, Riner and George Cleinow. *Turkestan, die politisch-historischen und wirtschaftlichen Probleme Zentralasiens*. Leipzig; n.p., 1900.

Ostroumov, N.P., ed. *Kaufmanskii Sbornik*. Moscow: n.p., 1910.

Parish, A. J. *Kansas Mennonites During World War I*. Hays, Kansas: Ft. Hays Press, 1968.

Penkin, Z. M. *The Transcaspian Province, 1866-1885*. St. Petersburg: n.p., 1888.

Poiovtsoff, A. *The Land of Timur*. London: Methuen and Co., Lts., n.d.

Radet, Georges A. *Alexandre le Grand*. Paris: n.p., 1950.

Reiner, Gustav and G. R. Gaeddert. *Exiled by the Czar: Cornelius Jansen and the Great Mennonite Migration*, 1874. Newton, Kansas: Mennonite Publishing Office, 1956.

Redekop, Calvin Wall. *The Old Colony Mennonites: Dilemma of Ethnic Minority Life*. Baltimore: The Johns Hopkins Press, 1969.

Reeves, Marjorie. *The Influence of Prophecy in the Later Middle Ages*. New York: Oxford, 1969.

Ryskulov, T. H. *Kirgiztan*. Moscow: Institute, 1929.

Samarkand. Tashkent: Verlag Usbekistan, 1971.

Schachermeyr, Fritz. *Alexander der Grosse*. Graz: Graz Press, 1949.

Schiller, Franz P. *Literatur zur Geschichte und Volkskunde der deutshen Kolonien in der Sowiet Union für die Jahre 1764-1926*. Pokrovsk: Pokrovsk Press, 1928.

Schock, Adolph. *In Quest of a Free Land*. San Francisco: San Jose State Press, 1964.

Smith, C. Henry. *The Coming of the Russian Mennonites: An Episode in the Settling of the Last Frontier, 1874-84*. Berne, Indiana: Mennonite Book Concern, 1927.

Smith, E. E. *A History and Record of the Schartner Family*. Newton, Kansas: Herald Printing, 1952.

Stahlin, Karl. *Russisch Turkestan gestern und heute*. Königsberg-Berlin: University of Berlin Press, 1935.

Stolypin, P. A. *Die Kolonisation Sibiriens: Eine Denkschrift*. Berlin: n.p., 1912.

Storms, Everek. *History of the United Missionary Church*. Elkhart, Indiana: Bethel Publishing Co., 1958.

Tarn, W. W. *Alexander the Great*. Cambridge, England: Cambridge University Press, 1948, 2 vols.

————. *The Greeks in Bactria and India*. Cambridge, England: Cambridge University Press, 1938.

Treadgold, Donald W. *The Great Siberian Migration: Government and Peasant in Resettlement from Emancipation to the First World War*. Princeton: Princeton University Press, 1957.

Triumph of Lenin's Ideas of the Cultural Revolution in Uzbekistan. Tashkent: Foreign Tourism Board, 1970.

238 *The Great Trek of the Russian Mennonites*

Triumph of Lenin's Ideas of the Cultural Revolution in Uzbekistan. Tashkent: Foreign Tourism Board, 1970.
Unruh, Benjamin H. *Die Niederländisch-niederdeutschen Hintergründe der menonitischen Ostwanderungen im 16, 18, and 19, Jahrhundert*. Karlsruhe: Privately published, 1955.
U.S.S.R. Uzbekistan. Moscow: Press Agency Publishing House, 1967.
Vambrey, Arminius. *Geschichte Bucharas*. Stuttgart: n. p., 1872.
Voeikov, A. I. *Le Turkestan Russe*. Paris: n. p., 1914.
Wiebe, David, *They Seek a Country*. Hillsboro, Kansas: The Mennonite Brethren Publishers, 1959.
Wilcken, Ulrich. *Alexander der Grosse*. Leipzig: n.p., 1931.
Yoder, John H. *The Legacy of Michael Sattler*. Scottdale, Pennsylvania: Herald Press, 1973.
Yoder, S. C. *For Conscience Sake*. Goshen, Indiana: Mennonite Press, 1940.

B. Special Studies: Articles

Andreas, W. C. "Highlights and Sidelights of the Mennonites in Beatrice," *Mennonite Life*, Vol. I, No. 2 (July, 1946), 21-23.
Belk, Fred R. "The Final Refuge: Kansas and Nebraska Migration of Mennonites from Central Asia After 1884," *The Kansas Historical Quarterly*, Vol. XL, No. 3 (Autumn, 1974), 379-392.
_____ "Turkestan: Russian Mennonite Promised Land," *Studies in Islam*, (January to April, 1973), pp. 58-79.
Bender, H. D. "Church and State in Mennonite History," *MQR*, Vol. XIII, No. 2 (April, 1939), 83-103.
Benzig, Johannes. "Das turkestanische Volk im Kampf um seine Selbständigkeit: I. von der russischen Eroberung bis zum Sturz des Zarentums," *Die Welt des Islams*, Vol. XIX (December, 1937), 94-137.
Bowman, H. M. "Jacob Y. Shantz, Pioneer of the Russian Mennonite Immigration to Manitoba," *Waterloo Historical Society Report*, Vol. XII, 1933, 85-100.
Braun, Peter. "The Educational System of the Mennonite Colonies in South Russia," *MQR*. Vol. III, No. 3 (July, 1929), 169-182.
Correll, Ernst. "Two Centuries of American Mennonite Literature: An Appraisal," *MQR*, Vol. IV, No. 4 (October, 1930).
_____. "The Congressional Debates on the Mennonite Immigration from Russia, 1873-74," *MQR*, Vol. XX, No. 3 (July, 1946).
Doerfer, Gerhard. "Die Usbekischen Lehnwörter in der Sprache der Araber von Buchara," *Central Asiatic Journal*, Vol. XII, No. 4 (1969), 296-308.
Dunn, Stephen P. and Ethel Dunn. "Soviet Regime and Native Culture in Central Asia and Kazakhstan: The Major Peoples," *Current Anthropology*, Vol. VIII, No. 3 (June, 1967), 147-298.
"Enquetes sur les vakoufs du Turkestan," *Revue du Monde Musulman*, Vol. XIII. No. 2 (1911), 276-311.
Fast, Gerhard. "Mennonites of the Ukraine Under Stalin and Hitler," *Mennonite Life*, Vol. XI, No. 2 (April, 1947).
Grigorieff, W. W. "The Relations of the Nomads with the Civilized States," *Russian Review*, Vol. VII, n.d., 321-50.
Hale, Douglas. "From Central Asia to America," *Mennonite Life*, Vol. XXV, No. 3 (July, 1970), 133-138.
Harder, M. S. "Contributions of the Russian Mennonites to the Culture of Kansas," *Proceedings of the Third Annual Conference on Mennonite Cultural Problems*, Vol. III, 1944, 101.

Hebberd, S. S. "Mohammedanism in Central Asia," *Mohammedan Religious Magazine,* Vol. 51, n.d., No. 118.

Herold der Wahrheit. 1940-1943.

Hoetzsch, Otto. "Russich-Turkestan und die Tendenzen der heutigen russischen Kolonialpolitik," *Schmollers Jahrbuch,* XXXVII (1913), 903-941, 1427-1473.

Kirchner, W. "Emigration to Russia," *American Historical Review,* LV (April, 1950), 552-566.

Krahn, Cornelius. "Some Social Attitudes of the Mennonites of Russia," *MQR,* Vol. IX, No. 4 (October, 1935), 164-177.

——————. "Faith of Our Fathers,". *Mennonite Weekly Review,* March-January, 1948-49.

Kuhn, Walter. "Cultural Achievements of the Chortitza Mennonites," *Mennonite Life,* Vol. III (July, 1948), 35.

Leibbrant, Georg. "Emigration of the German Mennonites from Russia to the United States and Canada in 1873-1880," *MQR,* Vol. VI, No. 4 (October, 1932), 205-226: Vol. VII, No. 1 (January, 1933), 5-41.

Manger, Edward. "Jung-Stilling," *Allgemeine deutsche Biographie,* Vol. XIV (1889), 697-704.

Majerczak, R. "Kaufmanskii Sbornik," *Revue du Monde Musulman,* Vol. XXVI (1914), 162-196.

Mandel, William. "Soviet Central Asia," *American Russian Institute Bulletin: Russia at War,* No. 26 (March 18, 1942).

——————. "Soviet Central Asia," *Pacific Affairs* (December, 1942).

Masal'skii, V. I. "Rural Industries and Forestry of Turkestan," *The Industries of Russia* (1893), 444-471.

Ostroumov, N. P. "Kistorii narodnago obrazovaniia v. turkestanskom kraie," *Konstantin Petrovich Fon Kaufmann, Ustroitel Turkestanskago kraia: Lichnye vospominaniia, 1877-81* (Tashkent, 1899).

Quiring, H. "Die Auswanderung der Mennoniten aus Preussen, 1788-1870," *Auslandsdeutsche Volksforschung,* Vol. II (1938).

Reimer, E. E. "Alma Ata": German Hymn Sets Tone," *Mennonite Mirror,* Vol. I, No. 4. (December, 1971), 16-20.

Rempel, D. G. "The Expropriation of the German Colonists in South Russia During the Great War," *Journal of Modern History,* Vol. IV (March, 1932), 49-67.

——————. "The Mennonite Migration to New Russia, 1787-1870," *MQR,* Vol. IX (April, 1935), 71-91.

Robinson, C. A., Jr. "Alexander the Great and the Barbarians," *Classical Studies Presented to Edward Capps* (Princeton, 1936), 298-304.

——————. "Alexander the Great and the Oecumens," *Hesperia,* supplement VIII (1949), 299-304.

——————. "The Extraordinary Ideas of Alexander the Great," *The American H...torical Review,* Vol. LXII, No. 2 (January, 1957), 226-244.

——————. "When Did Alexander Reach the Hindu Kush?" *American Journal of Philosophy,* LI (1930), 22-31.

Sallet, Richard. "Russlanddeutsche Siedlungen in den Vereinigten Staaten von Amerika," *Deutsch-Amerikanische Geschichtsblätter,* Vol. XXXI (1931), 5-126.

Schachermeyr, Fritz. "Die letzten Pläne Alexander des Grossen," *Jahreshefte des österreichischen archäologischen Instituts,* Vol. XLI (1954), 118-140.

Schmidt, C. B. "Reminiscences of Foreign Immigration Work." *Kansas Historical Collections,* Vol. IX, n.d., 484-494.

Schellenberg, D. J. "A Moses of Our Day — David Toews," *Mennonite Life,* Vol. V, No. 3 (July, 1950), 6-9.

Schultz, Harold J. "Search for Utopia: The Exodus of Russian Mennonites to Canada,

1917-23," *A Journal of Church and State*, Vol. XI, No. 3 (Autumn, 1969), 487-512.

Spuler, B. "Geschichte Mittelasiens," *Geschichte Asiens*, Munich: n.p., (1950), 309-360.

Strakhovsky, L. E. "Constitutional Aspects of the Imperial Russian Government's Policy Toward National Minorities," *Journal of Modern History*, Vol. XIII, No. 4 (December, 1941), 467-492.

Stumpp, Karl. "Deutsche Siedlungen in Mittelasian und im Amurgebiet," *Heimatbuch der Deutschen aus Russland* (1964), 14-22.

—————. "Das Deutschtum in Siberian v. Mittelasien," *Heimatbuch* (1959), 16-27,

Sudermann, Jacob. "The Origin of Mennonite State Service in Russia, 1870-1880," *MQR*, Vol. XVII, No. 1 (January, 1943), 23-46.

Tarn, W. W. "Alexander's Plans," *Journal of Hellenic Studies*, Vol. LIX (1939), 124-135.

Taylor, Lily Ross. "The 'Proskynesis' and the Hellenistic Ruler Cult," *Journal of Hellentic Studies*, Vol. XLVII (1927, 53-62).

Toews, John B. "The Social Structure of the Russian Mennonites," *Mennonite Life*, Vol. XXVI, No. 3 (July, 1971), 133-137.

Tylor, E. B. "Stone Age Basis for Oriental Study," *Smithsonian Report* (1893), 701-708.

Unruh, B. H. "The Mennonites of Russia," *MQR*, Vol. XI, No. 1 (January, 1937) , 61-67.

Young, Gertrude S. "A Record Concerning Mennonite Immigration, 1873," *American Historical Review*, Vol. XXIX, 1927, 518-522.

Zenkovsky, U. "Kulturkampf in Pre-Revolutionary Central Asia," *American Slavic and East European Review*, Vol. XIV (1955), 15-41.

C. General Works

Allworth, Edward, ed. *Central Asia: A Century of Russian Rule*. New York: Columbia University Press, 1967.

Bartold, V. V. *Four Studies on the History of Central Asia*. Translated by V. and T. Minorsky. Leiden: E. J. Brill, 1956-1962, 3 vols.

—————. *Istorija Kulturnoij Zhizni Turkestana*. Leiden: E. J. Brill, 1927.

—————. *Turkestan Down to the Mongol Invasion*. Leiden: E. J. Brill, 1956-57, 2 vols.

Brake, W. B. *Wheat Country*. New York: Duell, Sloan, Pierce, 1950.

Cressey, George B. *Asia's Lands and Peoples*. New York, 1944.

Drage, Geoffrey, *Russian Affairs*. London: 1904.

Dyck, Cornelius J. *An Introduction to Mennonite History*. Scottdale: Herald Press, 1967.

Etherton, P. T. (Col.). *In the Heart of Asia*. London: Longmans, Green and Co., 1925.

Horsch, John. *Mennonites in Europe*. Scottdale: Mennonite Publishing House, 1950.

Howorth, H. *History of the Mongols from the Ninth to the Nineteenth Century*. London: n.p., 1876-1888, 4 vols.

Kirchner, Walther. *An Outline History of Russia*. New York: Barnes and Noble, 1950.

Kononov, A. M. *Sovetskaia geografia*. Moscow: Gosigdatgeolit, 1960.

Lansdell, Henry, *Russian Central Aisa, Including Kuldja, Bukhara, Khiva, and Merv*. London: n.p., 1885, 2 vols.

Lensen, G. A., ed. *Russia's Eastward Expansion*. Englewood Cliffs, N.J.: Holt, 1964.

Lutskii, E. A. *Istoriia S.S.S.R., 1861-1917*. Moscow: n.p., 1956.

Mandel, William. *The Soviet Far East and Central Asia*. New York: The Dial Press, Inc., 1944.

Mazour, Anatole G. *Russia: Tzarist and Communist*. Princeton: D. von Nostrand Co.,

Inc., 1962. *Russian: Past and Present*. Princeton: D. von Nostrand Co., 1951.

Milivkov, Paul. *The Successors of Peter the Great*. New York: Funk and Wagnalls, 1968.

Mirov, N. T. *Geography of Russia*. New York: n.p., 1951.

Pares, Bernard, *A History of Russia*. New York: Alfred A. Knopf, 1960.

Pisarenski, G. G. *The History of Foreign Colonization in Russia in the Eighteenth Century*. Vol V. Moscow: Publications of the Moscow Archeological Institute, 1909.

Rogger, Hans. *National Consciousness in Eighteenth Century Russia*. Cambridge, England: University Press, 1960.

Rykin, Michael. *Russia in Central Asia*. New York: Collier Books, 1963.

Sarkisyanz, Emanuel. *Geschichte der orientalischen Völker Russlands bis 1917*. Munich: University of Munich, 1961.

Skrine, Francis H. and Edward Denison Ross. *The Heart of Asia: A History of Russian Turkestan and the Central Asian Khanates from Earliest Times*. London: Methuen and Co., 1899.

Smirin, M. M. *Weltgeschichte*. Vol. IV. Berlin: Deutscher Verlag der Wissenschaften, 1964.

Smith, C. Henry, *The Story of the Mennonites*. 4th Edition. Revised and enlarged by Cornelius Krahn. Newton, Kansas: Mennonite Publication Office, 1957.

Vambrey, Arminius. *Western Culture in Eastern Lands: A Comparison of the Methods Adopted by the English and Russians in the Middle East*. London: John Murray, 1906.

Vernadsky, G. *The Mongols and Russia*. New Haven: Harvard University Press, 1953.

Waltner, James H. *This We Believe*. Newton, Kansas: Faith and Life Press, 1968.

Wenger, John Christian. *Glimpses of Mennonite History and Doctrine*. Scottdale: Herald Press, 1959.

Wheeler, Geoffrey. *The Modern History of Soviet Central Asia*. London: Weidenfeld and Nicolson, 1964.

————. *Racial Problems in Soviet Muslim Asia*. London: Oxford University Press, 1962.

Wurm, Stefan. *Turkic Peoples of the U.S.S.R.* London: Oxford University Press, 1954.

INDEX

FRED RICHARD BELK was born in Kansas City, Missouri, in 1937. He received his education at William Jewell College (BA), Texas Christian University (MA), San Francisco Theological Seminary (Master of Divinity), and Oklahoma State University (PhD in history, 1973).

Dr. Belk is a member of the History and Political Science Department at Sterling College, Sterling, Kansas. During his graduate studies he held a variety of teaching assistantships.

In addition to his academic responsibilities the author has served numerous churches as pastor, including the First Presbyterian Church of Perry, Oklahoma, from 1966 to 1969, as well as the Zenith and Chase, Kansas, Presbyterian churches.

Dr. Belk and his wife, Nadine, are the parents of three children: Stephanie, Stephen, and Christopher.